D0169619

JERUSALEM
IN PROPHECY

RANDALL PRICE

HARVEST HOUSE PUBLISHERS
Eugene, Oregon   97402

Cover by Koechel Petersen & Associates, Minneapolis, Minnesota

Interior photos by Paul Streber

For a free copy of Dr. Price's newsletter about
biblical archaeology, biblical backgrounds,
and biblical prophecy, write to:

World of the Bible Ministries, Inc.
P.O. Box 827
San Marcos, TX 78667-0827
(512) 396-3799, FAX (512) 392-9080
www.worldofthebible.com
E-mail: wbmrandl@itouch.net

JERUSALEM IN PROPHECY

Copyright © 1998 by World of the Bible Ministries, Inc.
Published by Harvest House Publishers
Eugene, Oregon 97402

Library of Congress Cataloging-in-Publication Data
    Price, Randall.
        Jerusalem in prophecy / Randall Price.
            p. cm.
        Includes bibliographical references.
        ISBN 1-56507-783-0
        1. Bible—Prophecies—Jerusalem. 2. Jerusalem in the Bible. I. Title.
    BS649.J38P75 1998
    263'. 042569442—dc21   98-4079
                                                                                   CIP

Printed in the United States of America.

00   01   02   03   /BP/   10   9   8   7   6   5   4

CONTENTS

PART 1: THE DAYS OF DISCOVERY

PART 2: THE DAYS OF DARKNESS

PART 3: THE DAYS OF DELIVERANCE

PART 4: THE DAY OF DECISION

An Invitation to
Visit Jerusalem

There has been no better time for a book on the future
of Jerusalem than today, when the shadow of its future is
already heavy upon the city. It is especially appropriate to
consider Jerusalem in prophecy, for according to the Bible
it is the only city on earth that is guaranteed to have a
future! This is important to consider at a time when we've
just passed the milestones of Israel's fiftieth year as a
modern independent Jewish state and Jerusalem's 3,000-
year anniversary as the nation's capital. Then there's the
prospect of what's ahead in the new millennium!

Everywhere on earth, people who previously never gave
a thought to the city are asking, "What is going to happen to
Jerusalem?" Attempting a reply with only a look at Jerusalem's past and present will fail in the face of unanswerable
problems. For starters, the Israeli government has declared
that it will never allow Jerusalem to be redivided, and will
fight all foes to retain sovereignty over the entire city. However, Yasser Arafat has announced a Palestinian state with
Jerusalem as its capital and will continue in conflict until
the city is theirs. Then there are the leaders in the Temple
Movement, who believe the time is at hand to rebuild the

Jewish Temple, with or without the support of Israel's government. By contrast, the Arabs denounce the Temple as a Jewish myth and view such statements as attempts by the Israeli government to fabricate a Jewish history in Jerusalem. They have staunchly upheld their exclusive right of access to the Temple Mount, denying Jews even the privilege of prayer, and declaring that any incursion of their holy places for this purpose will be defended to "the last drop of blood!" How will these seemingly irreconcilable issues be resolved? Neither the past nor the present can help answer these questions about Jerusalem's future. Only those who can see infallibly into the days ahead can make sense of these contrary concerns, and with the prophetic Word of God you and I can have such an advantage.

Because of the constantly changing political scene, it is virtually impossible to write with relevance about the present-day history of Jerusalem. Previous works on Jerusalem (and the numbers are in the thousands) have concentrated primarily on the historical and political significance of the city. This, of course, is essential if we are to grasp how and why Jerusalem has come to occupy such a central place in the affairs of the world, and beyond this, the future of mankind. However, very few works have dealt with the future. This is unfortunate, for the Bible reveals that there are *two* Jerusalems that should occupy the thoughts and prayers of God's people. One is the earthly Jerusalem and the other the heavenly Jerusalem, both part of our promised future. The New Testament epistle to the Galatians reveals both of these when it speaks of "the present Jerusalem" and "the Jerusalem above" (Galatians 4:25-26). Likewise, the book of Revelation mentions both "the holy city" "given to the nations" to "tread under foot" (Revelation 11:2), as well as "the holy city, new Jerusalem, coming down out of heaven" (Revelation 21:2). It is with both of these that God's people past, present, and future will deal. For this reason I have focused in this work on the unchanging prophecies yet to be fulfilled concerning this city with an eternal destiny. In contrast to many recent books on Jerusalem in prophecy, in which the focus is on the dark days that will descend on the city, I have chosen to emphasize the glorious promises that will result in the city's revival and restoration, Messiah's return and reign, and the splendor of the New Jerusalem, where God's presence will so fill the city that its only light is the Lord. I have felt this to be important in order to avoid drawing disproportionate attention to the "doomsday scenarios" that are *temporal,* and remind us of the glorious days to come, which will be *eternal.*

While the facts are that a time of Tribulation is coming and "all nations of the earth will be gathered against [Jerusalem]" to do battle (Zechariah 12:2), it is also true that Jerusalem will be spared at Armageddon and that the city's deliverance will begin the day of blessing long awaited by the world. To me it appears to be in the order of the prophets to arm against the night by remembering we belong to the day (Romans 13:12-13), and that night's end and "His going forth [return] is as certain as the dawn" (Hosea 6:3; see also 2 Peter 1:19). Although it has been necessary for me to include examples from present-day events in order to show how the future is unfolding—examples that could well become outdated or irrelevant as time moves on—the prophetic Word stands sure, and we can be certain that Jerusalem will remain at the center of all the momentous events destined to transpire in the days to come.

This is also an appropriate time for Americans to become better educated concerning this far-off land. Our

military forces have battled in Iraq and exert a major influence in Middle Eastern prospects for peace, bringing our
country to become irreversibly entwined in the future destiny of the region.

The United States's involvement with Israel has been
condemned by Islamic terrorists, along with the "Zionist-
imperialists," as the "Great Satan." When the White House
hosted the signing of the Israeli-Palestinian Interim Agreement on September 23, 1993, in which President Bill
Clinton, who played no actual part in the process, stood
between the signers on that day, American intervention in
resolving the Middle-East conflict was clearly established.
That Interim Agreement placed Jerusalem on the agenda
for final-status negotiations and began the political battle
for Jerusalem—a battle with which America has yet to deal.
The intensity of this struggle now under way was illustrated
for me as I was completing this book in Jerusalem during
the celebration of *Yom Hatzmaut* ("Independence Day"),
the annual commemoration of the founding of the State of
Israel in 1948. As if to underscore the direction to which
half a century of conflict has pointed, the Palestinians were
concurrently commemorating the anniversary of the "Palestinian Catastrophe of 1948," vowing to renew the Intifada if peace negotiations failed, and holding pro-Saddam,
anti-American demonstrations.

America's involvement in the battle for Jerusalem has
deeply divided American opinion. On the one side are the
media elite and those influenced by their carefully controlled bias for the Arab agenda. On the other is a segment
of American-Jewry joined by Christian Zionists. Those
who support Israel must base their support more on Scripture than on sentiment. For this reason, it is imperative that

we search the Scriptures and accept their relentless request to "pray for the peace of Jerusalem." This book is also written to help guide us along a perilous path on which we find ourselves standing for or against world opinion concerning Jerusalem. Today the Christian world is divided between those who "Arabize" Jerusalem and those who "Judaize" it. But unless we know from prophecy the eventual outcome of the present political policy with Jerusalem, we may, as Rabbi Gamaliel once cautioned the Sanhedrin, "even be found fighting against God" (Acts 5:39). Since God has planned that future, He knows it well and has been pleased to inform those who will hear of what is needful for the journey. Prophecy is God's roadmap for roads only now under construction, and we are told that one day all roads will lead to Jerusalem (see Isaiah 2:2-3). Therefore, just as all eyes today have been forced to consider the city's conflict, we must look together to its tomorrows and consider its coming peace. While it's true that both horror and hope fill Jerusalem's future, they are necessary threads that, considered together, will present a proper portrait of God's love for His chosen city (Psalm 78:68). Will we then not love what God loves, and choose to learn about what He has chosen? That is a decision Christians in particular will have to make as they read this book.

There is yet another reason for this book—one that concerns the heirs of Jerusalem itself. Although primarily penned for Christians who desire to understand the promises made to the Jewish people, I am aware that many Jewish people, especially those who reside in Jerusalem, also need to know their future. This is literally a matter of life and death with regard to Jerusalem, for the prophet Jeremiah said: "She [Jerusalem] did not consider her future; therefore she has fallen astonishingly . . ." (Lamentations 1:9).

Jerusalem's past has been one of problems, yet it is has been rightly named the city of "Peace" (Hebrews 7:2). Down through the millennia the Jewish people have enjoyed only brief respites of peace, yet it is their destiny to be the larger part of God's plan to bring peace to this planet (Isaiah 2:4). It is my hope that this forward focus might encourage them to make their own individual future sure in present faith, even as their nation itself will one day do when Messiah comes (Zechariah 12:10-14). It is for this believing remnant and their promised Messiah that the city waits for its future at the present. Only then will the city have fulfilled its grand purpose, and there will be for both Jew and Gentile "His praise in Jerusalem" (Psalm 102:21).

Recently as I was surfing web sites on Jerusalem, I came across the testimony of a recent pilgrim to Jerusalem after a three-month stay:

> I would say "this is the most amazing place we've seen." In the end I decided it's all amazing. But nothing can compare with Jerusalem, especially the Old City. It is almost impossible to describe Jerusalem—you really have to go there. The whole of Jerusalem, new and old city, is made of Jerusalem stone, even the pavements. When the sun sets on Jerusalem, the stone looks like gold. Personally, I would say that Jerusalem is the best place in the world. . . . It was so easy to feel "at home" there. To me, Jerusalem is no longer just a place in the Bible, but a real city, an incredible city with an unforgettable past and present, and awaiting a glorious future. Jerusalem is a city struggling to survive while waiting for Messiah to come. My prayers for her will never be the same because she has become real. I will not forget you Jerusalem; hang in there, for Messiah will come to cleanse you, rebuild your

ruins and destroy your enemies. Then you shall be
a light to the nations, and they shall see your
glory. . . . [1]

This response is typical of those who have walked in the
path of the prophets in Jerusalem and found themselves on
fire for its future. In this book I want you, too, to see Jerusalem through the eyes of the prophets—not what it is, but
what it will be. The psalmist advised, "Walk about Zion,
and go around her; count her towers; consider her ram-
parts; go through her palaces; that you may tell it to the next
generation. For such is God, our God forever and ever . . ."
(Psalm 48:12-14).

To walk around Jerusalem today is to see ancient stones
that cry out concerning its past, and to see modern construction which affirms its present—though disputed—
status. But the events that have catapulted Jerusalem into
the international headlines are the seeds of a future rapidly
coming to flower. It is these things that I want us to consider
so that if our own generation is not the terminal one, we
may be able to pass on a witness to the next generation of
the unfailing faithfulness of our God, whose Word will go
forth from Jerusalem (Isaiah 2:3). The psalmist said it best
when he exclaimed, "Glorious things are spoken of you, O
city of God" (Psalm 87:3). Come join me in walking around
the Jerusalem that is and will be, and let us listen together to
those glorious things that are spoken of its future.

PART ONE

The Days
of Discovery

And so we have the prophetic word
made more sure, to which you do
well to pay attention as to a lamp
shining in a dark place, until the
day dawns and the morning star
arises in your hearts.

—2 Peter 1:19

1

WHY STUDY PROPHECY?

Prophecy's Relevance to Our Lives, Part 1

God gave prophecy to change our hearts, not to fill our heads with knowledge. God never predicted future events just to satisfy our curiosity about the future. Every time God announces events that are still future, He includes with His predictions practical applications to life.[1]

—Charles H. Dyer

I will always remember some 20 years ago seeing the Holy City for the first time. My family and I had arrived in Jerusalem in a hastily driven and overcrowded taxi late at night from the Ben-Gurion Airport in Tel Aviv. Our route to our new home in East Talpiot had bypassed the historic view of the Old City, so my initial glimpses of the city were only of endless rows of apartment complexes.

The next day came early (about 4:00 A.M.) with the sound of a Muslim Mu'azzin issuing the morning call to prayer from a nearby minaret. Jumping to my feet like an excited schoolboy, I had only one thought on my mind: get to the Mount of Olives and see the postcard view of Jerusalem! By the time I got there (on foot) the sun was already hot and camels and vendors were preparing for the impending tourist buses. But for that moment I was alone on the promenade with its great and glorious sight of the city. There, stretching across the horizon before me, was a panorama of history and prophecy. My eyes traveled down the Mount of Olives across the thousands of tombs filling in the Kidron Valley between myself and the ancient walls surrounding the Old City. There on the east was the sealed Golden Gate; to the west the Dome of the Rock, site of the ancient Temple; there to the south was the Dormition Abbey, site of the Last Supper; below me was the Garden of Gethsemane; and finally, on the skyline, was the Church of the Holy Sepulcher, the central site in Christianity.

Each site had played its part in Christian history: Jesus had entered the Eastern Gate on Palm Sunday, taught in the Temple during His last week, shared His last Passover with the disciples in the Upper Room, prayed in the olive-grove garden, and then had died, been buried, and had risen again at the site now marked by the church. Moreover, somewhere near to where I was standing Jesus had ascended with the promise of a return. This made my thoughts run forward to the things to come, and I looked again at the city before me with a vision of the future: There were the armies of the world surrounding the City of the Great King; there was the Great King Himself, returning in glory and triumph to deliver His own; there was the earthquake splitting the mountain on which I stood; and there was the transformed city with its resplendent new Temple calling the nations of the world to worship. Where else on earth could so much of the divine drama be placed on so small a stage? Where else on earth could a person see so much that is foremost to his or her faith? On that day prophecy became very real and practical for me. Here was a modern city like any other, but with a future that will affect the future of every person on earth! To understand this place and believe its promises is to find one's faith made more real and revitalized!

A Surprising Response

I have never forgotten that first experience with Jerusalem. It has remained with me through the years as I've shared the city's prophetic importance with hundreds of tourists and in conferences around the world.

Yet I will also never forget an experience I had with a group of pastors in the States shortly after writing my first book on prophecy and the Jerusalem Temple.[2] My co-author, Thomas Ice, and I had been included in the program at a local ministerial meeting to share on the subject of our book. So I enthusiastically delivered with words and slides our insights on an aspect of the prophetic destiny of Jerusalem. However, I wasn't prepared for my audience's reaction. When my brief presentation ended, one of the pastors said with an air of disdain, "Why are we bothering with this?! This has no relevance to our ministries." Unfortunately, he was not alone in his opinion, for it seemed to be shared by most of the ministers present. My enthusiasm diminished, I left that meeting wondering how men who were trained in the Scriptures could believe prophecy was so impractical. How could these ministers evade the plethora of prophetic passages while professing "to declare the whole purpose of God"? (Ironically, those words in Acts 20:27 are made in the very context of prophecy!)

I do not think that pastors (I myself have served as one for over 20 years) realize how such selective preaching can lead their parishioners to draw unwarranted conclusions about their views on prophecy. I well remember asking one woman in a church if her pastor ever preached on prophecy. She exclaimed, "Oh, our pastor doesn't *believe* in prophecy!" Of course he believed in prophecy, but she had interpreted his reluctance as rejection because in her 25 years at the church she had never heard him preach on the subject.

I have often asked pastors like this (whose numbers, blushedly, are in the majority) why they do not preach on prophecy. The answer I usually get is that the subject is too complex, too controversial, too divisive, too prone to turn some parishioners into date-setting fanatics. This attitude is often developed after exposure to sensationalists who make claims about prophecy that, in time, fail to be fulfilled. Some of these sensationalists may have good intentions, but frequently their efforts to warn people about the future are misguided. Their attempts may be ridiculed by the public and parodied by the press, such as that which appeared in a tabloid, with this statement: "The world is definitely coming to an end on *Wednesday*, December 11 at noon! Full report in *Friday's* edition."

A Definite Relevance

Just because there are people who *abuse* prophecy doesn't mean we have reason to *avoid* it. Then there are pastors who have told me that their calling is to save souls, help the poor, and restore values to society. They consider prophecy to be unimportant because they imagine that events that will take place in the distant future cannot have relevance for the here and now. They mistakenly assume that because they will never see these events unfold, they have no practical meaning for their lives, families, careers, or even worship.

But when we take a closer look at prophecy, we find that the preaching of it actually *fulfills* the various particulars of a pastor's calling. Prophecy answers the great questions of life: Where are we going? What will happen to us when we get there? And, how will we know when we have started the journey? In addition, prophecy tells us where we are at this juncture in history. When Paul learned that the tribulations suffered by the Christians in the Greek town of Thessalonica had caused some believers to question whether they might have entered the Day of the Lord (a predicted time of divine intervention that commences with tribulation) he taught them about prophecy, assuring them that that day had not yet come (2 Thessalonians 2:1-2). Many people are expressing the same concern today 2,000 years later. In 1991 when the Gulf War with Iraq broke out with its threats of nuclear and chemical weapons, the secular media frequently posed the question: "Could this be Armageddon?" As a result, many people became frightened that the end of the world might be at hand. What's especially interesting to observe is that it was not the students of prophecy who had said anything to fan such fears, but individuals who did not know Bible prophecy! Those who knew what the Bible said were aware that the world was not destined to end in this way. There were still many other events that had to precede Armageddon, and while the Gulf War might possibly have been one of the events leading to the grand finale, it was not the finale itself.

Ultimately, prophecy is practical because it is *a part of Scripture*. Consider for a moment these statistics: The coming of Messiah as King (in what we Christians call the *second coming)* is mentioned 1,845 times in the Bible. In the Old Testament it is the dominant theme of 17 books, and in the New Testament it is discussed in several New Testament epistles, with one entire book—the book of Revelation—devoted entirely to the subject. The 318 references to Christ's return appear in every New Testament book but three. This amounts to a prophetic reference in 7 out of every 10 chapters, or one out of every 12 verses (1 out of every 10 verses in the epistles). What's more, the first prophecy ever uttered by man in the Bible (Enoch) deals with the second coming (Jude 14), as does the last prophecy by John (Revelation 22:20). Given this preponderance of prophecy in the Word of God, it is incredible that any preacher would avoid it. Furthermore, given God's attention to prophecy, why would anyone want to avoid it? If we can talk about the first coming of Christ as good news, should we not talk about His second coming as *great* news?

Practical Benefits of Prophecy

Let's move beyond statistics and go to the Scriptures themselves, which demonstrate prophecy's relevance to an age that asks for application. I believe that prophecy is practical, or as we say in my hometown of Texas, "handy." Since our hands have ten fingers (and ten is also a "prophetic number"!), let us consider—in this chapter and the next—ten practical benefits of prophecy.

Prophecy Is a Proof of the Truthfulness of Scripture

We live in a day of doubt. From the presidency to church pulpits, people have grave doubts concerning the integrity of those who occupy our country's most influential offices. With the loss of a biblical heritage in American public schools and the invasion of dead-end philosophies that dismiss absolutes and values, Scripture has been reduced to the place of worthless myths. This generation wants what works, and demands to have proof that something is authentic and useful before it is given any consideration. Throughout the ages, *prophecy* is the means God has given to authenticate His truth before a watching world. In the Old Testament God threw out a gauntlet to the gods and announced to the nations that He alone could prove His power. In the book of Isaiah we read:

> "Present your case," the LORD says. "Bring forth your strong arguments," the King of Jacob says. "Let them bring forth and declare to us what is going to take place; as for the former events, declare what they were, that we may consider them, and know their outcome, or announce to us what is coming. Declare the things that are going to come afterward, that we may know that you are gods."... "Who is like Me? Let him proclaim and declare it. ... And let them declare to them the things that are coming and the events that are going to take place. Do not tremble and do not be afraid; have I not long since announced it to you and declared it?" (Isaiah 41:21-23; 44:7-8).

The test of a god (or his messengers) is whether or not he can accurately predict the future. Attempts have been made in our time to pierce the veil of the yet unknown through mystics, mediums, psychics, channelers, diviners, fortune tellers, and the like, but none have yet beaten the odds and proven they can meet the divine challenge. On the other hand, the God of the Bible has given hundreds of detailed prophecies which have come to pass exactly as predicted. These have concerned individuals, nations, places, and events, and their fulfillment is now a matter of historical fact. In the case of the Messianic prophecies of the first advent, the New Testament insists that the historical events it records as part of the gospel record are the written testimony of verifiable facts (see Luke 1:1-4; Acts 1:1-3; 1 John 1:1-3). Anyone who so desires can confirm most of these facts through the pertinent ancient and archaeological records. One example appears in the book of Isaiah, where the Persian ruler Cyrus is called by name 150 years before his birth and explicitly described as to his place of birth, his future military campaigns, conquest of Babylon, and his treatment of the Israelites (see Isaiah 41:25; 44:28–45:4).

The prophecies concerning the first coming of the Messiah are among the most precise in Scripture. They provide details about the place and time of His coming (Micah 5:2; Daniel 9:25), His unique character and nature (Isaiah 7:14; 9:6), and His unparalleled manner and message (Isaiah 53:2-8; 61:1; Zechariah 9:9). During the last day of Messiah's earthly life at least 33 prophecies were fulfilled in a single 24-hour period of time. Professor Peter Stoner has calculated that the probability of only eight of these prophecies being fulfilled in one man by chance is 1 in 10^{17} (100,000,000,000,000,000).[3]

To better grasp the immensity of this probability, Stoner offers this illustration: If we take 10^{17} silver dollars and lay them on the face of the state of Texas they would cover all of the state to a depth of two feet. Then, let's mark one of these coins and stir the entire mass thoroughly all throughout the state. What are the chances that a man with a blindfold would pick out the marked silver dollar? Allowing him to travel as far as he wished, the chance that he would correctly pick the marked coin on the first try is the same chance the biblical prophets would have had of having just *eight* of their prophecies fulfilled in one man. And because a hundred or more of the messianic prophecies were fulfilled in the first coming of Christ, think how much better the odds are for the fulfillment of the prophecies about His second coming!

There is a passage in the New Testament that affirms this truth. In 2 Peter 1:19 we read, "So we have the prophetic word *made more sure*, to which you do well to pay attention as to a lamp shining in a dark place, until the day dawns and the morning star arises in your hearts" (emphasis added). The prophetic word has been made more certain because, as this context contends, Christ has demonstrated the truthfulness of God's promises. Earlier in verse 16 Peter follows the pattern of historical verification when he declares, "We did not follow cleverly devised tales when we made known to you the power and coming of our Lord Jesus Christ, but we were eyewitnesses of His majesty." What Peter and the disciples saw was the fulfillment of the first advent prophecies. However, in many of the Messianic prophecies in the Old Testament, events involving the first and second advents are combined in the same text. Jesus Himself affirmed this important fact in Luke 4:17-21, correctly dividing between the two advents in His messianic career by stopping in mid-sentence as He read from Isaiah 61:1-2. Because Isaiah 61:1-2a had to do with events related to His first coming, Jesus could rightly say, "Today this Scripture has been fulfilled in your hearing" (Luke 4:21). But because Isaiah 61:2b concerned events that would take place at His second coming (the judgment of the nations), He "closed the book, and gave it back to the attendant, and sat down" (Luke 4:20). Peter recognizes in 2 Peter 1:19 that because the first coming prophecies were fulfilled, we can know that the fulfillment of the second coming prophecies is guaranteed! With such a certainty unfolding before us on the horizon of hope—the dawning day of Christ's return—it is no wonder that the apostle said, "You do well to pay attention." Then in 2 Peter 3:3-13 we read that among unbelievers in the last days, the prophetic hope would be not only disregarded but disdained: "Where is the promise of His coming?" people will ask (verse 4). Believers, by contrast, will be "looking for and hastening the coming of the day of God" (verse 12). Therefore, those who desire to defend the truthfulness of Scripture against the attacks of skeptics in these last days of the church age cannot afford to neglect the proof of prophecy.

Prophecy Presents a Proper View of Our Age

Back in the 1970s there was a public service announcement that aired on every television across the United States. It reminded parents: "It's ten o'clock. Do you know where your *children* are?" If such announcements had been carried over into the 1980s—the age of abandonment and latchkey kids—we might have heard: "It's ten o'clock. Do you know where your *parents* are?" And in the 1990s—the decade of delusion—the announcement might have said: "It's ten o'clock. Do you know where *you* are?"

As we look back upon the sixth millennia of human history and move into what may be our last, we find ourselves technologically blessed but theologically bankrupt. Jewish author Arthur Koestler put it this way: "Nature has let us down, God seems to have left the receiver off the hook, and time is running out." Yet despite such skepticism, God has sent out His own public service announcement to all who will hear. This announcement is found in the Bible in the form of prophecy, without which we could not know where we are in the course of the ongoing ages. Prophecy tells us where we are now and where God will take us and His world tomorrow. He alone knows the end from the beginning, and through prophecy has given us the last chapter (the book of Revelation) to allay our first fears. Until we understand God's overall plan, how can we relate our current activities to His ultimate realities? With this knowledge we can live wisely and responsibly, redeeming the time to reach out to an age whose time is almost run out (Ephesians 5:16; see also 1 Corinthians 7:31). Let's look now at several prophetic passages that enable us to pinpoint our location in God's master plan.

First we need to keep in mind that we are now in the church age—a period of time that began with the establishment of the church on the day of Pentecost (Acts 2) and will end with the translation of the church at the Rapture (1 Corinthians 15:51-54; 1 Thessalonians 4:16-17). And second, the various players and props for the prophetic drama are mainly in the Middle East. So if we know Bible prophecy, we will understand the turbulent events taking place in the Middle East and recognize our approximate place in time with respect to future events. If we want to understand what's ahead for Jerusalem, then we must also consider current events, for it is these events that will pave the way for the fulfillment of the prophecies relating to this city.

While there are no prophetic signs that relate specifically to the church, near the close of their earthly ministries the apostles were shown what conditions would be like for the church during the last days. In 1 Timothy 4:1 Paul uses the term "later times" and in 2 Timothy 3:1 he uses the phrase "last days." A similar term, "the ends of the ages," appears in 1 Corinthians 10:11. These expressions denote the period of time from the ascension of Christ until the second advent and distinguish within this stretch the "last days" of the church (the church age) and the "last days" of Israel (the Tribulation). This era will be marked by increasing apostasy ("some fall away from the faith"—1 Timothy 4:1). Paul declares that this apostasy will reach deep into the professing church, infecting its leadership as well as its laity (compare Acts 20:29-30; Matthew 13:24-30,37-43; Revelation 3:15-17).

This defection from what traditionally characterizes the church as distinct from the world is specifically stated as denials of the doctrines of the faith and devotion to the doctrines of demons (1 Timothy 4:1). In other words, at this point in the church age, professing Christians will not be people who are known for their thorough knowledge of the Bible and a selfless, sacrificial, biblically based life-style, but by their pursuit of worldly enlightenment and a self-centered, culturally based, entertainment-oriented existence (2 Timothy 3:2-4). And that, in fact, describes the state of the church today. Secular psychology's principles have influenced the church worldwide, Christians are divorcing in large numbers, Christian teens lack values, and Christians in general are abysmally ignorant about the teachings of Scripture. We are in the midst of a moral and spiritual decline unprecedented in church history for a people with free and abundant access to the truth.

In addition, heresy and error are becoming rooted in some Christian circles, producing people who appear to be godly but are godless inside (2 Timothy 3:5). The leaders of these lies will propagate their errors to eager followers who will listen passionately without ever learning the truth

(2 Timothy 3:7). They will manifest a controlling authority over their hearers, demanding of them strict obedience to select standards (1 Timothy 4:2-3), while themselves recognizing no authority and using their power to gain immoral advantages (2 Timothy 3:6; see also 2 Peter 2:2-3). Today the scandal sheet runs long with the names of professing Christian leaders who have betrayed their wives and worshipers.

Today, too, as in no other time, more and more books are warning the saints of spiritual seduction and counterfeit claims. The apostle John told us that's to be expected in "the last hour," for already the spirit of Antichrist is setting the stage for the Antichrist to come (1 John 2:18). His advice to those who are alert to the fact that false prophets will abound in the last days is to test for the spirit of Antichrist by examining a teacher's doctrine (1 John 4:1). And the most basic doctrines for which Christians should take a stand are those that relate to Christ. Do these teachers who claim to be prophets, manifest signs and wonders, and parade prosperity as their proof of blessing speak correctly concerning the doctrines of Christ's deity, His hypostatic union, His incarnation, His kenosis, His penal substitutionary atonement, and His bodily resurrection? Do they even understand these terms? The apostle Peter predicted that these false teachers will not only deny such doctrines, but they will also keep their hearers from realizing they are being deceived (2 Peter 2:1).

A flood of deception will fill the Tribulation period, making it easier for false prophets to persuade multitudes of what is false (Matthew 24:24; 2 Thessalonians 2:11). This, in turn, will make it possible for the Antichrist to receive universal worship in response to certain "signs and false wonders" (Matthew 24:5,23; 2 Thessalonians 2:9; see also Revelation 13:13-15).

Prophetic events tend to cast their shadows before them, therefore it stands to reason that the closer we come to the time of the Tribulation, the more we should see conditions surrounding the church age exhibiting the characteristics of that future ungodly era. We must remember, however, that as the shadow of that dark age draws nearer, it's more vital than ever that we live as children of "light and . . . of day" (1 Thessalonians 5:5), so the shadows can be seen and discerned. To be sure "night" is fast approaching "when no man can work" (John 9:4), but these are only "difficult times" (2 Timothy 3:1), not yet the "great day of . . . wrath" (Revelation 6:16-17).

Still, there is a great benefit in knowing what God has to tell us in prophecy, for it enables us to better live as lights in a darkening world (Philippians 2:15-16) until the dawning day when the light of the world Himself returns (2 Peter 1:19).

In the next chapter we will continue to look at the practical purposes of prophecy so that our own lights might shine more brightly as we wait for the return of "the sun of righteousness" (Malachi 4:2).

Blessed is he who reads and
those who hear the words
of the prophecy, and heed
the things which are written in it;
for the time is near.

—Revelation 1:3

2

FOCUSING ON THE FUTURE:

Prophecy's Relevance to Our Lives, Part 2

The dawn of a better tomorrow kept first-century people on their feet, just as it does twentieth-century people. Is not this the part played by the "blessed hope" in the lives of Christians of every age? Without it how quickly the early Christians would have been overwhelmed in the maelstrom of persecution, hardships and tribulation. How would we go another step if suddenly that hope should dim?

—Hershel Hobbs

In the previous chapter we began to show ten benefits of prophecy that demonstrate its practicality for the present. Here we continue that survey so that we might understand how the prophecies about Jerusalem's future are linked to our present lives and ultimate destinies. There is great encouragement to be derived from seeing how prophecy was provided by God to meet the pressing needs of our spiritual struggles and help direct our Christian conduct.

Prophecy Provides Comfort in Sorrow

Sorrow comes to all in this world; Jesus affirmed this would be true for His followers as well. Near the end of His earthly life Jesus told His disciples that they would soon be scattered both spiritually and physically (John 16:31-32). Yet to His prediction of coming sorrows Jesus added a word of comfort: "In the world you have tribulation, but take courage; I have overcome the world" (John 16:33). Tribulation comes in many forms—natural disasters, wars, abuses, loss of jobs, disease, death. Yet we as believers have the promise that we can, through faith, overcome the world (1 John 5:4).

There are times, however, when it doesn't seem that way. When we suffer, we may wonder why it is that ungodly people prosper and seem to be free of problems. And despite our faith, we know that all flesh will ultimately succumb to that great enemy, death. How, then, has Jesus overcome the world when it yet lies in the control of the devil and under the curse?

Our answer takes us to the future. Only then will the conquest of this world system be realized. John tells us in Revelation 17:14, "These [the Antichrist and his ten-nation confederation] will wage war against the Lamb [Jesus], and the Lamb will overcome them, because He is Lord of lords and King of kings." It is at this point in history that "the kingdom of this world has become the kingdom of our Lord, and of His Christ; and He will reign forever and ever" (Revelation 11:15). This prophetic promise of victory can comfort our sorrows over the eons of injustice, of crimes unpunished, and evils never avenged. How practical it is to know from prophecy that there will be a day of reckoning when all accounts will be settled and all wrongs made right! (2 Thessalonians 1:6-9).

Prophecy also promises that the last great enemy, death, will itself be abolished (2 Timothy 1:10) and that life will reign. The overcoming of death itself is the unique hope of the believer (1 Thessalonians 4:13-14). A disruptive intrusion into the original enjoyment of life, its threat hung over the first couple until it became the one great certainty of their lives, and through them of all mankind (Genesis 2:17; 3:19; see also Romans 5:12). Who has not stood at the graveside of a departed loved one and not hated death? It steals our best and brightest and leaves us with painful memories of the past. But for the believer there is the promise offered by prophecy. We have been assured that those who have died in the Lord will live again! But more than this, we who are now alive may not have to die at all! First Thessalonians 4:14-17 and 1 Corinthians 15:51-54 tells us that the translation of dead and living saints is both an imminent reality and an invaluable hope for those who grieve at the grave.

We may weep at the grave, but we need not fear the grave. At the moment that we are caught up (the rapture), every worldly worry will be forgotten instantly and our horizon will be full of an eternity with Christ (1 Thessalonians 4:16-17). Death will be swallowed up in victory and we will join in the anthem of true freedom: "We have overcome!" For this reason the prophecy in 1 Corinthians 15:51-54 is often recited at funeral services, for it is a practical comfort in the midst of our sorrows and a steadfast incentive for our toils. Beyond this, prophecy promises even the death of death itself (Revelation 20:14). That means our new beginning in eternity can never be threatened again by the spectre of either sin or separation. Prophecy, then, provides us the "living hope" of an "inheritance which is imperishable," which, despite the trials of life and death, will "result in praise and glory and honor at the revelation of Jesus Christ" (1 Peter 1:3-7).

Prophecy Proves God Is in Control

One popular philosophical idea that has been advocated in universities as well as seminaries for many decades is known as "process theology." This school of thought, which accommodates an evolutionary hypothesis, holds that God cannot see the future and therefore changes in response to human actions. In this philosophy, which views God as adapting Himself to man, it is man who appears to be in control and God who responds. This kind of God, however, offers little comfort to those who see their own lives and world as out of control.

For those who hold this view, the scandalous history of man's inhumanity to man in wars, inquisitions, pogroms, holocausts, and genocides may explain a wrathful God, but it cannot provide any hope God will change since His response is bound to man, whose tendency toward savagery has remained unchanged. This view leaves us with a future filled with uncertainties—both to us and to God. By contrast, the prophetic Scriptures portray and prove a God who is in control because He directs the future according to His perfect plan: "I am confident of this very thing, that He who began a good work in you will perfect it until the day of Christ Jesus"

(Philippians 1:6); "And we know that God causes all things to work together for good to those who love God, to those who are called according to His purpose" (Romans 8:28).

It is told that when the first American president, George Washington, was a boy, his father taught him a memorable lesson confirming God's control of the world. When his father was planting a flower garden he decided to plant some seeds in such a way that they would spell out the family name—Washington—right along a path where his son regularly walked. Some days later young George saw the budding plants spelling out his family name. He ran to his father to tell him about the amazing discovery. His father said, "George, do you think that happened by chance?" George replied, "No, I have never seen such a thing happen by chance before, but how could it have happened?" Then his father told him how he had planted the seeds to create the design, reminding him that everything with order in the world also had to have a Designer with a purpose. What a wonderful way for George's father to illustrate for his son the truth that God is in control of all life! We can be sure this lesson was remembered later when, as a soldier, George had to trust God with his life during the French and Indian War. After a very fierce battle Washington wrote his brother on July 18, 1755:

> But by the all-powerful dispensations of Providence, I have been protected beyond all human probability or expectation; for I had four bullets through my coat, and two horses shot out under me, yet escaped unhurt, although death was leveling my companions on every side of me![1]

Washington's report of God's control over His destiny was affirmed some 15 years later when he met the old

Indian chief who had fought against him and his soldiers in this battle. The chief told him:

> I am a chief and ruler over my tribes. . . . I called to my young men and said, mark yon tall and daring warrior? [Washington] . . . Quick, let your aim be certain, and he dies. Our rifles were leveled, rifles which, but for you, knew not how to miss—'twas all in vain, a power mightier far than we shielded you.[2]

The awareness of God's sovereignty is what helped to preserve the American nation at a crucial moment in its founding history. During the Continental Congress of September 17, 1787 the new U.S. Constitution was in jeopardy of not being ratified because of divisions among the delegates. Benjamin Franklin called for the group to pray, declaring that "the longer I live the more evidence I find that God governs in the affairs of men."[3]

When the church was in its infancy this same perspective was shared by its members, who faced much persecution. In Acts 4:23-29 we read that after being threatened by the religious establishment in Jerusalem, the apostles Peter and John reported to their fellow believers the warning they had been given. The collective response was that of praise and a prayer to God cast in the shape of fulfilled prophecy. In Acts 4:25-27 reference was made to a prophecy in Psalm 2 to explain the confrontation they were experiencing. In Psalm 2:1-2 it is predicted that the rulers of the nations would oppose the Lord and His Messiah. While that passage ultimately applies to the Tribulation period (compare Psalm 2:9 with Revelation 2:27), the prophets, the Lord Jesus, and the apostles understood that the nations would resist God and the Messiah as long as the Messianic era awaited fulfillment (see Zechariah 12:1-9; 14:1-11; Matthew 24:7; Luke 21:10; 2 Thessalonians 2:3-4,8-12; Revelation 17:14; 19:14-21).[4] Herod, Pontius Pilate, and all those who opposed Jesus and His followers were part of the prophetic program of resistance to God's rule that will finally be climaxed with the Antichrist and his confederation (Revelation 17:10-14). The persecuted believers in Acts 4 understood their circumstances as part of the divine plan; thus they could take confidence that what was happening to them was "whatever [God's] hand and . . . purpose predestined to occur" (Acts 4:28-29). Would not today's church likewise gain greater confidence for its mission if it adopted this aspect of the early church's perspective of prophecy?

We, too, can see God's hand at work governing world events by looking at prophecies that have yet to be fulfilled and seeing their preparation in the events unfolding in our day. We can show our children that God is in control of their lives as God answers their prayers or as circumstances develop in the direction of their requests.

If we want to see God's control demonstrated on a global level, we need to know where to look. Here is where Jerusalem comes into the picture. If a future Temple is to be rebuilt there (Revelation 11:1-2), the two witnesses will minister there (Revelation 11:4-14), the Antichrist will defile the Temple there (Matthew 24:15), and Christ will return there (Matthew 24:30), then it is to this city that we should turn our eyes to see God at work. To watch the evening news as a family and analyze world events in view of God's sovereign plan for history is to help increase our family's faith. For the God who is moving all of the kings of the earth to fulfill His great purpose (Proverbs 21:1) is the same God who is moving our lives in conformity with His perfect will.

Prophecy Produces Spiritual Stability

The early church also embraced the study of prophecy because it provided spiritual stability in the midst of uncertain and troubled times. The apostle Paul wrote to the church at Thessalonica an entire epistle on prophecy so that they would "not be quickly shaken from [their] composure or be disturbed" and that "no one in any way [would] deceive [them]" (2 Thessalonians 2:2-3). In like manner, after writing to the Corinthians about the rapture of the church, Paul concluded: "Therefore, my beloved brethren, be steadfast, immovable" (1 Corinthians 15:58). Knowing what will happen in God's tomorrow allows us to live today without fear of the future.

This relationship between prophecy and practice is evident in the order of presentation revealed in many of the New Testament epistles. For example, in Paul's epistle to the Romans, the practical portion of the book (Romans 12–16) follows immediately after the prophetic (Romans 9–11). The sequence is not unintentional. In Romans 12:1 Paul writes: "I urge you therefore, brethren, by the mercies of God, to present your bodies a living and holy sacrifice, acceptable to God, which is your spiritual service of worship." He calls us to separate ourselves to God, which affects our relationships with those in our community (Romans 12:3-8), society (Romans 12:9-21), government (Romans 13:1-10), and church (Romans 14–15). Paul's use of "therefore" connects our practice to the "mercies of God," which is the theme of his prophetic discourse in chapters 9–11. It is because God once showed mercy to faithless Israel (Romans 9:6–10:21), has now mercifully brought faithless Gentiles to faith (Romans 9:24-26,30;11:12,30), and promises yet again to show mercy to faithless Israel (Romans

11:1-15,23-27,31), that we should be caught up in awe of God's gift of salvation and gratefully submit ourselves to our Savior. In addition, we see at the end of the prophetic section of Romans that prophecy produces praise (11:33-36).

The reasoning that Paul uses here is this: If God will be faithful to the people of His first choice—the Jews (Romans 11:28), He will also be faithful to those who were once hopeless strangers to the covenants of promise—the Gentiles (Ephesians 2:12-13). Without the pledge that God would once again show His mercy to Israel, the largely Gentile church would have no ground for assurance about their future. Prophecy, however, assures us that God will perform as promised (for both Jew and Gentile), giving the church spiritual stability for the present.

Prophecy Promotes Evangelism

One criticism against the study of Bible prophecy is that it is thought to hinder evangelism. Some people believe that students of prophecy are "too theological" to be evangelistic. Yet one of the most fervent evangelists in Christian history, D.L. Moody, once declared: "There is no such incentive to evangelism as premillennialism [one school of prophetic interpretation]." This is borne out by the fact that on the day the church was born the first evangelistic message spoken was largely prophetic in content (see Acts 2:16-36). Shortly thereafter, the apostle Peter called the Jewish nation (represented by Jews from inside and outside the Land who had come to Jerusalem for Pentecost) to repentance and faith in their Messiah based on the prophecies of the second coming and the millennial kingdom (Acts 3:18-26). Then there is the gospel presentation found in Hebrews 9:26-27, which is often used as an outline for evangelistic messages. Here it is stated that Christ came to sacrifice Himself (verse 26) for sinners who are appointed to death and judgment (verse 27). The presentation is climaxed by the warning that Christ is returning—not to die again for sinners, but to save those who are waiting for Him (verse 28). The call to have faith in Christ is made all the more urgent by these last words, for without warning the opportunity to trust the Savior may end and the Judge will appear. Our faith that Christ came long ago must be joined to our confidence that Christ will come again at any moment. This was the pattern of preaching in the early church and what motivated thousands to become Christians despite the awful cost of social ostracization and probable martyrdom.

Of course there may be some people whose quest for prophetic insight may cause them to neglect evangelism, but such people are likely to be unbalanced in other areas of their spiritual lives as well. To the contrary, Titus 2:13-14 says that it is those who are "looking for the blessed hope [the rapture] and the appearing of the glory of our great God and Savior, Christ Jesus [the Revelation] who are *zealous for good deeds* [which includes evangelism]" (verses 13-14, emphasis added). What good is it to be able to understand the seven heads described in Revelation 13:1 if we don't use our own head? Of what profit is it to discern the ten toes of Daniel 2:42-44; 7:24 if we don't move our own two feet? And what value is it to know about the great mouth that speaks lies (Daniel 7:8; Revelation 13:5), unless we open our own mouth and speak the truth? In every generation where prophecy has been *properly* proclaimed, the results have been a harvest of souls to the glory of God.

My own testimony fits this pattern. Raised in a denominational church that had long ago left behind evangelical preaching, I was in the ranks of unsaved Christendom—religious, but lost. During my high school years one of my teachers, a Christian who wanted others to know his Savior, took me to a small evangelical church to hear a series of Sunday evening expository messages on the book of Revelation. I had never in my life heard what the Bible said about the end times, but as a science fiction buff I was already enthralled in fantasies about the future. Week after week I listened to these amazing messages, and by the time the preacher had reached the fifteenth chapter of Revelation, God's Word had seized me. After hearing descriptions of the horrible future plagues that were to engulf all mankind and of the Antichrist, whose mark would doom the deceived, Revelation 15:4 posed a question that seemed directed to me in particular: "Who will not fear, O Lord, and glorify Thy name? For Thou alone art holy; for all the nations will come and worship before Thee, for Thy righteous acts have been revealed."

Looking at my life in light of this passage I became filled with fear over the consequences of my sins because I had not glorified God, who alone was holy and had revealed His righteousness to me by Christ's death in my place. What's more, the preceding chapters of Revelation revealed God's wrath to come upon sinners such as I, and I knew I was not prepared to face His coming judgment. So I trusted Christ in that instant, and just as instantaneously my fears were removed and I became a part of that company who presently worships before Him. It was prophecy that brought me to praise Him, and that has always been one of the purposes of prophecy. Scripture states that the Lord is coming to judge the earth in righteousness, and His seeming delay in doing so is to bring unbelievers to faith: "The Lord is not slow about His promise, as some count slowness, but is patient toward you, not wishing for any to perish but for all to come to repentance" (2 Peter 3:9). And Paul's prophecy of the post-rapture judgment of believers adds, "Therefore knowing the fear of the Lord, we persuade men" (2 Corinthians 5:11). Let us then who know the certainty of coming judgment use prophecy to persuade those who have yet to make a decision to follow Christ.

Prophecy Promises Spiritual Purity

One of the great deficiencies among professing Christians today is their failure to observe scriptural standards of purity. From churchgoing politicians whose moral behavior has disgraced some of the highest offices in the land to high-profile televangelists whose ethical antics have brought reproach to the name of Christ, the image of the American church worldwide has never suffered more. Perhaps one cause of this failure is the absence of prophetic teaching and preaching in today's church. Prophecy, which reminds us of what is to come, is to motivate us toward pure living. The apostle John underscored this fact by saying that when Christ appears, we shall be like Him: "Everyone who has this hope fixed on Him purifies himself, just as He is pure" (1 John 3:3). When we are translated and transformed at the rapture, we will be holy like Christ the Holy One. Until that day, however, the prophetic promise ("hope") of holiness is to have a refining and purifying effect in us.

I like to illustrate this by sharing how I motivate my own children to correct behavior while I am away from home. When I travel I help my wife maintain family order by promising my children a special present upon my return if they keep their rooms clean. Because they are not always privy to the exact time of my return, they have to keep their rooms as clean as possible in case I arrive "unexpectedly" and they lose their reward. When the apostle John talks about prophecy as a purifying hope in 1 John 3:3, he reminds us that we are "children of God" (1 John 3:1-2). His prophecy of the Lord's return is to motivate us to "keep our rooms clean" until the day we are rewarded at the judgment seat of Christ (2 Corinthians 5:10) for both our work (1 Corinthians 3:13-14) and our waiting for Him (2 Timothy 4:8).

Prophecy and personal purity are also mentioned together in Titus chapter 2. In verse 13 we find a prophecy about "the blessed hope," which is sandwiched between verses 12 and 14, which deal with the imperative of purity. In fact, verse 12 is tied to verse 13 in such a way as to connect prophecy and purity: "instructing us to deny ungodliness and worldly desires and to *live* sensibly, righteously and godly in the present age, *looking* for the blessed hope and the appearing of the glory of our great God and Savior, Christ Jesus" (emphasis added). How are we to live? Verse 13 provides the answer: We are to live . . . looking!

Titus 2:12-14 further exhorts us to live godly in an ungodly age. How this can be accomplished is described to us in a similar sounding text in Romans 13:11-14. The opening and closing verses of this passage contain the clues: "it is already the hour for you to *awaken* from sleep," and "*put on* the Lord Jesus Christ, and make no provision for the flesh." These exhortations remind me of yet another illustration from my family. When we take a car trip, I have noticed that as we near the end of our journey all five women (my wife and four daughters) wake up and grab for the mirrors. Out come brushes, hairspray, and makeup. Each is getting ready to emerge from our cramped car and meet her family and friends looking her best. Similarly, all of us who are believers are on a journey in the program of God. And according to prophecy, we are far down the road and about to end our trip and meet our Maker. Knowing this, what are we to do? We are to *wake up* and *makeup!* That is what Romans 13:11-14 tells us, and it is sage advice if we are to live responsibly in the light of Christ coming. Such a perspective compels us to pure living because it focuses our faith on Christ, who is pure. In a day like ours where purity is at a premium, that which produces it—prophecy—is surely practical!

Prophecy Procures Social Responsibility

One misunderstanding some people have with regard to prophecy is that they think it produces pessimism: They believe it is discouraging for Christians to hear that we live in an age of increasing apostasy; that a global government is inevitable; that the Antichrist is coming; that the world will fall into deception and follow the Antichrist; that the Tribulation is ahead with its plagues, pestilence, and cosmic catastrophes; and that finally Armageddon will follow. Add to this the tiresome warning that time is short, and the fear is that some Christians will begin to wonder if it's even worthwhile to be involved in social redemption, missionary outreach, various relief organizations, or even politics. However, the proper attitude for us to adopt is not, "The time is so short and the world so corrupt that I *can't do anything!*" but, "The time is so short and the world so corrupt that I *must do something!*"

It's this latter attitude—accepting the dire predictions of prophecy for our secular society while being committed to working for its redemption—that we find in Romans 13:11-14. Verse 11, which begins: *"This do, knowing the time . . .* for now salvation is nearer to us than when we believed" (verse 11), appears in the context of the Christian's responsibility to human government (Romans 13:1-14). It reveals that what we are supposed to do we must do, and even more so in view of the lateness of the hour. While we should remember that the church's commission is to proclaim the gospel and not to govern the political order, still, if we are not involved in reclaiming our society for Christ, it is not the fault of prophecy, but of our priorities. Prophecy is designed to motivate us to work with a greater urgency and commitment during what is left of the day, knowing that night is coming—when man's work is done and he will be judged.

Prophecy Presents a Prepared Student of Scripture

To be a student of the prophetic scriptures is to be a student of the Scriptures in their entirety. In order to comprehend prophetic passages, we must have a good grasp of the Old Testament and its relationship to the New Testament. For example, to properly interpret the book of Revelation we must take into consideration the Old Testament books of Daniel, Isaiah, Ezekiel, Jeremiah, Zechariah, and Zephaniah. It is necessary to have an understanding of God's overall prophetic plan as well as the particulars that make up God's program. This requires thorough study of the Bible as well as interpretive principles, a process described in 1 Peter 1:10-11, where we learn that even the prophets themselves had to study their own prophecies:

> As to this salvation, the prophets who prophesied of
> the grace that would come to you made careful

> search and inquiry, seeking to know what person or
> time the Spirit of Christ within them was indicating
> as He predicted the sufferings of Christ and the glo-
> ries to follow.

Because prophecy originates in the mind of God, the prophets, like the rest of us, had to make "careful search and inquiry." God revealed to Paul the prophecy that eventually the church would be raptured—an event not revealed in the Old Testament, and Peter confessed that Paul's prophetic statements were "hard to understand" (2 Peter 3:16). That prophecy is sometimes difficult to understand is one excuse people use to neglect their study of it. However, rather than be dissuaded, we are simply to work harder at understanding prophecy (see 2 Timothy 2:15). It is vital that we do so, for immediately after acknowledging prophecy to be "hard to understand," he warns about those who have a wrong or incomplete understanding: "which the untaught and unstable distort, as they do also the rest of the Scriptures, to their own destruction." Peter implies that if people can misunderstand and distort prophecy, imagine what they can end up doing to the rest of the Bible!

If we want to preserve the integrity of Scripture and properly defend the faith against the attacks of the untaught, we ourselves must be taught (and teach) prophecy. As a result, we equip ourselves to handle the Scriptures correctly and carry out our confession of faith, which has as its climax the coming of Christ (1 Timothy 6:13-14).

Prophecy Provokes a Sincere Love for Christ

Prophecy was not given by God in order for us to merely produce charts or provoke controversy. Prophecy was not given primarily to produce anticipation for the coming of Christ, but to provoke in us a love for Christ, who is coming. As a heavenly angel professed to the apostle John after the latter received his revelation of the second coming, "the testimony of Jesus is the spirit of prophecy" (Revelation 19:10). We could not say it any plainer: Prophecy is about Jesus. Therefore, the more we involve ourselves with prophecy, the deeper our relationship will become with Christ.

The early church was given two mandates as a result of their turning to God: They were "to serve a living and true God, and to wait for His Son from heaven, whom He raised from the dead" (1 Thessalonians 1:9-10). In the Bible, the resurrection is tied to the second coming because each event represents the last and next appearances of Jesus to those who loved Him on either side of the church age (see Acts 1:11). After the resurrection, Jesus said to those disciples who had seen Him, "Because you have seen Me, have you believed? Blessed are they who did not see, and yet believed" (John 20:29). That blessing is directed to each of us who live between the resurrection and the rapture. It has been our *responsibility* to believe that which we have not seen; it will be our *reward* to see that which we have believed.

According to Peter, because prophecy assures us that our faith will be fulfilled at the revelation of Christ, we are provoked to an overflowing love for Christ: "Though you have not seen Him, you love Him, and though you do not see Him now, but believe in Him, you greatly rejoice with joy inexpressible and full of glory" (1 Peter 1:8). This truth was made real to me during a visit in the home of a friend. My eyes were drawn to a beautiful picture frame standing on a coffee table. From where I sat, I could not see the front of the frame, so I waited for an opportunity to move and get a better look. Based on the beautiful quality of the frame I expected it held a favorite family portrait or treasured old photo. But to my surprise, there was no picture at all! Then I noticed a small inscription at the bottom of the frame: "Though you have not seen Him, you love Him." That simple testimony to the truth of 1 Peter 1:8 impressed me. The apostle Paul must have also been impressed by the same truth, for in some of the very last words he ever wrote he spoke of the reward that would be granted to "all who have loved His appearing" (2 Timothy 4:8).

We cannot very well condemn those who, because of neglect or ignorance of the prophecies of Christ's first appearing, "did not recognize the time of [their] visitation" (Luke 19:44) if we are no better equipped to recognize the time of Christ's second coming. We should not simply *look* for that appearing, but look with eagerness and love, for Christ's return will bring us together with the One we love. And if prophecy provokes us to nothing more than a sincere love for the Savior, then its purpose has been proven to be immensely practical.

Jerusalem in Prophecy

Now that we have seen the practicality of prophecy, let's look at the specific prophecies related to Jerusalem, the city of the Great King, Jesus. It was the city of His choice, it was the first place He visited after His birth, and it was the site in which He, as a prophet, was destined to die (Luke 13:33). And, according to the heavenly prophecy spoken to His disciples at His ascension, it is the place to which He will return in glory (Acts 1:11; see also Isaiah 59:20; Zechariah 14:4). Is prophecy practical? Yes, and more so, for to understand prophecies related to Jerusalem is to understand the plan and program of God. Come, join with me as we look at *Jerusalem in Prophecy!*

The Practical Purpose of Prophecy

Practical Purpose	Biblical Reference
Prophecy is a part of Scripture	2 Peter 1:19-21; Revelation 1:3; 22:18-19
Prophecy is a proof of the truthfulness of Scripture	Isaiah 41:21-29; 42:9; 44:7-8,24–45:7; 46:8-11; 2 Peter 3:4-13
Prophecy presents a proper view of our age	1 Corinthians 7:31; Ephesians 5:16; 1 Timothy 4:1; 2 Timothy 3:1-5; 1 John 2:18
Prophecy provides comfort in our sorrow	1 Thessalonians 4:13-18; 1 Peter 1:7-9
Prophecy proves God is in control	Daniel 9:27; Acts 4:25-29; Philippians 1:6
Prophecy produces spiritual stability	1 Corinthians 15:58; 2 Thessalonians 2:2
Prophecy promotes evangelism	Acts 3:18-24; Hebrews 9:26-27
Prophecy promises spiritual purity	Philippians 4:5; 1 Thessalonians 3:13; 5:23; Titus 2:12-13; James 5:7-9; 1 Peter 1:3-7; 2 Peter 3:11-12; 1 John 3:3
Prophecy procures moral and social responsibility	Romans 13:11-14; 1 Thessalonians 5:6-11
Prophecy presents a prepared student of Scripture	2 Timothy 2:15; 1 Peter 1:10-12; 2 Peter 3:16
Prophecy provokes a sincere love for Christ	2 Timothy 4:8; 1 Peter 1:8

Thus says the Lord GOD,
"This is Jerusalem; I have set her
at the center of the nations,
with lands around her."

—Ezekiel 5:5

3

JERUSALEM AT THE CENTER:

The Recipient of Worldwide Attention

Jerusalem, the center of world interest centuries after other capitals have disappeared; Jerusalem, destined to be completely renewed after Washington, Moscow, Paris and London have joined the other centers of power in the cemetery for dead bodies; Jerusalem, future site of the "holy city, the new Jerusalem, coming down from heaven."[1]

—Arnold Olson

It was the evening of the last day of February. Turning on my car radio, I heard a broadcaster giving the usual rundown of the weather for several local cities. Then he added: "And the weather in Jerusalem today was sunny with a high of 65 and a low of 46." Hearing a report about Jerusalem's weather would not have been odd had this been a radio station in Israel, but it was not. The station was in Texas. It might not have even seemed odd for Texas had the station been Jewish, but it was not. It was Christian. What impressed me then, as it has countless times before, is that a city that most people in the world will never visit occupies such a place in our interests that even its daily weather is considered news!

Jerusalem. In the United States alone there are more than 30 cities which bear its name in one form or another.[2] Say the word *Jerusalem* to almost anyone—even in our geographically illiterate American culture—and it is instantly recognized. Whether in Sunday school lessons or on the evening news, the name *Jerusalem* regularly appears.

A Special Significance

Down through history Jerusalem has been regarded with a special significance not reserved for any other city. The Jewish Babylonian Talmud boasts that: "of the ten measures of beauty that came down to the world, Jerusalem took nine" (*Kidushin* 49b), and that "whoever has not seen Jerusalem in its splendor has never seen a beautiful city" (*Succah* 51b). A Christian hymn confesses: "No people blessed as thine, no city like Jerusalem." And an Islamic saying declares: "One prayer in Jerusalem is worth 40,000 elsewhere." To Jews it is the eternal capital of Israel, to Christians it is the city of the Great King, to Moslems it is *Al-Quds* ("the Holy"). Medieval cartographers pictured Jerusalem as the center of the then-known world based on Ezekiel 5:5: "This is Jerusalem; I have set her at the center of the nations, with lands around her" (see photo 1). A similar orientation is found in the New Testament, with Jerusalem at the geographical (as well as spiritual) hub of the gospel outreach to the world: "You shall be My witnesses both in Jerusalem, and in all Judea and Samaria, and even to the remotest part of the earth" (Acts 1:8). The Babylonian Talmud made it explicit: "Israel lies at the center of the earth, and Jerusalem lies at the center of the Land of Israel" (Tanhuma 106).

The novelist Mark Twain marveled at the affection shown to the city when he visited it during the 1860s—one of the more bleak periods in the city's history: "We toiled up one more hill, and every pilgrim and every sinner swung his hat on high! Jerusalem! . . . [Yet] Jerusalem is mournful and dreary and lifeless."[3] This feeling of awe and euphoria over the city today has a name: "Jerusalem Syndrome." That is the medical or psychological diagnosis applied to tourists and pilgrims who are overcome by the significance of the city and exhibit extreme behavioral traits in response.

No people, however, have a greater regard and sense of appreciation for the centrality of the city than the Jews. As Chaim Hazaz observes:

> Jerusalem was the stuff of our growing up in our homes, from the cradle on, accompanying us all along our way through life . . . so close, so intimate, heart of our heart, an integral part of both our sacred and secular time, the essence of our study, the very substance of our thrice-daily prayers, the culminating benediction over our meals, the stuff of all our emotions, feelings and longings. Jerusalem of the Prophets, Jerusalem the destroyed, Jerusalem of the Time-to-Come. There is not a single city in the world . . . not Athens, not Rome, nor any other city . . . on which has been lavished so

> much love, so much poesy, so much heavenly rhet-
> oric, so many so-human words of the Living God.
> And there is not another city in the world that has
> been so elegized as Jerusalem.[4]

There can be no doubt that for multitudes, Jerusalem is at the center of faith and fascination. As a city "at the center," and a sacred city as well, Jerusalem is desired, adored, prayed for, and argued over by a disproportionate number of the world's population. It has played a role in history that is out of proportion to its geographic location, economic importance, political significance, or military clout.

Like fragments of metal drawn to a magnet, so the nations of the world have been attracted to Jerusalem. This is especially true in our present day. Threats to global unity, international relations, and political stability are all blamed on Jerusalem, and the city occupies the foreign policy agendas of governments the world over. Why this attraction? In the ancient world, Israel's geographical location at the crossroads of Europe, Asia, and Africa was of strategic importance. But today, this is no longer true in our world of supersonic aircraft and internet communication. Furthermore, Jerusalem's economic situation is poor even by comparison with other Israeli cities. A survey taken in 1998 revealed extensive migration from the city; only 4 percent of the large immigrant population that arrived in the city in 1990 still remains.[5] The primary reason for this is the lower economic standards in the city (lack of housing, jobs, etc.).

The center of Israeli government is at Jerusalem, with the Knesset and Supreme Court on Mt. Herzl. Israeli politics, which are complex and confusing, are rife with corruption and rival factions. The world has little respect for the Israeli government, which has traded its hard-won land to its enemies time and again with no guarantees of peace or protection. Neither can Israeli military might, though impressive in past successes against overwhelming odds, make her attractive to nations whose superpower status commands arsenals far superior. Israel's army is made up of national reserves whose sole interest is national security, not imperialistic conquests. Thus no nation feels any threat from Israel's military.

So why does tiny Jerusalem command so much of the world's attention? The answer goes beyond natural causes—it is supernatural. Whether perceived or not, Jerusalem is at center stage because of God's prophetic plan for the future. The nations of the world will eventually be gathered together against Jerusalem for an end-time battle as predicted in Scripture (as we'll see later in chapters 7 and 8).

There can be no question today that Jerusalem is at the center of controversy as the stage is being set for the final conflict. The now-failed "peace process" between Israel and its neighbors was unsuccessful because the issue of who would control Jerusalem could not be broached. When Israel signed a peace accord with Jordan, King Hussein of Jordan made the proviso that "Jerusalem is the essence of peace between us."[6] For the Islamic terrorist organization Hamas, the issue has been "Jerusalem first."[7] Yitzhak Rabin, who succeeded in peace negotiations with Jordan and the Palestinians, never considered Jerusalem negotiable. He said: "Jerusalem is a different issue for us. For us it's *the* symbol . . . Jerusalem is a living city, but also the heart, the soul of the Jewish people and the state of Israel."[8] Jerusalem's mayor, Ehud Olmert, argues for the unity of the city on these grounds when he states, "Now we are in Jerusalem, never to be divided, never to split again, never to pull out from the most ancient and sacred place in Jewish history. Jerusalem is a commitment to our history. Jerusalem is also a commitment to our future. Jerusalem is the symbol of Jewish resurrection. And as such it will survive forever in the hearts, in the minds, in the dreams, and in the actual life of the Jewish people."[9]

Rabin's successor, Benjamin Netanyahu, was elected into the Prime Minister's office primarily on his commitment to never negotiate on Jerusalem. He stated, "If we give in on Jerusalem, then we give in on everything. If we stand on Jerusalem, we'll be able to achieve the peace that we've always dreamed of."[10]

A Scriptural Focus

Why does Jerusalem have such a central place in the plan of God? Why has it always been at the center of the struggle for peace in the Middle East? Why does it still have a place in biblical prophecy even 2,000 years after Jesus predicted its destruction by the Romans in A.D. 70? The answer to these questions is as simple as one, two, three: 1) God loves her; 2) Satan hates her; and 3) Christ will not come without her. What God loves, Satan hates and seeks to destroy. What Satan attempts to destroy, Christ came to redeem and is coming to restore. Let's look now at the evidence that establishes Jerusalem's centrality in God's plan for the past, the present, and the future.

God Loves Jerusalem

The psalmist declared in his praise of Jerusalem, "The LORD loves the gates of Zion more than all the other dwelling places of Jacob" (Psalm 87:2). Why should God have a greater love for Jerusalem than the rest of Israel? Before we answer this, let's remember that the love of God is not a capricious emotion based on received affection, but a steadfast determination of the will toward the well-being of another. When God's love is directed toward a chosen people in a chosen place, like Jerusalem, its demonstration must be evaluated from the perspective of both the past and the present in order to understand the nature of it.

God's Love in the Past

The apostle Paul states plainly that the Jewish people, and especially the city of Jerusalem, have received particular blessings from God: "Theirs is the adoption as sons; theirs the divine glory, the covenants, the receiving of the law, the temple worship and the promises. Theirs are the patriarchs, and from them is traced the human ancestry of Christ" (Romans 9:3-5 NIV). Concerning God's love of Jerusalem the Old Testament proclaims: "He . . . rejected the tent of Joseph, and did not choose the tribe of Ephraim, but chose the tribe of Judah, Mount Zion [Jerusalem] which He loved. . . . The LORD loves the gates of Zion more than all the other dwelling places of Jacob" (Psalms 78:67-68; 87:2). Why should God set His love on Jerusalem above others? The answer may be found in Deuteronomy 7:6-8:

> The LORD your God has chosen you to be a people for His own possession out of all the peoples who are on the face of the earth. The LORD did not set His love on you nor choose you because you were more in number than any of the peoples, for you were the fewest of all peoples, but because the LORD loved you.

God's love is a *sovereign* love—it acts for the good of the one loved even if that one is no good. In other words, God did not love the people of Israel because of what they were, but because of what He is—not because of what they had done, but because of what He would do. This sovereign love chose Israel and Jerusalem for a purpose within His plan irrespective of their ability to perform it. This is in accord with God's overarching purpose to rightly receive and reveal glory (see Psalm 29:2; Isaiah 40:5; Romans 11:36; Ephesians 1:6-18).

We may find it helpful to consider an analogy from sports. In sports we do not give glory to the coach who picks a first-draft team and then goes on to win the championship; rather, our praise goes to the team. But, if a coach gets last pick and takes the worst players and trains them to be the best, then their win is to his glory (see 1 Corinthians 1:26-29). For the same reason God chose a desert site in a pagan land as the place where His name would dwell (2 Kings 21:4), His glory would shine forth (Jeremiah 3:17), and to which He would draw all the world in worship (Isaiah 2:2-3). While this select relationship gave Jerusalem a greater *access* to God (the Temple), it also gave it a greater *accountability* to God (the covenant—see Luke 12:48). Our standards are applied more strictly to those whom we love than to strangers. For example, if our children were to hold a party at our house without permission, we would discipline our kids, but not the neighbors' kids. It's because of God's special relationship with Jerusalem that the city has received such special promises and such severe punishments. Both are an evidence of God's love and are the means to create a vessel that would more greatly glorify God (see Deuteronomy 8:16-17).

God's Love in the Present

While most people will agree that God chose and loved Jerusalem in the past, many of them would say that this is no longer true in the present. How could God continue to love the people and the place where His Word was rejected, His Son scorned and crucified, and His church opposed and persecuted? From this standpoint, all of the promises made to Israel lost their validity when Israel rejected Christ, who was to fulfill those promises. Fortunately, God did not leave us to depend upon our own feelings in this matter, but has revealed His unconditional care based on His unchanging character. In Romans 11:28-29 Paul points out the enduring nature of God's promise to Zion: "From the standpoint of the gospel they [the unbelieving Jews] are enemies for your sake, but from the standpoint of God's choice, they are beloved for the sake of the fathers; for the gifts and calling of God are irrevocable." While the Jewish rejection of Jesus as Messiah has brought resistance to the gospel of the Messiah, God's promise to the patriarchs is unfulfilled and not forgotten (Genesis 12:2-3; 17:7-8). God will always be true to Himself.

Moses affirmed the same truth when he stood in the gap between Israel's God and ungodly Israel (Exodus 32:13). If we claim that God's promises to Israel have been abrogated, then we end up making God's mercy provisional—limiting His love to those who love Him, and His faithfulness to those who remain faithful. But Romans 11 argues just the opposite. The disobedient Gentiles were not chosen nor as loved by God as Israel, nor did they as nations respond to the light available through Israel, but attacked it. Yet they were still shown mercy (Romans 11:30). Isaiah prophesied that a day would come when even Israel's greatest enemies, Egypt and Assyria, would be called "My people" and "the work of My hands," and worship the Lord (Isaiah 19:25). If God has shown such mercy to Gentiles who were less loved, will He not restore His mercy to Israel, who He still calls beloved? This, in fact, is just what the text says will happen—mercy will again be shown to disobedient Israel (verse 31). Therefore, we must conclude that

God has chosen His love, and will love His choice. Whether we Christians like it or not, we must accept our present role in relation to Israel's present rejection and future return (Romans 11:25-27). We must expect and endure hostility as we seek to persuade Jews of their Messiah, while at the same time affirming God's love for them as a chosen people.

Just as God was faithful in the past to bring the Savior to His City (Jerusalem), so He will be faithful in the future to bring Him back again. This plan requires that Jerusalem remain and be restored to a greater glory than it has previously known. Thus we must avoid getting caught up in "the controversy of Zion" (Isaiah 34:8) while at the same time be constantly praying for the city and God's plan to bring peace and prosperity to it (Psalm 122:6-9).

Satan's Hate for Jerusalem

Because the world opposes God's plan for Jerusalem, we can be sure that the controversies over the city will continue. In fact, the "controversy of Zion" goes back to the beginning of the world itself. Satan's attempts to attack Jerusalem's Messiah have been prophesied from as early as Satan's invasion of the Garden of Eden (Genesis 3:15). From that time forward Satan is seen as the adversary of Jerusalem.

Satan as the Adversary of Jerusalem

Satan is a Hebrew word that means "adversary." By nature, Satan is the opponent of God and all things dear to Him. Because Jerusalem is God's chosen place for the fulfillment of His Messianic program for redemption, restoration, and rule, Jerusalem has been opposed by Satan since its earliest mention in Scripture. In Genesis 22:14-18, it was prophesied that a Redeemer would come to Mount Moriah, and that He would come from Abraham's seed. Satan's response was to attack the descendants of Abraham by attempting to corrupt the 12 tribes of Israel and plunder the path that led to Jerusalem (Genesis 37:20; 38:1-10). But God raised up an intermediate savior for the Savior's seed by the name of Joseph (Genesis 50:20). Joseph, in turn, prophesied that Israel would return to the Promised Land (Genesis 50:24), and his bones preserved that prophecy for 430 years and saw its fulfillment (Genesis 50:25; Exodus 13:19; Joshua 24:32).

Satan as the Attacker of Jerusalem

Satan is not only an adversary of Jerusalem, but an attacker. While Joseph's brethren waited for his prophecy to come to pass, Satan—through Pharaoh—attacked the Jewish remnant resident in Egypt (Exodus 1:8,22). Once again God sent a savior (Moses) with a prophecy that God's people would one day be planted in Jerusalem (Exodus 15:17-18). When God raised up David to fulfill Moses' prophecy (2 Samuel 5:7-12), God also gave him a prophecy for Jerusalem that his seed would fulfill (2 Samuel 7:10-16): an eternal descendant on an eternal throne (the Messiah). So Satan, in an effort to disrupt David's dynasty and bring down Jerusalem, incited David to sin by counting the military men of Israel. The text that records this pivotal point in Jerusalem's history is 1 Chronicles 21:1-30 (see also 2 Samuel 24:1-25). There, we read that "Satan stood up against Israel and moved David to number Israel" (1 Chronicles 21:1). Satan knew that taking a census of David's military was an offense to God because it exhibited a reliance upon human strength (numbers) and could have influenced the Israelites to trust in themselves rather than God (verses 2-4; 2 Samuel 24:3-4). As a result, "God sent an angel to Jerusalem to destroy it" (verse 15; 2 Samuel 24:15). But God's plan had already anticipated this attack of Satan (2 Samuel 24:1a), and brought about through it the purchase of the site for the Temple on Mount Moriah (1 Chronicles 21:18-26; 2 Samuel 24:18-25). This incident reveals that throughout history Satan and men's sinful attempts to destroy the city have only served to advance God's program for it.

Though Satan's attacks continue today through those who desire to remove the Jewish presence from Jerusalem, change its capital status, or redivide the city, God will continue to protect and defend Jerusalem for His name's sake (Isaiah 37:35). During the Tribulation period Satan will launch his final assault against Jerusalem, defiling the Temple Mount (Matthew 24:15; 2 Thessalonians 2:4; Revelation 11:1-2) and bringing the armies of Antichrist against Jerusalem at Armageddon (Zechariah 12:2-9; 14:1-5). This final attack will be met by God's final victory over Satan at the Second Advent of Christ (Revelation 19:19-20; 20:1-3), and, as before, will move the city forward in God's purposes to fulfill its glorious destiny.

Christ Will Not Come Without Jerusalem

In light of what we have just seen concerning the city, it is evident that the Second Advent of Christ cannot take place without Jerusalem. The New Testament declares that "Christ has become a servant to the circumcision [Jewish people] on behalf of the truth of God to confirm the promises given to the fathers" (Romans 15:8). Christ took upon Himself not just flesh, but circumcised flesh, in order to fulfill the prophecies made to the Jewish people. Not only is

Jerusalem indispensable because the first and second comings take place in the city, but also because Christ's return will directly fulfill specific prophecies concerning Jerusalem's future.

Christ Will Come to Save Jerusalem

In Matthew 24:15-21, we read about Satan's future attack on the Jewish people, which will take place during the Tribulation and begin in Jerusalem. There are many Christians today who interpret Matthew 24 as having been fulfilled at some point in past history. For them Jerusalem has lost any future significance; it has relevance only for historical or archaeological studies of the past. The problem for people who hold this view is this: Why does this section of the Olivet Discourse, which climaxes with the second coming of Christ (verses 30-31), focus on Jerusalem? The answer is that Christ will return there in the future. This is in harmony with other texts in the Old and New Testaments which also speak of Christ's return to Jerusalem (which we'll study more in chapter 9 of this book). Christ's purpose, according to these texts, is to save the city and the Jewish people, who will be brought to recognize the Deliverer from Zion as the Messiah and repent over Him in faith (Isaiah 59:20-21; Zechariah 12:10-14; 14:3-11; Matthew 24:30; Romans 11:26-27). As the Savior who also loves Jerusalem, He could not complete His saving purpose if it were not delivered for the future He has planned for it.

Christ Will Come to Sanctify Jerusalem

The salvation Christ will bring to the remnant of Israel will be complemented by a sanctification of the entire city of Jerusalem. Jerusalem will be set apart (sanctified) to serve as the center for the world's worship of the reigning Messiah. The prophet Jeremiah portrayed future Jerusalem as "the Throne of the LORD" (Jeremiah 3:17). Ezekiel saw it as the place where God's glory will return and remain (Ezekiel 43:5-7). Zechariah said that the city will become so dedicated to the Lord that even the common cooking pots in Jerusalemite homes will be as holy as those used in the Temple's ceremonial services (Zechariah 14:20-21). Thus Jerusalem—betrayed by its people, defiled by the nations, and attacked by Antichrist—will become what God intended it to be when Christ comes to deliver and rededicate the city.

A Certain Destiny

Jerusalem is the city at the center. It is at the center of mankind's hopes and God's purposes. God loves it, Satan hates it, Jesus wept over it, the Holy Spirit descended in it, the nations are drawn to it, and Christ will return and reign in it. Indeed the destiny of the world is tied to the future of Jerusalem. However, before we can see where God will take Jerusalem tomorrow, we need to first see where He has taken it until today. That's what we'll do next, with a look at how Jerusalem has occupied a place in God's prophetic program in the past and present in preparation for the future.

Glorious things are spoken of you,
O city of God. . . . And the Most
High Himself will establish her.

Psalm 87:3, 5

4

JERUSALEM'S PLACE IN PROPHECY:

A Central Theme in Scripture

In our time, men have stepped on the moon seeking new Jerusalems in foreign galaxies, but so far the old Jerusalem has not been replaced. She retains an extraordinary hold over the imagination, generating for three hostile faiths, in perfectly interchangeable phrases, the fear as well as the hope of Apocalypse.[1]

—Amos Elon

When we consider Jerusalem's place in prophecy, one of the most obvious facts of the prophetic record is that no matter where we start or end, Jerusalem is there. Starting at the beginning 3,000 years ago, if you were to take the winding road that began at the shores of the Mediterranean Sea and go some 30 miles east, you would have eventually come to a cluster of unimpressive hills and a Canaanite city known as *Salem* (see Psalm 76:2). *Salem* was the Canaanite name for the Babylonian god *Shalmanu*, the god of evening twilight. The more familiar name *Jerusalem* (Babylonian *Urusalim*) means "the foundation of the god Salem." Knowing this connection, one would have thought it doubtful that it would have ever been chosen by God to occupy one of the most sacred places in His plan for the ages.

Today, traveling the ascent to Jerusalem on that same road, your entrance to the city would weigh heavily with 3,000 years of accumulated history. The remains of David's City, the Herodian Temple Mount, the Western (Wailing) Wall, and the walls of the Old City—wearing the dress of Hasmoneans, Jews, Christians, Romans, Crusaders, Turks, and Arabs—all supply an awesome sense of antiquity. And if you know the prophecies related to Jerusalem you will sense something much greater, for its place in the past will be nothing in comparison to what lies ahead in the future.

A Comprehensive Survey

Jerusalem's Place in the Bible

Take Jerusalem out of the Bible, and it will immediately become apparent that something major is missing. Moody Bible Institute professor Harold Foos, who wrote a doctoral dissertation about the prophecies concerning Jerusalem, says,

> Jerusalem, by that name alone, is expressly named over eight hundred times in the biblical record, besides its many occurrences under various other names. Under one name or another Jerusalem appears in about two-thirds of the books of the Old

and almost one-half of the books of the New Testament. [2]

Researchers have found 660 verses in the Old Testament and 142 in the New Testament that speak of the city. Of these, 465 in the Old Testament and 24 in the New refer to prophecies about Jerusalem subsequent to the time of their utterances. In addition, we can include the thousands of passages that have Jerusalem as their context and unfold the events that have taken place or will take place there in the future.

In the Bible, Jerusalem occupies a strategic position with respect to two major prophetic periods: "the times of the Gentiles" (Luke 21:24) and the seventy weeks of Daniel (Daniel 9:24-27). In the case of "the times of the Gentiles," the city prophetically marks the beginning and ending of this period, which stretches from the Babylonian destruction (586 B.C.) to Christ's second advent. As for Daniel's "seventy weeks" prophecy, Jerusalem marks both the beginning and ending of this period as well as the time between the sixty-ninth and seventieth week.

Jerusalem's Place in Redemptive History

Jerusalem is at the heart of redemptive history. In fact, we could say that God's redemptive plan could not have been revealed apart from its presence. God, as a God of order (1 Corinthians 14:40), works out His purposes from beginning to end, setting forth a discernable pattern that can be followed through the Scriptures and history. This order of redemptive revelation was evident in the first appearing of the Redeemer, and it will also characterize His final appearing. If we trace the progressive unfolding of the redemptive plan we will find that both advents have their climax in Jerusalem.

Jerusalem was indispensable to the preparation of Christ's first coming. Though spiritual defection led to the city's destruction and the captivity in Babylon some 2,500 years ago, Jerusalem was later restored from ruin (Isaiah 52:7-12) to fulfill her role when the Messiah came to earth (Galatians 4:4-5). Following this pattern, Jerusalem's subsequent destruction in A.D. 70 because they "did not recognize the time of [their] visitation" (Luke 19:44) has been reversed and the city is now being readied for the events associated with the second advent. Even Jerusalem's status as a place that will be "trampled under foot by the Gentiles until the times of the Gentiles be fulfilled" (Luke 21:24) is part of the end-time drama, which will climax at the end of the Tribulation with Christ's coming (Matthew 24:21-31).

Jerusalem's Place with Greater Israel

Although Jerusalem is an indispensable part of God's prophetic program, its destiny is linked with that of greater Israel. That's why we don't see any prophecies concerning Jerusalem being fulfilled during the church age. However, as the church age draws near to an end and Israel's end-time drama begins, we should see various elements related to Jerusalem's future falling into place to herald the beginning of the seventieth week of Daniel. Israel's return to Jerusalem in 1967, the annexation of East Jerusalem, and the unified city's declaration to be Israel's capital in 1980 are all believed to be part of the stage-setting taking place in preparation for the fulfillment of prophecy during the Tribulation. According to Scripture, during the Tribulation Jerusalem will be a Jewish city, the Jewish people will have control of East Jerusalem, and the Temple will be rebuilt (see Daniel 9:26; Matthew 24:15; 2 Thessalonians 2:4; Revelation 11:1-2).

Before we look at the specific details of what will happen during that time, we need to see where God has taken Israel up to today.

Jerusalem's Key Points in History

For 1,000 years before God revealed that Jerusalem was His chosen city, Jerusalem was under Canaanite rule. Even after God's purpose for the site of Mount Moriah was made clear, the city continued to remain under Canaanite control for another 1,000 years. This past history stands in sharp contrast to God's future plans: "There will no longer be a Canaanite in the house of the LORD of hosts in that day" (Zechariah 14:21).

Though the city was in Canaanite hands for many centuries, it is clear that from the very beginning the city belonged to God. When the Lord first gave Abraham the boundaries of the Promised Land, they included Jerusalem (Genesis 13:14-17). These boundaries were reaffirmed with greater specificity in Genesis 15:18-21 when God gave to Abraham the land of the Jebusites (the Canaanites who lived in Jerusalem—see the end of verse 21).

When Abraham later met a representative from the city he found that God was already there, for the representative was the Canaanite king Melchizedek, who was "a priest of God Most High" (Genesis 14:18). Think of the prophetic associations here for Jerusalem's future role with the Messiah: *Melchizedek* means, in Hebrew, "King of Righteousness," and this historic king of Jerusalem came to present a gift to the forefather of all Israel. This association was not lost on later Jewish writers in the Old Testament (see Psalm 110:4), nor in the New

Prophetic Events Concerning Jerusalem in Jewish Eschatology

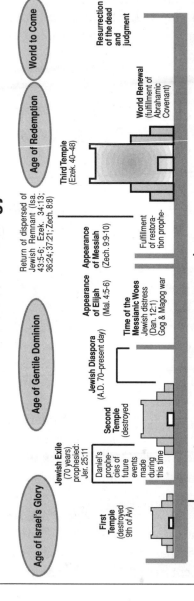

Age of Israel's Glory

Age of Gentile Dominion

Age of Redemption

World to Come

First Temple (destroyed 9th of Av)

Jewish Exile (70 years) prophesied: Jer. 25:11

Daniel's prophecies of future events made during this time

Second Temple (destroyed

Jewish Diaspora (A.D. 70–present day)

Time of the Messianic Woes (Dan. 12:1) Jewish distress Gog & Magog war

Appearance of Elijah (Mal. 4:5-6)

Appearance of Messiah (Zech. 9:9-10)

Fulfillment of restoration prophe-

Return of dispersed of Jewish Remnant (Isa. 43:5-6; Ezek. 34:13; 36:24; 37:21; Zech. 8:8)

Destruction of Gentile nations that come against God and His Messiah (Psa. 2; 110)

Third Temple (Ezek. 40–48)

World Renewal (fulfillment of Abrahamic Covenant)

Resurrection of the dead and judgment

Return from captivity after 70 years fulfillment of prophecies of Jer. 25:11 and Dan. 9:25. Rebuilding of Temple under leadership of Zerubbabel and Ezra fulfillment of prophecies of Jer. 27:19-22 and Isa. 41:25; 45:1-3; 52:11-12.

Prophecies of Israel's national ruin, symbolized by the desecration and destruction of the First Temple, are balanced by prophecies of Israel's national restoration (Jer. 31-33) and the rebuilding of a Restoration Temple that supercedes the former (Ezek. 37:27-28; 40-48; Hag. 2:7-9). Israel is promised to repent (Hosea 3:5; Zech. 12:10-13:1), be regathered (Ezek. 36:18-24), revived (Ezek. 36:25-27; 37:1-14), and restored in a Davidic Kingdom (Ezek. 37:24-25) that will be recognized by all nations as blessed (Isa. 2:2-4; Zech. 8:20-23).

Jerusalem is enlarged and made glorious by the return of the Divine Presence (Jer. 3:17; Ezek. 43:1-7; Zech. 8:3-8). It is made the center of the world with the Temple Mount as the source of universal religious instruction and worship (Isa. 2:2-3; 56:7). The Temple is built by Messiah with Gentile assistance (Zech. 6:12-15; Isa. 56:5-6), and the Gentile nations learn Torah and worship the One True God (Zech. 14:16-19).

Sources

Based on Seder Olam, Talmud, Midrash Rabbah, Commentaries by Rashi, Maimonides, Abarbanel, Targum Onkelos and Jonathan on the Torah, Targum Jonathan on the Prophets, and Urbach, *The Sages*.

Testament (Hebrews 7:1–8:13), where Melchizedek is presented as a type of the Messiah, who as Priest will give the gift of salvation to Israel and as King will reign in righteousness from Jerusalem. So, when God later sent Abraham to Mount Moriah in Jerusalem, Abraham was headed to a place which had been prepared with a purpose (Genesis 22:2).

Abraham's test of faith (the evidence of his unreserved devotion to God) and the prophecy of Christ's substitutionary sacrifice both take place in Jerusalem. Isaac was the son of promise because in him were bound up all the prophetic promises made to Abraham for the future of Israel and the nations. Similarly, all of God's promises for Israel and the nations are bound in Christ, the Promised One, "the son of Abraham" (Matthew 1:1).

Going back to Abraham, never before and never again until Jesus would God ask someone to take their only beloved son to be sacrificed. Though Abraham most likely did not understand God's command, he understood God's character, and believed that with God, life would result from death. This is evidenced in Abraham's statement to his servants at the foot of Mount Moriah: "I and the lad [his son Isaac] will go yonder; and *we* will worship *and return to you*" (Genesis 22:5, emphasis added). Either Abraham was staging a cover-up or he was staying himself on God's character. The New Testament opts for the latter, stating, "He [Abraham] considered that God is able to raise men even from the dead" (Hebrews 11:19). Isaac did not die, but his return from sacrifice was as if he had returned from the dead. In Isaac's place a ram was offered, and Mount Moriah from that day forward had prophetic significance as the place where God would provide (Genesis 22:8,14).

The next step along the prophetic path that led toward Jerusalem came with the prophet Moses. After Moses saw the salvation of the Lord and His great power in the parting of the Red Sea during the exodus, Moses prophesied to Israel in his praise to God: "Thou wilt bring them and plant them in the mountain of Thine inheritance, the place, O LORD, which Thou hast made for Thy dwelling, the sanctuary, O Lord, which Thy hands have established. The LORD shall reign forever and ever" (Exodus 15:17-18). The identification of these words with Jerusalem is made certain by the reference to the Temple (sanctuary), also prophesied in detail in Deuteronomy 12:1-32. Moses' words in Exodus 15:17-18 revealed two things that had never been previously revealed: that Israel and the Temple would be established on Mount Moriah. Abraham, the father of Israel, had gone to the mountain; now Israel the nation would follow there. Abraham had offered the first sacrifice there; now Israel would offer sacrifices there for centuries to come.

Yet another step further along Jerusalem's road of divine destiny came with King David, whose own rise to fame was clearly a part of God's prophetic plan. In one key Scripture verse we are told about God's specific choices for a place and a person: "I have chosen Jerusalem that My name might be there, and I have chosen David to be over My people Israel" (2 Chronicles 6:6). David himself recognized God's sovereignty at work, as the author of David's history explains: "And David realized that the LORD had established him as king over Israel, and that He had exalted his kingdom for the sake of His people Israel" (2 Samuel 5:12). Moses' prophecy in Exodus 15:17-18 began to be fulfilled when David captured Jerusalem from the Jebusites (2 Samuel 5:6-10) and united the 12 tribes apportioned throughout the Land. He did this by moving his capital and the Ark of the Covenant to Jerusalem (2 Samuel 5:5; 6:1-17). By his action David made the city uniquely the political and religious center of Israel, forcing every person through-out his realm seeking civil justice or ceremonial worship to make a visit there.

Whereas God gave Abraham and Moses prophecies that were specifically related to Jerusalem, when He spoke to David He went a step further and repeated the promise made to Moses, including with it a new Messianic element: "I will also appoint a place for My people Israel and will plant them. . . . He shall build a house for My name, and I will establish the throne of his kingdom forever" (2 Samuel 7:10,13).

These words are part of the Davidic Covenant (2 Samuel 7:12-16), in which God unconditionally promised David a son who would build the Temple and whose throne would never end. David purchased the site for the Temple and made preparations for its construction (1 Chronicles 21:25-26; 28:11–29:19) because he understood Jerusalem and the Temple Mount as the spiritual center for God's salvation story. Just as God promised, David's son (Solomon) did indeed build the First Temple 2,500 years ago. And although Solomon ruled on David's throne, later he died, and God's presence departed from the Temple (Ezekiel 11:23). Afterward, the Temple was destroyed in 586 B.C. Therefore, it is ultimately David's *greater* son, Jesus (Matthew 1:1), who will fulfill both aspects of this prophecy when He builds the Messianic Temple of God's glory in Jerusalem (Zechariah 6:12-15) and reigns on David's throne in Jerusalem during the millennial kingdom (Psalm 2:6; 110:2; 132:11-18; Isaiah 2:2-4; 24:23; Jeremiah 33:15-17; Micah 4:7; Zephaniah 3:15; Zechariah 2:11; 14:9). However, before these prophecies related to David could be fulfilled, the prophecy connected with Abraham had to be fulfilled—the cross before the crown. Jesus came and was crucified on Mount Moriah in literal fulfillment of this (John 8:56). Jesus was promised David's throne forever (Luke 1:31-33), yet at this time Jesus is not sitting on David's throne in Jerusalem but on Messiah's throne in heaven (Hebrews 12:2). In the same manner as in the first advent, Jesus will come again to Jerusalem and literally fulfill the promises inherent in the Davidic covenant (Matthew 19:28; Acts 15:15).

Our next and final step on the road of Jerusalem's divine destiny comes with one of David's descendants, King Hezekiah. According to the parallel accounts in 2 Kings 18–20, 2 Chronicles 29–32:23, and Isaiah 37, King Hezekiah was unequaled among the Judean kings of the Divided Kingdom for his devotion to the Lord (2 Kings 18:3-7). When Hezekiah recognized that the people of Judah were in a sorry spiritual state, he enacted national spiritual reforms in Jerusalem as well as throughout Judah (2 Chronicles 29:2–31:21). During his reign (722–721 B.C.) God fulfilled His prophecy of judgment against the Northern Kingdom of Israel (Isaiah 28:1-13; Hosea 5:8-15) by sending the Assyrian army to besiege and destroy their chief cities and deport their citizens (2 Kings 18:9-12; 1 Chronicles 5:26).

In 701 B.C., the Assyrians, who had already conquered the Northern Kingdom, moved south to conquer Judah as well (2 Kings 18:13). Hezekiah was outnumbered and outgunned by the Assyrians (2 Kings 18:17; 19:10-13), and all of his efforts to maintain peace failed (2 Kings 18:14-16). Then, when all hope seemed gone, Isaiah the prophet and Hezekiah prayed, and God prophesied the Assyrian king's withdrawal and death (2 Kings 19:32-33) based on His promise that "I will defend this city [Jerusalem] to save it for My own sake and for My servant David's sake" (2 Kings 20:6). The account in the book of 2 Chronicles implies that God delivered Jerusalem on this occasion because the Assyrians had spoken of "the God of Jerusalem as of the gods of the peoples of the earth, the work of men's hands" (2 Chronicles 32:19). A similar idea is implied in 2 Kings 19 when Hezekiah prays, "Deliver us from his hand [the Assyrian king Sennacherib] that all the kingdoms of the earth may know that Thou alone, O LORD, art God" (2 Kings 19:19). Jerusalem, then, was spared from the Assyrians so that God would be honored and because of the prophetic promises made in the Davidic Covenant.

God's miraculous intervention in Hezekiah's day provides a pattern for Jerusalem's deliverance from her enemies in the last days. With even greater arrogance and blasphemy than the Assyrian king, the Antichrist will exalt himself above all gods and seek to usurp the worship that rightfully belongs only to God (Daniel 11:36-37; 2 Thessalonians 2:4; Revelation 13:5-8,15). The Antichrist's actions, combined with his persecution of the Jewish people (Matthew 24:16-22; Revelation 12:13), his attack on Jerusalem (Zechariah 12:3; 14:2), and his opposition to Christ and those who follow Him (Revelation 11:7; 17:14) will threaten both God's honor and the fulfillment of the Davidic Covenant. In response, God will once again intervene in a miraculous way to deliver Jerusalem (we'll see more on this in chapter 9).

Jerusalem's Preparation for the Future

Those who study the Messianic prophecies in Scripture and the conditions leading to their fulfillment are aware that the world was prepared in various ways for the first coming of Christ. The New Testament affirms this fact when it says, "When *the fulness of time* came, God sent forth His Son, born of a woman, born under the Law" (Galatians 4:4, emphasis added). The term "fulness of time" indicates that God had prepared, in advance, the time for Messiah's incarnation into history. Indeed, a number of factors worked together in a unique way to make this the right time to send the Savior: 1) the moral and spiritual condition of society was so bad that even the pagans cried out against it; 2) the spiritual state of the Jewish people and political oppression of Israel by the surrounding nations provoked the people's desire for a Messianic deliverer; 3) the Greek language had become the universal language, which made it possible for the message of the gospel to spread everywhere rapidly; 4) the Romans had built a wonderful system of roads that linked the world under Roman rule, enhancing the spread of the gospel; 5) the Roman *pax Romana* extended to most of the civilized world, making travel and the exchange of ideas possible on a scale as never before; and 6) there was an unparalleled yearning for the Messiah that characterized much of Judaism during the Second Temple period, making the time of His coming also an answer to Jewish prayers (see Luke 2:25; 24:21; Acts 5:34-39). All of these factors were pivotal in the timing of Christ's first coming, bringing together the Jewish leadership (the Sanhedrin), the Judean ruler Herod Antipas, and the Roman official Pontius Pilate, all of whom had a role in God's plan to redeem the world through Christ.

In like manner, God is at work behind the scenes today, allowing for different factors to prepare the world for the second coming of Christ. Just as Galatians 4:4 affirms the God-ordained timing of Christ's first coming, so the New Testament uses similar language to announce a divine preparation for the second coming: ". . . the appearing of our Lord Jesus Christ, which *He* will bring about at *the proper time*" (1 Timothy 6:14-15, emphasis added). God's proper timing has been affirmed prophetically and will parallel the conditions present in the first century. The world of the last days will have the following elements:

1. *A moral and spiritual vacuum* of competing religions that offer little value. Today, Eastern religions have swept into Western society, and New Age thinking and the mind sciences have infiltrated conventional Christian denominations, contributing to growing apostasy in the church worldwide.

2. *The Jewish people will face unparalleled spiritual and political persecution* during the Tribulation. Today, anti-Semitism is increasing worldwide and the Land of Israel, the only refuge for the Jewish people, is at odds with most of the nations of the earth.

3. *A new universal "language"* will unite the world under the dominion of Antichrist to receive his mark (Revelation 13:17). Already in our day the universal language of the computer has linked the globe via satellite digital technologies. We are now able to communicate instantly verbally and visually with anyone on earth through both television and the worldwide web. I am constantly amazed that on the web I can see the Western Wall plaza at the Temple Mount in Jerusalem 24 hours a day via Visual Jerusalem's Kotel Kam, a video camera, positioned directly opposite the wall in the Jewish Quarter. Such technology will make it possible for the whole world to witness live the execution and resuscitation of the two witnesses in Revelation 11:7-12—enabling the fulfillment of yet another prophetic statement related to Jerusalem!

4. *Global transportation* will make possible a more rapid immigration of Jews to Israel as well as of the armies of the world, which will assemble at Megiddo and march against Jerusalem. Today we have witnessed the entire population of Ethiopian Jewry being airlifted to Israel, and we have seen the speedy deployment of troops for engagement in the Gulf War. The means therefore now exist to fulfill the prophetic military scenario of the last days.

5. *A global pseudopeace* will prevail (Revelation 6:4), making possible the spread of both the Antichrist's deception (Revelation 12:9; 13:8,14) and the truth of God's Word, which will be proclaimed by the Lord's chosen witnesses (the 144,000 Jewish believers mentioned in Revelation 7:1-8).

6. I*srael will cry out for Messiah* in repentance and faith (Zechariah 12:10-13; Matthew 24:30; Revelation 1:7). This cry will be provoked by the military efforts to annihilate the Jews at the end of the Tribulation. Indeed, in the past decade there has been an unparalleled Messianic revival in Orthodox Judaism in response to the Gulf War and the fear of impending Arab attack on Israel and anti-Semitism in America and Europe. The Hassidic group known as the Lubavitchers identified their own 92-year-old Rebbe Menachem Mendel Schneerson as the King Messiah. They believe that he was a prophet and that supernatural signs attended his doings. When he died, his faithful followers, which number into the hundreds of thousands, believed he was fulfilling the prophecy of Isaiah 53 and still continue to believe that he will be resurrected before the general resurrection (Daniel 12:2) and return to Israel as Messiah. They say that at present his spirit (the *Guf*) continues to guide them, and their faith is preserved and proclaimed throughout Jerusalem and the world by posters, banners,

books, and music that announce, "Messiah is coming . . . prepare for the coming of Messiah!" Deception of this kind will pave the way for the deception propagated by the false prophet of the Antichrist, who as a Jew (Revelation 13:11, where "the earth" can be understood as "the Land [of Israel]") will counterfeit the works of Messiah and seek to deceive the Jewish people and the world through great signs and miracles (Revelation 13:12-15).

A Definite Promise

The parallels between the events preceding Christ's first and second comings reveal to us that just as the prophecies of the first coming were fulfilled literally, so will the prophecies of the second coming be fulfilled literally. And just as Jerusalem occupied a pivotal place in the events surrounding Christ's first advent, so it will also occupy a central role in the events that are part of the second advent. With this understanding, Jerusalem's place in prophecy is assured.

British Prime Minister Sir Winston Churchill, who understood Jerusalem's place in prophecy, once stated, "Jerusalem must be the only ultimate goal. When it will be achieved it is in vain to prophesy; but that it will someday be achieved is one of the few certainties of the future."[3] The reason for such certainty concerning the city of Jerusalem is that it, unlike all the other cities on earth, is uniquely God's City. In the next chapter we will explore why this is so and examine why there has been and continues to be such great conflict among competing rivals for sovereignty over the site.

―――――――――

"Great is the LORD, and greatly
to be praised, in the city of
our God . . . is Mount Zion. . . .

—Psalm 48:1-2

The LORD has chosen Zion;
He has desired it for His habitation.

—Psalm 132:13

―――――――――

5

ZEALOUS FOR ZION:

Recognizing Jerusalem as God's City

Whose Jerusalem? . . . This issue is bound, sooner or later, to appear on the international agenda and dominate it as the most intractable problem of all.[1]

—Eliyahu Tal

The day that Eliyahu Tal predicted—in which the question would be raised about who rightfully owns Jerusalem—has come sooner rather than later. Today any renewed effort toward bringing peace to the Middle East hangs on the resolution of this central issue. More than 50 possibilities and sub-possibilities for this resolution have been proposed, with various geopolitical models ranging from the status quo to a radical change in the existing situation and division of the city between Israel and the Palestinian Authority. And as Meron Medzni points out, every possible claimant has made their demands for negotiating a piece of the whole:

> Israel has accorded Jordan status in the Moslem holy places. By signing an agreement with the Vatican, Israel acknowledged the role of the Vatican in the negotiations. The Russian Federation reminds Israel constantly that it sees itself as the representative of Russian Orthodox interests. Greece speaks for the Greek Orthodox Church, Egypt for the Copts, Britain for Anglican Church interests, Ethiopia for the Ethiopians. Armenia may demand a say on behalf of the Armenians. There are doubts as to who represents the Moslem world, let alone the Jewish and Protestant worlds.[2]

Throughout time Jerusalem has been in the possession of most of these nations and more. But what do we do with a city that today is called "holy" by one billion Catholics, one billion Muslims, 400 million Orthodox Christians, 400 million Protestants, and countless members of numerous pagan sects? No city can be peacefully divided to satisfy once and for all the religious claims and demands of so many diverse and conflicting groups. As Deputy Mayor David Cassuto has asserted, "You don't make peace by divding cities; and at any rate, we have already tried that. . . ."[3] And it is a curious fact of history that despite the fervency shown the city by the adherents of various religions, its place in their history is not overly prominent. For example, the Koran never mentions Jerusalem by name, nor was it ever in any Islamic period the capital of any province. The same may be said for Christianity, for Jerusalem was never accorded the central status that went to Constantinople, though it was under Christian control throughout the Byzantine period. Yet both Muslims and Christians have fought bitter Crusades and wars through the centuries for the right to possess the city.

Whatever claims might be made upon Jerusalem, it is first and foremost the city of God. Before we consider the biblical evidence that supports this conclusion, let's consider the Land of Israel as a whole, of which Jerusalem is a special part.

What the Bible Says

God Owns the Land

God's perspective of this Land is that it's His, even though it was in the possession of as many as ten national entities before He gave it to Israel (see Genesis 15:19-21). The territorial claims of men mean little to the Most High God, the Possessor of heaven and earth (Genesis 14:19,22; see also Psalm 50:10; Isaiah 40:15). As Lord of the Land, He made it His covenant land and leased it to the Jewish people as the chosen tenants: "The land . . . shall not be sold permanently, for the land is Mine; for you are but aliens and sojourners with Me" (Leviticus 25:23). The witness to this lease is in their flesh—circumcision (Genesis 17:10-11), but also in the covenantal documents found within the legal sections of the Torah, the original of which still is deposited inside the Ark of the Covenant (Deuteronomy 31:26).

However, because the Jewish people are but lessees of the Land, we must not wrongly conclude that God, in casting them out at times, intended to give their Land to others. From the beginning the grant of the Land was unconditional and meant to endure despite periods of covenantal failure and consequent exile. This is plainly stated in Leviticus 26:44-46:

> Yet in spite of this, when they are in the land of their enemies [exile], I will not reject them, nor will I abhor them as to destroy them, breaking My covenant with them; for I am the LORD their God. But I will remember for them the covenant with their ancestors, whom I brought out of the land of Egypt in the sight of the nations, that I might be their God. I am the LORD.

In other words, God has bound Himself by covenant to do what He promised for His people. To do otherwise would be impossible, for God by nature is immutable (Malachi 3:6; see also 1 Samuel 15:29; Hebrews 7:21).

Israel's privilege of possession depended on each generation's faithfulness to the covenant; however, Israel's position as possessors did not change even when they were exiled from the Land. Even while the Jewish people were in exile Ezekiel called the Land "your own land" (Ezekiel 36:24), and qualifies it in terms of the covenant by also identifying it as "the land that I [God] gave to your forefathers" (Ezekiel 36:28) and "the land that I gave to Jacob [Israel] My servant, in which your fathers lived" (Ezekiel 37:25). In those passages the context speaks prophetically of Israel's future return, and so confirms Israel's right to the Land through the present Diaspora and the end times. Israel's failure to adhere to the terms of the covenant with God did not deny them possession of the Land; rather, the covenant stipulated the conditions they had to meet if they wanted to "live securely on the Land" (Leviticus 25:18).

It is because of God's covenant of promise that He forbade the Land from being permanently sold to anyone. Israelites could sub-lease portions of the Land under their possession to their fellow Israelites, but such agreements expired in the Year of Jubilee (Leviticus 25:10,13). The

Land was to be understood and treated as God's Land and as the place to which the Jewish people would return after they had been scattered. It was this understanding that, among the Orthodox Jews, provoked violent opposition to the "land for peace" negotiations between Israel and the Palestinian Authority, and remains the problem for any form of peace process in the Middle East. The Land is simply not negotiable, and Israel has no right to relinquish its position as its appointed tenants and caretakers. But beyond that, the Land has a prophetic purpose that involves the fulfillment of Israel's future destiny. This destiny cannot be compromised or traded for even a temporary treaty with the nations, for the nations' own destinies depend on what happens to Israel.

God Specified the Boundaries

Currently all of the territory that comprises modern Israel is disputed by Arab nations, and by Palestinian-Arabs in particular. However, the Scripture unambiguously declares that God gave this territory to the Patriarchs of Israel:

> I will establish My covenant between Me and you and your descendants after you throughout their generations for an everlasting covenant, to be God to you and to your descendants after you. And I will give to you and your descendants . . . all the land of Canaan, for an everlasting possession; and I will be their God (Genesis 17:7-8).

> He has remembered His covenant forever, the word which He commanded to a thousand generations, the covenant which He made with Abraham, and His oath to Isaac. Then He confirmed it to Jacob for a

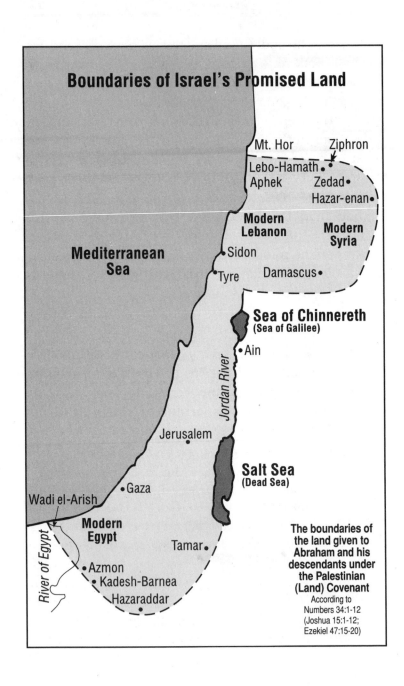

Boundaries of Israel's Promised Land

Mt. Hor   Ziphron

Lebo-Hamath •   • Ziphron
Aphek   Zedad •
    Hazar-enan •

Modern Lebanon   **Modern Syria**

• Sidon

• Tyre   Damascus •

Mediterranean Sea

Sea of Chinnereth
(Sea of Galilee)

• Ain

Jordan River

• Jerusalem

Salt Sea
(Dead Sea)

• Gaza

Wadi el-Arish

River of Egypt

Modern Egypt

Tamar •

• Azmon
• Kadesh-Barnea
Hazaraddar •

The boundaries of
the land given to
Abraham and his
descendants under
the Palestinian
(Land) Covenant
According to
Numbers 34:1-12
(Joshua 15:1-12;
Ezekiel 47:15-20)

statute, to Israel as an everlasting covenant, saying,
"To you I will give the land of Canaan as the portion
of your inheritance" (Psalm 105:8-11).

If we look at current maps of Israel, we will see that the
nation comprises only a small portion of the area originally
promised to the Patriarchs for their future descendants (the
12 tribes of Israel) as an everlasting possession. When
Abraham received the title deed to God's Promised Land
the geographical boundaries were significantly greater than
those occupied by the modern state: "from the river of
Egypt as far as the great river, the river Euphrates" (Genesis
15:18).[4] Later these boundaries were made even more specific to Moses (Numbers 34:2-12).[5] This land grant encom-
passed most of modern Lebanon and Syria as well as all of
the land known as modern Israel, including the West Bank
(biblical Judea and Samaria) and the Gaza Strip.

Except for a brief time during the reigns of David and
Solomon, very little of the original boundaries have ever
been fully occupied by Israel. Therefore, the prophetic fulfillment of this land grant will not take place until the future
Messianic Age. However impossible this fulfillment may
seem at this time, God's promise is that He will not fail to
bring it to pass. When Jacob fled for his life from his family
and his future seemed bleak, he settled one night in the
vicinity of Jerusalem and received this assurance from God:
"The land on which you lie, I will give it to you and to your
descendants. Your descendants shall be like the dust of the
earth. . . . and [I] will bring you back to this land; *for I will not
leave you until I have done what I have promised you*" (Genesis
28:13-15, emphasis added). What God starts, He finishes
(Philippians 1:6). When God gave the Land to Abraham's
descendants, it came with a guarantee that the Jewish people

could not perish nor be permanently scattered from the Land until they had returned to possess their inheritance.

However, Israel's prophetic purpose is greater than simply that of possessing a part of the Middle East. God's program for *all* of the nations of the world hinges on His program with Israel:

> When the Most High gave the nations their inheritance, when He separated the sons of man, He set the boundaries of the peoples according to the number of the sons of Israel. For the LORD's portion is His people; Jacob is the allotment of His inheritance (Deuteronomy 32:8-9).

This passage explains that in God's division of the Gentile peoples, He providentially accounted for the number of Jews who will affect the history of each nation.

God Has Chosen Jerusalem

God's special relationship with Israel is more dramatically pronounced in His relationship with Jerusalem: "The LORD has chosen Zion; He has desired it for His habitation. This is My resting place forever; here I will dwell, for I have desired it" (Psalm 132:13-14). This divine desire for the city is portrayed through the prophet Ezekiel in the parable of the unfaithful wife, recorded in Ezekiel chapter 16. The story illustrates God's personal possession of the city— taking a pagan place, making it His own, and blessing it beyond measure (verses 1-14). After cataloging its sins and the judgments it would receive (verses 15-34), God promises its restoration and repentance because of His goodness (verses 53-63). The promised restoration reveals the enduring nature of God's commitment to the city He brought up from birth. Jerusalem may break God's covenant (a legally binding contract); nevertheless, [He says] "I will remember My covenant with you in the days of your youth, and I will establish an everlasting covenant with you" (verse 60).

God's commitment to Jerusalem is connected to His plan to not only make Himself known to Israel (Ezekiel 16:62), but to all the nations as well (Ezekiel 36:23; 37:28). The means God chose for accomplishing this was to make Jerusalem "His habitation . . . His resting place" (Psalm 132:13-14). That became a reality with the construction of the First Temple in Jerusalem. Even so, God's intention was already broadcast some 450 years before, when on more than five occasions in Deuteronomy chapter 12 He referred to Jerusalem as the place He had chosen to place His Name, or divine presence. Therefore, from the beginning God's special purpose for Jerusalem has been to make it the spiritual center of the world, where all the nations would come to know Him (Isaiah 2:2-3; Jeremiah 3:17). However, because of the Jewish people's rebellion, the fulfillment of this purpose has been postponed until "the . . . restoration of all things about which God spoke by the mouth of His holy prophets from ancient time" (Acts 3:21).

Jerusalem, the Focal Point

From the time that Jerusalem first belonged to the nation of Israel, it has always been regarded as a unique part of the Land upon which possession of and blessing for the rest of the Land depended. When the Northern and Southern Kingdoms were in exile, they looked to the restoration of Jerusalem as the answer to their prayers for a return to the Land. We see this in Daniel's three daily prayers for Jerusalem (Daniel 6:10). If Jerusalem did not retain its sanctity or purpose with the expulsion of the

Jewish people, as some people argue, then why should Daniel have opened his windows toward Jerusalem and prayed so fervently for its restoration (Daniel 9:16-19)? Though in ruins and under the rule of Gentile powers, Jerusalem, for Daniel, was still "Thy city Jerusalem" (Daniel 9:16) and "the holy mountain of my God" (Daniel 9:20). That being the case, we cannot say that the Jewish people's expulsion from Jerusalem in A.D. 70 severed it from God's past promises for the future. If God's future prophetic program centers on Jerusalem, then Jerusalem must remain. In order for the specific prophecies relating to Jerusalem's future to be fulfilled, the city must once again come under Jewish control yet remain in a vulnerable position under the greater dominion of the Gentile nations.

Is Jerusalem God's City Today?

The Error of Replacement Theology

Jerusalem has what no other city has: the scriptural confirmation that it was chosen by God (1 Kings 8:48; 11:13). But does that choice continue on through today? The renowned biographer of Rome's decline and fall, Edward Gibbon, dogmatically declared that it did not: "The Jews, their nation and their worship" have been "forever banished" from Jerusalem and its environs.[6] Jerusalem, according to this view, is no longer the "holy city" and does not have any continuing theological significance. This view has been shared and stated throughout church history by such notables as Eusebius Pamphilus, the third/fourth-century bishop of Caesarea and ecclesiastical voice of the pre-Constantinian era, and Martin Luther, the sixteenth-century father of the German Reformation from which Protestant Christianity developed. The reasons for these views were largely based on theological interpretations originating from the Roman Catholic Church as well as the physical condition of Jerusalem at the times Eusebius and Luther were alive.[7] When Eusebius formulated his statement toward the end of the third century, Jerusalem and the Temple Mount were in ruins and a Hadrianic edict had forbidden Jews from entering or even setting their eyes upon the city, thus leaving it, for a time, without any Jewish population.[8] To the Roman Catholic Church and Eusebius, Jesus' prophecies about the city's destruction and Israel's supersession by Christianity were proof that God's promises to the Jewish nation no longer applied. They say that in God's plan, the old earthly Jerusalem has been replaced by the new heavenly Jerusalem. Therefore, they believe that focus on the physical city was to look backwards and act more like a Jew than a Christian.[9] According to Luther, who was trained in this thinking known as Replacement Theology, the unruly political power and religious apostasy manifested by the Roman Pontiff were evidence that the people of his day were living in the end times. He concluded that because the Jews had not yet repented and embraced their Messiah, they were, by their continued rejection, clearly beyond redemption.[10]

The Permanence of God's Covenant

Those scholars whose views were not prejudiced by the social, political, and religious conditions of Israel in their day believed that Christ's second coming could not occur until the Jews returned to Jerusalem. In other words, they believed God's promises to Israel had not been nullified on account of Israel's unbelief. For example, the Puritans, who were among the scholarly heirs of the Reformation, studied Hebrew and even the Talmud in an effort to better grasp the long-neglected teachings of the Old Testament.[11] One of their premier divines, the Reverend John Owen, whose works of 17 volumes are still in print today, stated the following view, which was representative of most of his colleagues:

> The Jews shall be gathered from all parts of the earth where they are now scattered, and brought home into their homeland before the end of all things prophesied by St. Peter can occur.[12]

Such thinking had an influence upon many people in Europe. There is even some evidence that Napoleon Bonaparte intended to issue a proclamation on April 20, 1799 offering "Palestine" to the Jews as a national homeland. The offer, however, was contingent upon Napoleon's conquest of Jerusalem and Jews from Africa and Asia responding to his call to join his army "for the restoration of Jerusalem." Although Napoleon did not take Jerusalem, and the proclamation was lost, the historian Salo W. Baron noted that it "symbolized Europe's acknowledgment of Jewish rights in Palestine."[13]

In the nineteenth century, evangelical Christians in Europe awakened to the Old Testament prophecies concerning Jerusalem and began to express sympathy—both in religious and political circles—toward the Zionist movement, which came to full flower in 1897. Evangelical Christians joined with Jewish leaders in gaining public support for and urging political action toward the formation of a homeland for the Jews in what was then called "Palestine." Among these individuals were Lord Shaftesbury and Lord Alfred James Balfour, both outstanding British Christian social reformers and statesmen who, influenced by Bible prophecies, worked in their respective spheres of influence to help achieve Zionist (or pro-Israeli) objectives.

At the same time, similar sentiments were stirring in the United States. David Larsen notes one expression of this when he records that "M.M. Noah, an American Jewish lawyer and American Counsel in Tunis, became burdened for the Jews and shared his views with James Madison, Thomas Jefferson, and John Quincy Adams, who wrote in 1825, 'I really wish the Jews again in Judea, an independent nation.'"[14] This aggressive stance was necessary in order to counter an entrenched anti-Semitism in the United States as well as political tides that were bent on washing away the hope for a Jewish homeland. One such tide was directed by President Woodrow Wilson, who on August 28, 1919 presented the King-Crane Report, which proposed merging "Palestine" with Syria and putting all the holy places under international and interdenominational (but not Jewish) guardianship. Fortunately, the view of Jewish restoration prevailed, even in the face of Arab threats, and President Harry S Truman (who had led the American people in support of the creation of the Jewish nation) led the United States in 1948 to become the first nation to recognize the newly reborn State of Israel.[15]

Today there are a substantial number of evangelical Christians who are supportive of Jewish nationalism, providing testimony to the modern Israeli government that a segment of American Christianity believes that Zion still has a future.

Among the many prophecies that have compelled Christians—as well as politicians—to rally support for a return to Zion were those of the prophet Isaiah, who states in the strongest terms the unconditional character of God's purposes for Jerusalem:

> Zion said, "The LORD has forsaken me, and the LORD has forgotten me." Can a mother forget her nursing child, and have no compassion on the son of her womb? Even these she may forget, but I will not forget you. Behold, I have inscribed you on the palms of My hands; your walls are ever before Me. . . . For a brief moment I forsook you, but with great compassion I will gather you" (Isaiah 49:14-16; 54:7-8).

Not only had God not forgotten His people, He had also constituted them to be a "kingdom of priests" (Exodus 19:6). His purpose was to bring sanctity into a fallen world. How, then, can this purpose ever be realized if the Jewish nation does not possess the Holy City and the Temple Mount where the priesthood functions? Indeed, the very road to restored Zion is called "the Highway of Holiness" (Isaiah 35:8) and Mount Zion, "My holy mountain" (Joel 3:17). That's why Jewish prayers in both home and synagogue have daily entreated God for the restoration of Jerusalem. For instance, the *Mussaf*, a service that follows the Sabbath day liturgy, petitions the Almighty for renewed worship in a restored Zion. The 13 benedictions of the *Amidah*, recited daily, include a request to rebuild the Temple, and a Sabbath benediction prays, "Have pity on Zion, which is the home of our life. . . . "

That all this might become a reality seemed more plausible when, on June 7, 1967, Jewish control of Jerusalem was restored with the capture of the Old City and the city's reunification. Then in 1980, with the annexation of East Jerusalem, despite an almost universal recognition of Jerusalem as an "international city," the capital status of the united city was officially declared. Today, the continued affirmation of its indivisible nature under Jewish sovereignty has been maintained by Israel throughout the attempted peace with the Palestinians.

God's Plan at Work

Is the Jewish return to Jerusalem, now over three decades old, simply to be dismissed as a historical accident or as a socio-political consequence of the Holocaust with no scriptural significance? For the past two millennia, every prophetic interpreter who took seriously God's promises to Zion had expected this event to occur. True, the great end-time regathering and spiritual return has not yet taken place, but then the prophets depict that taking place with an unbelieving Jewish remnant already resident within Jerusalem and observing Jewish laws (Zechariah 12:10–14:4; Matthew 24:15-20,29-31). Reflecting on such a fulfillment under present conditions, Israeli Pastor Noam Hendren states:

> As we look at the situation of today and anticipate what may take place, I believe that we are reaching a point of no return where, in fact, the pressures that are coming against the Jewish people will require us to come to that point of national repentance. . . . All the events that we have seen with the restoration of the land of Israel, the restoration of Jewish national life in this land, of a normalcy which belies the threats which lie around this small country, I believe that we are reaching a point where no longer can we anticipate an exile of the people from the land. But ultimately that God is bringing our people together, as it says in Ezekiel chapter 20, bringing us together out of the peoples into a desert

> into an isolated place into this land. And in this
> land God will pour out the judgment, which will
> ultimately bring about the national repentance of
> Israel.[16]

The one reason that some people are hesitant to accept this conclusion is because they doubt whether the present State of Israel will prevail. However, despite gains and losses in the half-century-old state, and the threat of Jerusalem's being redivided, most Orthodox Jews have affirmed this is indeed the return predicted by the prophets. An example of this confidence may be illustrated from an incident that occurred at the conclusion of the Six-Day War on June 7, 1967. The Israeli army that had taken the Old City of Jerusalem assembled together at the Western Wall. The call to prayer at this historic wall was sounded, with a shofar (a ram's horn), by Israel Defense Forces Chaplain Rabbi Shlomo Goren. The men stood in reverent silence as Rabbi Goren recited the first Jewish prayers heard at the Wall in almost two decades. Then he declared: "We have taken the City of God. We are entering the Messianic era for the Jewish people." However, one month later, Rabbi Goren was forced to relinquish the Temple Mount to Arab jurisdiction, and he had cause to reconsider whether it was yet the Messianic era. But he did not and could not change his mind about the fact that Jerusalem was the City of God. It will always be God's City no matter who has temporary control, for its permanent Possessor is the Lord of heaven and earth, whose control cannot be commuted or contradicted.

We have closed this chapter with reference to the Six-Day War, a recent event that some people may feel has no place in the context of prophecy. Since many individuals wonder if current events can help us predict the future, we will take time in the next chapter to examine the relationship between current events, prophecy, and Jerusalem . . . and see whether present-day happenings can help us to discern the nature and nearness of prophetic fulfillment.

She [Jerusalem] did not consider
her future; therefore she
has fallen astonishingly.

—Lamentations 1:9

About the time of the end a body of
men will be raised up who will insist
upon the literal interpretation of
the prophetic scriptures among
much clamor and opposition.

—John Newton

6

THE ZION FACTOR:
Jerusalem, Current Events, and Prophecy

With the political world in utter confusion as it is today; the economic world in a hopeless tangle; suicidal wars being prepared; Palestine looming up as the cockpit of a terrible "holy war," and world diplomats trying to partition a land that God said cannot be parted without bringing a curse upon the perpetrators (Joel 3:2)—how can we doubt that we stand at the very consummation of the age? Never has it been clearer than now that the movements of the Jews furnish a key with which we may unlock the meaning of world events.[1]

—Keith L. Brooks

Everyone who has been a parent has sought to guide their children with respect to the future. Having been down the path before, they want to prepare the ones they love for what is ahead. While it is impossible to explain all the details, they attempt to impart as much as can be understood without having actually been experienced. And what child, after going down the path, has not been grateful for such counsel? How many fortunes have been acquired and failures avoided because a loving parent pointed out the things to come?

God calls Himself our Father. He, too, loves His children and wants to guide them into the future He is preparing for His world. He knows it is impossible to impart the details to children whose faith is frail, but He still wants to ready them for each step into the future in a world that will be caught unaware. To do this our Father has shown us the things which are to come and encouraged us to be watching for the signs of the times, which will tell us where we are along the way. And because the signs of the future involve people, places, and events present today, should we not be looking at these things in order to see where God will take them tomorrow?

Recently I traveled to Lynchburg, Virginia, for a speaking engagement and saw a billboard erected by a prominent real estate chain. The billboard pictured a row of houses in a neighborhood, each with the trademark *Sold* sign of that particular real estate agency. The headline on the billboard read: "How do you tell the greatest name in real estate? . . . The signs are everywhere!" As I thought about that ad I couldn't help but see a spiritual analogy. The Lord, who owns the cattle on a thousand hills (and the hills to boot!), is the greatest name in real estate. Furthermore, He has announced that He is coming soon to claim and close on His property. How do we know? The signs are everywhere! These signs are, of course, the prophecies of

Scripture, which, as we have said, tend to cast their shadows before them into our age.

Another way of saying this is that events occurring today are setting the stage or preparing the way for the prophecies that will come to fulfillment in the Tribulation period and beyond. Dr. John F. Walvoord, the Chancellor of Dallas Theological Seminary and one of the world's foremost prophetic scholars, has stated:

> Never before in history have all the factors been present for the fulfillment of prophecy relating to end-time religious trends and events. Only in our generation have the combined revival of Israel, the formation of a world church, the increasing power of Muslim religion, the rise of the occult, and the worldwide spread of atheistic philosophy been present as a dramatic setting for the final fulfillment of prophecy. As far as world religion is concerned, the road to Armageddon is already well prepared, and those who will travel to their doom may well be members of our present generation.[2]

That the road to the future is now being prepared should be expected. God has announced that Israel has a future, that Jerusalem will be the center of international controversy and conflict (Zechariah 12:2-3; 14:2) and then at Christ's return (Isaiah 59:20; Zechariah 14:4), it will be elevated above every city on earth (Isaiah 2:2-3; Jeremiah 3:17; Zechariah 14:17). If we believe that God is active in the affairs of His world, directing people and events according to His plan, then we should be looking at the *people* (the Jewish people) and the *place* (the Land of Israel) where the fulfillment of these things will occur. Since God is at work daily (Jeremiah 23:23) moving the world toward that final day (Acts 17:31; Romans 13:11; 1 Timothy 6:13-14), we should expect to see in the details of the daily news the pieces of the prophetic picture slowly taking shape. Our study of Bible prophecy should include current events as the means to behold the hand of God in history and to understanding how and when He will bring His prophetic purposes to pass.

Interpreting Current Events

There are many events filling the news nowadays that seem to be preparing the stage for the final drama as prophesied in Scripture. The advent of globalism and technologies linking our communications and cash systems, the growing spiritual apostasy worldwide, and the longing for a leader who can unite the diverse religious and political factions are just a few examples. Although these may be setting the larger stage for the Antichrist and his one-world government, our concern in this book has to do more specifically with the Middle East, the Land of Israel, and especially the city of Jerusalem. How can the events taking place today in this region be interpreted in relation to the prophetic scriptures?

Current events must be rightly interpreted in order to be properly applied. For example, when in 1998 the fiftieth anniversary of the founding of the State of Israel was celebrated, many Christians mistakenly assumed that this jubilee year was the biblical Jubilee in which the Land was to revert to its original owners. They believed that this year would fulfill a prophetic event during which God would return all the Promised Land to the Israelis. Because the principal message of the Jubilee Year is proclaiming liberty throughout the Land (Leviticus 25:10), many expected the freedom of the "Year of Release" to come to Israel and end "the times of the Gentiles." In harmony with this thinking, I received letters from well-intentioned people warning that, based on Romans 8:18-21, the rapture of the church would take place this year, and that we would "be set free from [our] slavery to corruption into the freedom of the glory of the children of God" (verse 21). However, these expectations reveal significant misunderstandings of both the biblical Jubilee and the identification of it on our present calendar.[3]

The Year of Jubilee, as defined in the Old Testament book of Leviticus, was to serve as a check-and-balance on social institutions. Returning tenant land to its owners, indentured servants to their families, and giving rest to the land justly regulated the social institutions of family property, slavery, and agriculture, while teaching a valuable lesson about God's ownership over all things and the necessity of trusting Him as the source of all provision. The Day of Atonement was especially significant in the Jubilee Year, for the trumpet sounding the jubilee was blown on that day, the tenth day of the month Tishri, in contrast to other years, when it was blown on the first of Tishri (*Rosh Hashanah*—the New Year). Therefore, on the same day that physical land and liberty were restored, the high priest also offered a sacrifice to free the nation from its spiritual debt.

Today the biblical Jubilee Year cannot be determined with accuracy because the records that preserved the exact date were presumably lost with the destruction of the First Temple. For this reason, during the Second Temple period (the time of Christ), Jewish sources such as Maimonides report that the Jubilee Year was not observed. So it is unwarranted to argue that because the State of Israel has existed for 50 years that it fulfills any prophetic purpose. Furthermore, the biblical Year of Jubilee prophetically portrays the

future restoration of Israel through full ownership of the
Land (including Jerusalem's Temple Mount) and uncontested independence (politically and spiritually). This kind
of Jubilee will be possible only after the time of Gentile
domination has ended and the Messiah has returned to
spiritually revive the nation and restore its God-given
boundaries.

Thus, while it is significant that a "chronological jubilee" for Israel has occurred, the prophetic events portrayed
by the biblical Year of Jubilee have yet to occur.[4]

The Modern-Day Return to the Land

The modern-day return of Jewish people to Israel, the
country's national independence, and the government's
sovereignty over Jerusalem have all been considered such
significant events that some scholars who formerly questioned the prophecies of a literal return have advised their
colleagues:

> . . . with the surprising geographical and political
> fact of the establishment of the State of Israel, the
> moment has come for us to begin to watch for
> political and geographical elements in God's activ-
> ities, which we have not wanted to do in our
> Western dualism, docetism, and spiritualism.[5]

There is no question that, to the majority of Israelis and
most Jews throughout the world, the establishment of the
Third State of Israel in 1948 and of Israeli control over all of
Jerusalem in 1967 has fulfilled Jewish prayers and expectations as formed by the Bible's prophecies. While there are
differences of opinion among the Orthodox as to whether
the Messianic era has begun, all recognize that what has
happened was meant to happen. Thus, for Jews, an era of

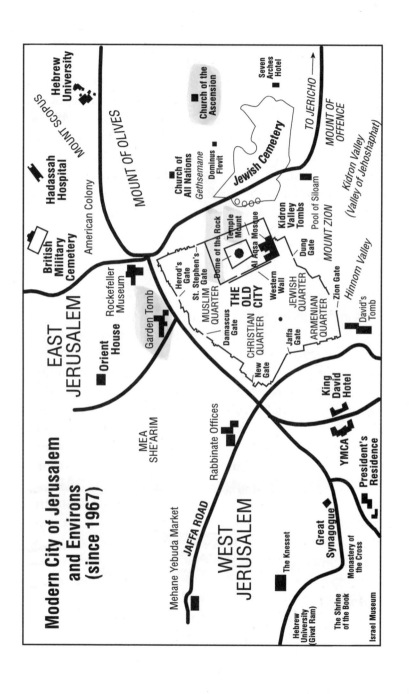

Modern City of Jerusalem and Environs (since 1967)

Hebrew University
MOUNT SCOPUS
Hadassah Hospital
British Military Cemetery
American Colony
MOUNT OF OLIVES
Church of the Ascension
Seven Arches Hotel
Church of All Nations
Gethsemane
Dominus Flevit
Jewish Cemetery
TO JERICHO
MOUNT OF OFFENCE
Kidron Valley (Valley of Jehoshaphat)
Rockefeller Museum
Garden Tomb
Orient House
EAST JERUSALEM
Herod's Gate
St. Stephen's Gate
MUSLIM QUARTER
Dome of the Rock
Temple Mount
Al Aqsa Mosque
Kidron Valley Tombs
Pool of Siloam
Dung Gate
MOUNT ZION
Hinnom Valley
Damascus Gate
CHRISTIAN QUARTER
THE OLD CITY
Western Wall
JEWISH QUARTER
ARMENIAN QUARTER
Zion Gate
David's Tomb
New Gate
Jaffa Gate
King David Hotel
MEA SHE'ARIM
Rabbinate Offices
YMCA
President's Residence
JAFFA ROAD
Mehane Yebuda Market
The Knesset
Great Synagogue
WEST JERUSALEM
Monastery of the Cross
Hebrew University (Givat Ram)
The Shrine of the Book
Israel Museum

waiting has ended—a wait that for ages was symbolized in the acclamation at the closing section of the Passover *lashanah haba'ah birushalayim* ("Next year in Jerusalem!").

However, for some Christians, and Jewish academics, the prophetic significance of what took place in 1948 and 1967 is obviated by their interpretation that the prophecies related to the people's return and the city's restoration were already fulfilled in past history. Before we can move onward in our attempt to determine how current events are relevant to prophecy, we must first take a moment to understand this major objection.

Were the Prophecies Already Fulfilled?

The Perspective

Isaiah had prophesied that Israel would "rebuild the ancient ruins . . . raise up the former devastations, and . . . repair the ruined cities" (Isaiah 61:4). A prevalent view today known as historicism (and preterism) generally interprets this and other similar prophecies as having had a *past* fulfillment. For this reason, historicists and preterists do not attribute any prophetic significance to the masses of Jewish people returning to Israel and Jerusalem. They contend that the return occurred at some point in past history, literally in the return from the Babylonian exile in 538 B.C., or spiritually with Christ's fulfillment of the Messianic predictions, or through the Roman conquest and destruction of Jerusalem in A.D. 70. When Jesus came to earth during the Second Temple era, the city of Jerusalem and the Land of Israel had already been in the process of restoration for 500 years. Even so, ancient Jewish records reveal there was widespread belief that this restoration was not a fulfillment of what the prophets had predicted.

The Problems

One problem is that in the "return" that occurred in 538 B.C. under Zerubbabel only a relatively small number of exiles (50,000) actually returned, while the majority of the Jewish people remained in the lands of their captivity (Egypt and Babylon/Persia). Those who did return showed no commitment toward the rebuilding of the Temple (Ezra 3:6; 4:4) and the walls of the city (Nehemiah 1:2-3). In addition, the low spiritual state of the resident population and priesthood (Ezra 9:1-4; Nehemiah 5:1-9; 13:7-11,23-29), and the continued domination by foreign powers (Persian, Egyptian, Syrian, Greek, Roman) made it difficult for the returnees to accept that their journey back to Jerusalem fulfilled the grand vision God had given to the prophets. One "solution" that historicists have offered for this seeming contradiction is that the prophecies related to the return used hyperbolic (exaggerated) language. However, any attempt to interpret these prophecies less than literally fails when we measure today's large return (presently six million) against the comparatively minuscule returns that took place in the past.

Another solution offered by some is to take the "return" prophecies as symbolic of spiritual realities fulfilled in Christ and by His church. This helps resolve the problem that the "return" prophecies failed with respect to literal fulfillment. But it creates another problem: If you say that all such prophecies are merely symbolic, then you have to say that Jesus' future return is also merely symbolic. Prophecies related to the second advent are part of return and restoration passages; the two cannot be separated. What's more, the Old Testament restoration prophecies are basically repeated in the New Testament with a literal application to the Jewish people (Acts 1:6; 3:18-21; Romans 11:11-32). Why shouldn't the Old Testament, in which we originally find these prophecies, be used as the standard for interpreting similar passages in the New Testament rather than vice versa? Such a reverse standard has reduced the Old Testament to a place of irrelevancy (the *Old* Testament) in much of Christendom today.

More significantly, an objection to the past fulfillment view is raised by one of the prophets himself.[6] Zechariah, whose future predictions of Jerusalem's ruin and restoration stand at the forefront of such prophecies, issued his message *after* the exiles had returned to Judah (518 B.C.). His prophecies spoke of a yet future increase in population and material and spiritual prosperity unparalleled in the nation's history (Zechariah 2:4-5,17; 8:3-5,11-12; 14:1-21). For example, his prophecies are not merely of a return of Judah (two tribes), but also of Israel (Zechariah 10:6). He prophesied a return not just from Babylon, but from *all the earth* (Zechariah 8:7-8; 10:9-11). Furthermore, not only will Jewish people come to the Land, but also the Gentile nations, who will seek the favor of the Jews (Zechariah 2:11; 8:20-22) and their Messiah, who will build the Temple and establish a worldwide rule of peace (Zechariah 6:12-13; 9:10). Again, all of this is viewed as future *after* the return and beginning of restoration in Jerusalem.

Now let's go back to Isaiah's prophecy that Israel would "rebuild the ancient ruins . . . raise up the former devastations, and . . . repair the ruined cities" (Isaiah 61:4). The context of those words tells us that the restoration will not occur until after the advent of the King Messiah (verses 1-3). Even though Jesus, reading this text in the synagogue in Nazareth (Luke 4:16-21), interpreted this prophecy as being fulfilled in His day, He was careful to make it clear that only a partial fulfillment had taken place. That's why He stopped His reading of the passage in mid-sentence (at Isaiah 61:2a; see Luke 4:17-21), thereby dividing His Messianic work into present and future aspects. As "the Lord's anointed" (Messiah), Jesus at the first advent would "bring good news to the afflicted," "bind up the brokenhearted," "proclaim liberty to captives," "freedom to prisoners," and "proclaim the favorable year of the LORD" (verses 1-2a). What remained unfulfilled was the great day of King Messiah's vengeance and of Israel's revival (verses 2b-3), which would attend the second advent.

Zechariah again offers us evidence that the prophesied return to Jerusalem must be future to any previous historical event. Through the prophet, God sets His own standard for the final restoration, against which every lesser restoration must be weighed:

> "But now I will not treat the remnant of this people as in the former days," declares the LORD of hosts "... just as you were a curse among the nations, O house of Judah and house of Israel, so I will save you that you may become a blessing" (Zechariah 8:11,13).

If the return of the remnant under Zerubbabel and the restorations led by Ezra and Nehemiah were the fulfillment of this promise, as the historicists and preterists say, then how is it that God subjected the Jews to another destruction of Jerusalem and the Temple and a more prolonged exile? Where does the Bible predict another judgment after the final eschatological restoration? Up until the Roman desolation that occurred in A.D. 70, it was possible for the return of the Jewish people and Israel's restoration to world dominance to take place with the coming of the Messiah. But after the Roman destruction, this possibility was ended with the loss of Jewish sovereignty and even of access to the Land. Therefore, the Jews looked to the future for the fulfillment of Zechariah's words. Until the State of Israel was established and East Jerusalem was captured, there was nothing that had occurred in the past that could have been construed as fulfilling Zechariah's prophecies. But with the modern return and the annexation of East Jerusalem, it is legitimate to look to these recent events as having a part in prophecy, and very possibly leading us toward the final events scheduled to take place in Israel during the last days.

How, then, can we benefit from examining current events without abusing prophetic interpretation? Here are some suggested guidelines that can be used to avoid making careless claims that certain prophecies have been fulfilled while, at the same time, recognizing those events that could have a hand in shaping the future.

Suggested Guidelines for Examining Current Events

1. *Interpret current events in light of the Bible, not the Bible in light of current events.*

This general principle is a necessary corrective to discourage what has been called "newspaper exegesis," or interpreting Bible prophecies based on stories that appear in the media. Just as we should not use extrabiblical writing (such as Josephus or the Dead Sea Scrolls) in order to interpret the Bible, we should not let current events shape our understanding of Scripture. Rather, the other helps enable us to better understand historical context and the minutiae of the Bible text. So current events can help us to discern how some of the undefined details of prophecy may transpire, but they should not cause us to read certain ideas into the prophetic text. For example, the terrestrial and cosmic plagues described in Revelation chapters 6–19 are written in first-century language. Not until recently have we come to see what these plagues might have comprised—global pollutants, environmental disasters, comets and asteroids colliding with the earth, and chemical and biological weapons.

2. In the Bible, the fulfillment of prophetic events related to Israel will not take place until after the age of the church.

We need to maintain a balance here. On the one hand, considering all details provided for us in the prophetic texts, we can conclude that no prophecy related to Israel's possession of the Land and promised burdens and blessings have yet taken place. On the other hand, the present possession of the Land and the conflict within the region is evidently a preparation for the fulfillment of these prophecies in the near future. It is exciting to think that the events of 1948 and 1967 have fulfilled prophetic promises to Israel, but it is no less exciting, and more accurate, to say that these events have *made it more than ever possible* for Zechariah's prophecies to be fulfilled. There is no doubt that the return to the Land and re-establishment of sovereignty over Jerusalem are necessary prerequisites to the fulfillment of Tribulational and millennial prophecies, but inasmuch as they have not fulfilled all aspects of the prophecies, they serve as "signs of the times" indicating that fulfillment is near. Another way of saying this is that the stage is being set today for the drama that will be acted out tomorrow. If the scenery (the Jewish people in the Land and Jerusalem at the center of world attention) is in place, and the prophetic players in the nations are waiting in the wings, how close might we be to the curtain call?

3. *Be sure the biblical text provides enough data to draw a correspondence with current events.*

The responsibility of anyone who seeks to compare current events with the biblical text is to first understand thoroughly the context and meaning of the biblical text. This simple procedure will help to preclude the possibility of premature interpretation. What we are trying to avoid is the temptation to say, "This is that," which we have already determined is impossible to do because no specific prophecy is being fulfilled today! It's easy for us to look at phenomenal or unexplained events occurring today and compare them with particular prophetic passages. We may find some very compelling correspondence between the details of current events and certain prophecies. But even then, since exact correspondence is lacking, we must be open to alternate explanations or we may end up building prophetic interpretation upon a wrong premise.

Let's take, for example, two conclusions people have made today, and see what kinds of questions we should ask to test their validity:

a. *The demonic invasion in Revelation 9 describes extraterrestrial activity.* Do the details of reported alien sightings and abductions provide sufficient evidence to identify extraterrestrial beings as the "sons of God" of Genesis 6 who will return to plague the world in Revelation 9? Does the exegesis of these passages warrant such an identification? Are other interpretations possible or more likely in the context?

b. *The increase in number of earthquakes these days is a sign of impending Tribulation judgment.* Is the evidence of increasing global earthquake activity accurate, and if so, how does it fit with the heaven-sent earthquakes described as judgments that occur at definitely ordained times (Revelation 6:12; 11:13; see also Matthew 24:29)? These are the kinds of questions we need to ask before we attempt to connect current events with prophecies about the future.

4. *Distinguish between the last days of the church and the last days of Israel.*

This distinction is often missed among those who look at the events of the last days. Just because the Bible refers to the "last days" or "latter days" does not mean that in every usage it's referring to the same period of time.[7] With reference to Israel such terms speak of that time in which the prophecies about Israel will finally be effected. But for the church, the terms refer to the present age, which will conclude with the rapture. This distinction appears in 1 John 2:18 (written in the first century), where we read: "It is the last hour . . . antichrist is coming" (in the future during Israel's "last days" in the Tribulation period), yet "even now many antichrists have arisen"—a reference indicating that we are in the age that is seeing the preparation take place for the fulfillment of the future event. Since there were no prophecies given concerning the church in the Old Testament (Romans 15:25-26; Ephesians 3:5-10), its "last days" were described as experiencing an increasing spiritual apostasy and deception in connection with the prophetic truth promising Christ's return (1 Timothy 4:1; 2 Timothy 3:1; 2 Peter 3:3-4). Being aware of this distinction helps us to avoid taking prophecies designed for Israel and applying them to the church or taking present signs related to Israel's future and applying them erroneously to some aspect of the church's hope (the rapture).

Now, the prophecies concerning Israel's "last days" indicate that the Jewish people would return to the Land

before the Tribulation (Ezekiel 20:33-34), during which
God will "enter into judgment" with the nation (Ezekiel
20:35-38). In Ezekiel 22:17-22 we see a pattern for this
future punishment of Israel in the gathering of unbelieving
Jewish people into Jerusalem for judgment (as happened in
the Babylonian destruction). Again, this return and gathering is said to take place *before* the time of Israel's judgment (Zephaniah 2:1-3). The modern-day regathering and
return of the Jews to Israel and Jerusalem, as a secular state,
in unbelief, certainly fits the prophetic picture of a people
being readied for judgment, through which they will finally
be brought to faith (Isaiah 59:20; Romans 11:26). Even
though this will occur within the last days of the church age,
it is a sign of Israel's prophetic last days.

5. *Be sure the prophetic interpretation of a current event does not imply date-setting.*

Since the last-day prophecies of the Old Testament concern Israel and not the church, the signs that point to the
nearness of their fulfillment cannot be used to calculate
events expected at the end of the church age.[8] The rapture
of the church, therefore, is a "signless" event, since nothing
must happen (such as a sign) before it can occur (1 Corinthians 1:7; 16:22; Philippians 3:20; 4:5; 1 Thessalonians
1:10; Titus 2:13; Hebrews 9:28; James 5:7-9; 1 Peter 1:13;
Jude 21; Revelation 3:11; 22:7,12,17,20). In like manner,
since the events related to the church and Israel are distinct,
we cannot use the prophetic calendar for Israel (the Feasts)
to predict the rapture of the church. Any use of current
events that results in being able to set a date for the Lord's
return is in conflict with the statements of Scripture that "it
is not for you to know times or epochs which the Father has
fixed by His own authority" (Acts 1:7; see also Matthew

25:13). If Christ would not inform His apostles, why should He make an exception with us?

Date-setting can also occur unintentionally when prophetic events are painted too brightly with modern colors. For example, consider the locust described in Revelation 9. If someone interprets these locusts as being Blackhawk helicopters or Scorpion fighter-helicopters, then they are dating the fulfillment of this future passage within the time-frame of these present aircraft. But we do not know when the rapture of the church will occur, nor how much time will pass between the rapture and the beginning of the Tribulation, nor how radically aircraft technology might change in the time leading up to the Tribulation, when the world goes to war. The only thing we can safely say is that *if* the events of Revelation 9 were to occur *today,* these helicopters might resemble what's being described in the text.

A Cause for Anticipation

In the final analysis, we can say that the proper use of current events indicates that we are living in very exciting times. The alternative is to neglect the "signs of the times" that are on every hand, and thereby be unaware of God's power to perform His promises and unprepared for the judgment seat of Christ (2 Corinthians 5:10). This excitement does not depend on our having to demonstrate that the return of the Jewish people to Jerusalem is a fulfillment in part or in whole, but only that the conditions now exist for that prophetic promise to be fulfilled in the future.

Israeli Pastor Noam Hendren, speaking from the living context of the Land of prophecy, explains his convictions concerning these present conditions:

As we look at the prophetic literature as it relates to
the world coming against Jerusalem, we today can
see how that can really happen. It is no longer far-
fetched, it is no longer "Well, one day all these
things will come to pass." We could see exactly how
it could be in our land and in our time as we think
about the place of the Palestinian and Israeli peace
talks at the present time. Many things seem to have
been solved, and yet we've come to a point of break-
down in the resolution of the key issues—things
are moving again closer and closer to the focus on
Jerusalem. Who will control the city? To whom
does the city belong? Will it be a Palestinian capital?
Will it be the capital of Israel? Will it be divided in
some way? The politicians are having their discussions. But we know that these very discussions and
the difficulties that are facing the negotiators as
they deal with these issues are the kinds of discussions or the kinds of problems which ultimately are
going to lead to Jerusalem becoming that burden-
some stone. So as we look, whether it's in the general sense of the Jewish presence in the land of Israel
and particularly in the city of Jerusalem or if we're
looking at the current state of negotiations and the
question as to whom will this city belong ultimately, we see that the stage has been set for the fulfillment of the predictions of the prophets and of
Jesus Himself in Matthew 24. Jerusalem will be at
the focus, and ultimately the events that we see
today will lead to the fulfillment of the prophetic
events leading to the second coming of Jesus.[9]

The greatest name in real estate is indeed coming to
reclaim His world—the signs are everywhere! They are
present for us at this time in history because our loving
Father knows the path ahead and wants us, His children, to

walk wisely. These are the times of the signs—take note of them and have a pleasant journey!

PART TWO

The Days
of Darkness

The LORD has commanded
concerning Jacob that the ones
round about him should be
his adversaries. . . .

—Lamentations 1:17

With cunning they conspire against
your people; they plot against
those you cherish. "Come," they
say, "let us destroy them as a
nation, that the name of Israel be
remembered no more." With one
mind they plot together; they form
an alliance against you. . . .

—Psalm 83:3-5 (NIV)

7

DARK BEFORE THE DAWN:
The Rise of
Jerusalem's Enemies

Israel lives in a bad neighborhood. One reason it is bad is that the Palestinian people have had a long run of execrable leaders, leaders who supported Adolf Hitler in World War II, the Soviet Union during the Cold War and Saddam Hussein in the Persian Gulf War.[1]

—George Will

"The future isn't what it used to be!"

This paradoxical saying, which captures the feelings of failed expectations in troubled times, might well voice Jerusalem's present dilemma. The Bible prophecies of a brighter tomorrow for Jerusalem, which since 1967 have seemed to be moving toward fulfillment, have today been dimmed by the failure of the peace process and a growing international opposition to a Jewish-controlled Jerusalem.

On every side the enemies that historically opposed a Jewish return to Jerusalem have now been joined by many of Jerusalem's former friends. And recently, for the first time, the superpowers of civilization have interceded, demanding that the Israelis relinquish their sovereignty over the city, even as the Arab states stand ready to invade Jerusalem and remove its Jewish presence. This removal may appear to focus mainly on the Muslim holy places in East Jerusalem,* but ultimately the Palestinian goal is for the Jewish people to be driven from the entire country as well. These dark clouds seem to cast a shadow of doubt over the promises of peace and prosperity made by the prophets, leading many people to ask, "Has prophecy failed? Is the dream about to become a nightmare?"

In truth, prophecy has not failed, but is about to be fulfilled. With prophecy, as with life, the darkest hour is just before the dawn, and the rise of Jerusalem's enemies is a difficult but assuring prelude to the accomplishment of God's promises. Let us, therefore, first look at how the Scripture presents the drama of Jerusalem in the end times, and then from there look at what will happen when God's promises are fulfilled.

Jerusalem and International Opposition

Scripture has predicted that initially Jerusalem will face mounting opposition by the Gentile nations of the world.

---

* At this point, I would like to point out to politically sensitive readers that the use of terms such as *East Jerusalem* and *West Bank* have anti-Semitic or anti-Israel connotations. I personally believe that the West Bank is biblical Judea and Samaria, and that Jerusalem is an indivisible Jewish city. These terms are used only out of convention because in some instances they communicate more clearly than the more accurate but less-conventional terms. In like manner, in the case of the site of the Jewish Temple I have attempted to strictly use *Temple Mount* rather than the Islamic signification, *Harem es-Sharif* ("Noble Enclosure"), even if it would be more accurate when discussing the Islamic viewpoint, because it is the more conventional term.

Psalm 2 prophesies concerning this end-time conflict prior to the second advent:

> Why are the nations in an uproar, and the peoples devising a vain thing? The kings of the earth take their stand, and the rulers take counsel together against the LORD and His Anointed [Messiah]. . . . But as for Me [the LORD], I have installed My King upon Zion, My holy mountain (verses 1-2,6).

This psalm presents God's plan to have the Messiah return to earth and reign over the world from Jerusalem (verses 4-6). The nations have always opposed this plan because they do not want Messiah's rule, but their own (verse 3). As time runs out in the last days, the nations will unite to launch an assault upon the city. This is predicted in Zechariah 12–14:

> Behold, I am going to make Jerusalem a cup that causes reeling to all the peoples around. . . . in that day I will make Jerusalem a heavy stone for all the peoples; all who lift it will be severely injured. And all the nations of the earth will be gathered against it. . . . for I will gather all the nations against Jerusalem to battle (Zechariah 12:2,3; 14:2).

These verses announce that a time is coming when the long history of hostility against Jerusalem will have caused the Gentile nations to become intoxicated with possessing the city. They will all want to internationalize and legislate its future, but those who attempt to drink of it will only find disaster. Attempting to carry off Jerusalem for their own purposes, they will instead find it a heavy and jagged burden that will cut them to pieces. However, the nations that attack Jerusalem will not realize these consequences until it is too late and God's judgment falls heavy upon them (Zechariah 12:9; 14:3,12; see also Daniel 2:44).

Jerusalem in the Tribulation

Whatever happens to Jerusalem affects the rest of the world. God's plan for the future of the earth hangs upon His purpose with Israel, and the timetable for God's purpose with Israel hangs on Jerusalem. This timetable is a predetermined period of domination over Israel that Scripture calls "the times of the Gentiles" (Luke 21:24). The beginning and ending of this period are governed by events that occurred and will occur in Jerusalem. This Gentile rule began in 586 B.C. when the Babylonian army invaded the city. Ever since, except for brief periods of independence, Jerusalem has been under Gentile control. The seventieth week of Daniel's prophecy of the 70 weeks (each week being a period of seven years) will end the "times of the Gentiles" with the coming of the Messiah to defeat the Gentile armies of earth at the climax of this week in the campaign of Armageddon (Revelation 19:11-16). Daniel's seventieth week is referred to by many terms in both the Old and New Testaments,[2] but the term Jesus used in His Olivet Discourse, "the Tribulation," is the one that's used most often when speaking of this period.

The Old Testament presents at least five purposes for the Tribulation:

1. The Tribulation will complete the decreed period of national Israel's judicial hardening as punishment for her rejection of the Messianic program, which the partial return from exile did not remove, and which culminated in the national rejection of Jesus (Isaiah 6:9-13; 24:1-6; see also John 12:37-41; Romans 11:7-10).

2. The Tribulation will produce a Messianic revival among the Jewish people scattered throughout the world

(Deuteronomy 4:27-30; Revelation 7:1-4), and also will result in a massive return of Jews to the Land of Israel (Ezekiel 36:24; 37:21; Zechariah 8:7-8) in preparation for national repentance.

3. The Tribulation will convince the Jewish nation of their need for the Messiah in order to produce a national repentance and regeneration (Daniel 12:5-7; Isaiah 59:20-21; Jeremiah 31:31-34; Ezekiel 20:34-38; 36:25-27; 37:1-14; Zechariah 12:9–13:2).

4. The Tribulation will effect the deliverance of the Jewish people from Gentile dominion by bringing about the judgment of the nations and ending their rule in the coming of Israel's Messiah as Universal King (Isaiah 24:21-23; 59:16-20; Matthew 24:29-31; Mark 13:24-27).

5. It will purge the earth of wicked people in preparation for the coming Messianic kingdom, which will be characterized by righteousness (Isaiah 11:9; 13:9; 24:19-20; Ezekiel 37:23; Zechariah 13:2; 14:9). This violent reduction of the world's unbelieving population will result from the divine judgments unleashed throughout the Tribulation (Revelation 6–18), climaxing with the battles of Armageddon under King Messiah (Revelation 19) and His purge of both rebellious Jews and Gentiles at the end of the Tribulation (Ezekiel 20:33-38; Matthew 25:31-46).

Jerusalem and the Antichrist

During the Tribulation Jerusalem will occupy a prominent position that will cause its enemies to multiply against it. According to Daniel 9:27, at the beginning of the Tribulation, a covenant will be made with the Antichrist which will initiate a three-and-a-half year period of pseudopeace

(1 Thessalonians 5:3; Revelation 6:4) and provide for the rebuilding of the Jewish Temple and the restoration of Jewish worship (more on that in chapter 12). At this time Jerusalem will not only serve as Israel's capital, but most likely as the center of governmental authority for the Antichrist. We can only speculate that his seemingly benevolent occupation of the city will be in keeping with the international concerns stipulated in the covenant.

Those in Jerusalem who sign this covenant, according to Daniel 9:27, are "the many," which refers to the Jewish leadership of Jerusalem. Like the Jewish rulers in the past who unwisely rejected Jesus as Messiah because they felt it would threaten national security (John 11:47-50) and those in the present who have traded the Promised Land for the promise of peace, these leaders represent the city and effect consequences for it. Isaiah 28:14-15 calls these future rulers of Jerusalem "scoffers" rather than leaders because they will "have made a covenant with death, and . . . made falsehood [their] refuge, and have concealed [themselves] with deception." However, there will be a remnant of Jerusalemites (since "the many" does not mean "all") who will reject the covenant, despite its benefits, as an unwise and unbiblical compromise. They will be proven right, for by peace "he [Antichrist] will destroy many" (Daniel 8:25).

That the Antichrist appears to occupy Jerusalem from the time of the signing of the covenant finds support in a text dealing with Antichrist's war with the ten kings (the ten-nation confederation) at the midpoint of the Tribulation: "He will pitch the tents of his royal pavilion between the seas and the beautiful Holy Mountain" (Daniel 11:45). The two "seas" referenced here most likely are the Mediterranean Sea to the west and the Dead Sea to the east, since between them is the "beautiful Holy Mountain." No other place qualifies as the "Holy Mountain" but the Temple Mount in Jerusalem. The "royal pavilion" in Daniel 11:45 refers to the military command center of the Antichrist in Jerusalem. Why in Jerusalem? Because apparently he will already be there. It is for this reason that the attack by the other kings will be aimed at Jerusalem (Daniel 11:44) and why the Antichrist will be killed there—only to be resuscitated and promoted by the False Prophet (Daniel 11:45; Revelation 13:11-14).

It is probably the outbreak of this midtribulational war that ends the period of pseudopeace and causes the Antichrist to break his covenant (Daniel 9:27; Isaiah 28:17-18) and put Jerusalem under his military command (Daniel 11:41). Because the rebuilt Temple appears to be a pivotal part of the peace agreement, it makes sense that the Antichrist's desecration of the Temple at that time will be prompted by his decision to end the Jewish worship and sacrifices that his covenant made possible in the first place. In bringing about this defilement, the Antichrist, following the precedent of earlier Gentile conquerors (Antiochus, Pompey), will enter the Temple's Holy of Holies (Daniel 9:27; 11:36-37; Matthew 24:15). However, the Antichrist's actions will involve more than simply desanctifying the Temple and thereby stopping its sacrifices (Daniel 9:27; 12:11). At this same time a war will break out in heaven between the forces of the Archangel Michael and Satan, and Satan will be confined to earth (Revelation 12:7-9). Consequently, Satan will go after Israel (Revelation 12:13-17). One way he will do this is by having the Antichrist usurp the place of Israel's God in the Holy of Holies. By this act the satanically empowered Antichrist will deify himself, magnifying himself above the gods of every religion (2 Thessalonians 2:3-4; Revelation 13:5-6) and forcing idolatry ("abomination") upon the Jews (Daniel

9:27; Matthew 24:15) by requiring them, and all the world, to participate in satanic worship centered on his image (Revelation 13:2-4,15-16). The Jewish remnant will resist this policy, which from this point onward will result in the Antichrist's persecution of these Jews, starting in Jerusalem (Matthew 24:16-21; Mark 13:14-19) because now it seems that the Antichrist has made the city his religious as well as governmental capital.

Jerusalem and the Two Witnesses

The Antichrist's persecution of the Jewish people will be thwarted by two Jewish prophets who will be raised up at the beginning of the Tribulation (Revelation 11:3-4). Like the two olive trees and menorah (lampstand) in Zechariah's prophecy (Zechariah 4:11-14), they will be lights in the world in testimony to the Lord. However, they will also have the power to do miraculous works similar to those of Moses and Elijah (Revelation 11:5-6).

Unlike the 144,000 Jewish witnesses whose ministry is to both Jews and Gentiles worldwide (Revelation 7:1-17), these two prophets seem to have a ministry centered in Jerusalem and connected in some fashion to the Temple. In Revelation 11 this is implied by the word "and," which connects their appearance in verse 3 with the desecration of the Temple in verse 2. It is also implied in that the two witnesses will be put to death in "the great city... where also their Lord was crucified" (verse 8), which can only be Jerusalem. Their ministry is stated to be three-and-a-half years in duration (verse 3). The same time period is given in the previous verse for the duration of the Temple's desecration, and would imply that they begin their unique ministry at the midpoint of the Tribulation and continue it during this period (the last half of the Tribulation).[3] This might also be supported by the fact that the seventh trumpet is sounded immediately after their translation from earth (verses 14-15). If this is the case, their appearance would come in response to the Antichrist's desecration and the Temple's return to Gentile domination, and continue in a protected state in opposition to the Antichrist's persecution and the False Prophet's miraculous acts of deception. This would give a reason for their being in Jerusalem, especially at the time of their deaths.

If my chronological placement is correct, the two prophets' being resuscitated and translated after three-and-a-half days in full view of the city's inhabitants (verses 9-12), simultaneous with a devastating earthquake, fits Jerusalem's prophesied time of regathering and regeneration. Support for this may be seen in verse 13, where those in Jerusalem, assumed to be mostly a Jewish city, repent as a result of these two events. This repentance would correspond to the national repentance of Israel, centered in Jerusalem, to which the Messiah returns at His second advent (Zechariah 12:10-14; 13:4; Romans 11:26). In this case, the death of the two witnesses coincides with the final assault on Jerusalem, which will be one of the last battles of the Armageddon campaign (Zechariah 14:2).

Jerusalem's Enemies Today

Our progression toward these future events is evident today as the enemies of Israel continue calling for its destruction. Every Arab country is in a declared state of war with Israel except Egypt and Jordan, and even with these two exceptions, the "peace" is only on paper and just as thin. Both Egypt and Jordan support the PLO and their

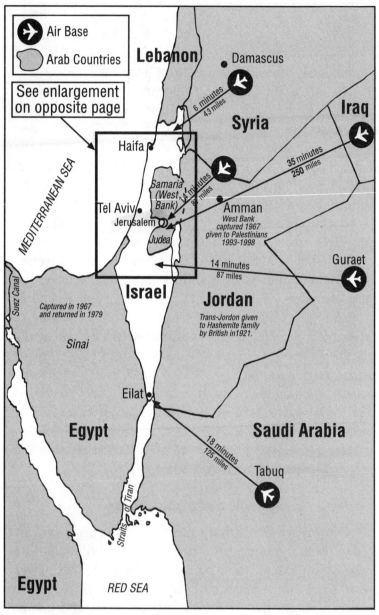

Map showing proximity of Israel's enemies to the State with respect to military engagement.

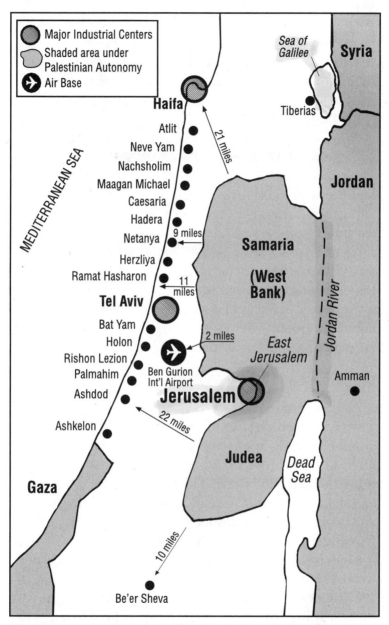

Legend:
- Major Industrial Centers
- Shaded area under Palestinian Autonomy
- Air Base

Syria

Sea of Galilee

Haifa

Tiberias

Atlit

21 miles

Neve Yam

Nachsholim

Jordan

Maagan Michael

Caesaria

Hadera

9 miles

Netanya

Samaria

Herzliya

(West Bank)

Ramat Hasharon

11 miles

Tel Aviv

Jordan River

Bat Yam

Holon

2 miles

Rishon Lezion

East Jerusalem

Palmahim

Ben Gurion Int'l Airport

Amman

Ashdod

Jerusalem

Ashkelon

22 miles

MEDITERRANEAN SEA

Judea

Dead Sea

Gaza

10 miles

Be'er Sheva

Close-up map showing vulnerability of major Israeli cities to attack from Palestinian Authority in West Bank and access for other enemy nations.

proposed Palestinian State, and most certainly are aware
that the PLO has never revoked the clause in their charter
calling for Israel's destruction. The PLO also sides openly
with Iraq's Saddam Hussein, who has repeatedly sought
Israel's annihilation.

Historically, Israel has not had many friends. To Islam,
Israel is one of the foremost friends of Satan. Then there are
Christians who believe Israel has been rejected by God and
replaced with the church. In addition, there are the White
Supremacists, Neo-Nazis, Nation of Islam, and other assor-
ted anti-Semites who perpetuate the nonsense found in *The
Protocols of the Elders of Zion*, a false document which
teaches that all bankers and media elite are Jewish or are controlled by a conspiratorial, Rothschild-funded, secret Jewish
society. To all of this applies this observation from Josh Bill-
ings: "The trouble with most folks isn't so much their ignorance as their knowing so many things that aren't so!"

Understanding Jerusalem's Enemies

It has been said that you cannot appreciate what
another person feels until you wear his skin and walk
around in it. It is one thing to hear about the hatred
directed at the Jews, Israel, and Jerusalem, but another
thing altogether to have that hatred pointed at you. I have
had the unique experience of identifying with the Jewish
and Israeli people on this level, even though I am neither
Jewish nor Israeli. During the time I was living in Israel I
was among a handful of Israelis who journeyed into Egypt a
few days after the borders were opened for the first time in
1980 after peace was made between Egypt and Israel. I was a
student at the time and finances were in short supply, so I
made the trip by hitching a ride with the Arab newspaper

carrier who made the run between the Old City's Damascus Gate and downtown Cairo. The car was rusty, dirty, and of course had no air conditioner. I shared the backseat with newspapers stacked to the ceiling. The papers were being delivered to destinations along the way (via the Gaza Strip), so stops—and stares from the locals—were frequent. But it was not until I began to walk around in Cairo and talk to Egyptians that I began to realize that I was not perceived as a tourist but as trouble! When merchants asked me where I came from and I answered, "Israel," they made me understand what it feels like to be the object of so much hatred and fear. Added to the prejudice taught from birth toward Jews, the Egyptians had suffered significant defeats in their wars with Israel. I was probably the only person from Israel they had ever met outside the battlefield, and I remember especially the mixed look of loathing and suspicion in their eyes as they sarcastically said, "Well, now we are brothers!" After repeated encounters like this, I felt not only like an unwelcome stranger in this city of 40 million, but as if every eye was watching and plotting against me.

This experience, in a small way, helped me to appreciate what it must be like for the Jewish people to have enemies shouting on every side for their destruction and to have a watching world either turn away from or against their cries for support. So before you decide where you stand in the conflict, listen to what Jerusalem's enemies are saying.

Jerusalem's Enemies Speak

Many of Jerusalem's enemies today have gone on record with their hatred and hostility. The following statements are only a small sample of what is being said quite openly, but ignored quite willingly by the modern media:

We are announcing a war against the sons of apes and pigs [the Jews] which will not end until the flag of Islam is raised in Jerusalem[4] (Hamas leaflet, September 1, 1993).

Our first goal is the liberation of all occupied territories . . . and the establishment of a Palestinian state whose capital is Jerusalem. . . . It is the only basis for interim solution and the forerunner to a final settlement, which must be based on complete withdrawal from all occupied Palestinian lands. . . . The Palestinian state is within our grasp. Soon the Palestinian flag will fly on the walls, the minarets, and the cathedrals of Jerusalem[5] (Yasser Arafat, January 1994, and repeated frequently ever since).

We Palestinians will take over everything, including all of Jerusalem. . . . We plan to eliminate the State of Israel and establish a Palestinian state.[6] (Yasser Arafat to Arab ambassadors in Stockholm, January 30, 1996).

The Muslims say to Britain, to France, and to all the infidel nations that Jerusalem is Arab. We shall not respect anyone else's wishes regarding her[7] (Sheikh Ekrima Sabri, Palestinian Mufti of Jerusalem at the Al-Aksa Mosque, July 11, 1997).

Our Palestinian nation will never forget Jerusalem, and will sacrifice half of its number to sanctify the holy name of Allah for the Arab, Palestinian, Islamic and Christian character of occupied Jerusalem (*Voice of Palestine* broadcast, September 26, 1997).

If Israel persists in not recognizing Palestinian sovereignty in the eastern part of Jerusalem, it is the Palestinian side's right to demand its rights from the [Jordan] river to the [Mediterranean] sea[8] (Feisal Husseini, November 28, 1997).

I am sounding the alarm against the Jewish scheme, which aims to establish the Solomon Temple in the place of Al-Aksa Mosque, after removing the mosque.... Delivering holy Jerusalem from the monster represented by this continuous and advancing settlement [Har Homa] and the threat of Judaization is a duty imposed upon all of us by Allah . . . [9] (Yasser Arafat, speech to the Organization of Islamic Conference Summit in Teheran, Iran, December 9, 1997).

Everything within the Palestinian area [in Jerusalem] will be subject to Palestinian sovereignty, no matter who lives there[10] (Feisal Husseini, December 26, 1997).

I have come to personally understand the accuracy of such quotes by my own conversations with Feisal Husseini, the Minister for Jerusalem Affairs in the Palestinian Authority, and Adnan Husseini, Administrator of the Wakf. I have also been at the Palestinian "governmental" offices located in the Orient House in Jerusalem. There I found a large, framed wooden map of Palestine, which depicted the entire country from the Mediterranean Sea to the Jordan River. However, the map depicted not a single Israeli city or town! (See photo #22.) In addition, the whole of the city of Jerusalem was referred to by its Arabic name *Al-Quds*, showing not only the intentions of the Palestinians to occupy all of the Land (including that now defined as Israel), but that Jerusalem as a sacred city is above all other locations on the map as the real source of strife.

Finally, in seeking to understand Jerusalem's Arab enemies, we must ask why they are so intent on taking the city and why diplomacy and negotiation has failed in the political arena. For an explanation I went to a 25-year resident of East Jerusalem, the International Director of the organization Bridges for Peace, Clarence Wagner. He replied:

> The agenda for Jerusalem in the Arab world really comes from a Muslim ideology. It has nothing to do with economics, it has nothing to do with tourism, it has everything to do with how the different peoples read their scriptures. While Jews and Christians read the Bible to understand what God has to say about the city of Jerusalem and the significance both in the Old and New Testaments, the Muslims read the Koran.

> The city of Jerusalem is not in the Koran, and the only allusion to it is to a mystical night ride of Muhammad. Interestingly, before this century, Jerusalem was not as significant in the Muslim world as Mecca and Medina. When the Muslims come to pray on the Temple Mount, which they have now built a mosque over, they pray facing Mecca. Muslims have to go on a Haj as one of their tenets of faith and they must visit, it is said, Mecca, Medina, and Jerusalem. However, the Haddith, the writings of the Muslims, state only that they must visit Mecca and Medina. Jerusalem has been brought into the picture in this century as a direct opposition to the Jewish people's return to Zion, and the Land of Israel. Under Muslim authority... since the seventh century right up until 1917, Jerusalem was never a significant city, it was never a capital city, it wasn't even an important city in the Muslim world. In fact, we find that the main Muslim trade center was Ramleh, which is a small town very near to today's Ben-Gurion airport. Jerusalem was a

misbegotten little side street and in the 1830s we find that Jerusalem only had a little population of about 15,000 people. Already by the 1840s the majority of the population was Jewish and that population has increased.

Zion is significant to the Jewish people. Jerusalem was not significant to the Muslims until the Jews began to return and the Muslims saw, theologically if you will, that they were beginning to lose a hold over some territory which before then had been Muslim.

Now, if we try to understand the Muslim theology or the Muslim tenets of faith, they spread their religion by territorial conquests. And, therefore, we find that the Muslim world has reached out even into Europe in centuries past—up the Iberian peninsula and through the Balkans up towards even to Vienna. They stopped the Muslims at the gates of Vienna and the red flag of Austria is supposed to represent the blood of the Muslims, which they stopped at the gates of Vienna and the Muslim hordes coming up centuries before into the European continent. However, in the last decade a book was written in the Muslim world called *Spain, the Emerald of the Muslim World, the Jewel of the Muslim World.* And when you read this, you find that the Muslims have never let go of the Iberian peninsula, even though they have not been there since 1492. To them, the land is still Muslim because it was once Muslim. And it will therefore again be Muslim if they wait patiently for Allah to give them an opportunity. Therefore, when you come to what they call the land of Palestine, what the Bible calls Israel, as the Jews began to return, as

prophecies began to be fulfilled and we see that
Jewish sovereignty was granted over a land that was
formerly Muslim, this is an affront to Allah. It is an
affront to the Muslim people and their mission in
life is to avenge the cause of Allah and to establish
for themselves a Muslim presence and sovereignty
over all the land of Israel—all the land west of the
Jordan River. And the reason they are focusing
upon Jerusalem is that it is a holy site for Muslims.
It wasn't as significant throughout history, but it is
the most holy site for the Jewish people. Therefore,
if they can reach out and capture Jerusalem, then
they have fairly well defeated the ideology of the
Jewish people that seized Jerusalem.[11]

Jerusalem, a Source of Strife

The question of the city of Jerusalem has been the most
difficult point of contention in the Israeli-Arab peace negotiations: Jordan's King Hussein made it clear that his
country's peace with Israel was conditioned upon the resolution of Jerusalem's ownership. He declared: "Jerusalem is
the essence of peace between us."[12]

Contention over Jerusalem is nothing new. Jerusalem
has been the center of strife all throughout its history. The
city has attracted its enemies by virtue of its unique identification as the capital of God's country. As the symbol of
political and spiritual power, Jerusalem became the final
prize of every conqueror. During the 2,545 years between
the loss of the city to the Babylonians in 587 B.C. and its
recovery by the Israelis in 1967, more than 20 conquerors—
from different empires—have ruled over Jerusalem. These
rulers, however, came from countries which had their own
capital cities. Only for the Jews alone, for more than 650

years during the First and Second Commonwealths, and for the State of Israel since 1948, has Jerusalem served as a capital city. While the Crusaders attempted to make Jerusalem the capital of their Latin kingdom for the 87 years that they held the city (beginning in A.D. 1099), they were not a national entity, so technically it could not have been their "capital." This means that despite Muslim dominance over the city for 1,122 years and the insistence today that Jerusalem is the third holiest site in Islam, the city was never in all of this history ever made the capital of any Arab government. By contrast, for the Jewish people, it has been the only capital of their nation, the central point of their prayers, the subject of their songs, and the most sacred spot on earth. With the fiftieth anniversary of Israel's independence in 1998, Jerusalem passed the half-century mark as a city that has been partly or entirely under Jewish sovereignty as Israel's capital.

Today the historic Jewish right to the city continues to be a source of strife. The Palestinians claim it as the capital of their proposed Palestinian state. However, like the Crusaders, the Palestinians are not a nation and cannot claim a national right to the city or even its Eastern part or declare it their capital. In addition, the Catholic Church opposes both Jewish and Arab control of Jerusalem, recognizing only those sites which they claim for the Vatican as the arbiter of Christendom. They want Jerusalem to be an "internationalized" city—a city for all the world, the very Gentile world which has been prophesied at present to be the enemy of Israel.

The Pattern of Pseudopeace

We have seen that when the Tribulation commences in the future it will begin with the signing of a covenant that produces a false peace for Jerusalem and permits the Jewish people to fulfill their ambition to reestablish worship on the Temple Mount (Daniel 9:27). While we do not know the factors that will make this future covenant possible, the paradigm for this treaty has already been produced. The "peace" agreements between Israel and the Egyptians, Jordanians, and the Palestinians have all illustrated the type of covenant that will be made with the Antichrist. For one, those agreements show Israel's willingness to enter into a covenant with a Gentile power (Antichrist will most likely be a Gentile power—Daniel 11:37; Revelation 13:1). For another, they have all been pseudopeace treaties. Although Egypt and Jordan have not directly fomented aggression, both have forbidden their citizens to travel to Israel or carry on economic trade with the country. Both have also actively supported Israel's enemies, including Saddam Hussein.

The PLO has not only openly supported Saddam Hussein and the Hamas terrorists (the suicide bombers), but has enlisted terrorist leaders in their Palestinian Police Force, fired upon Israeli soldiers and civilians, and continued other acts of aggression. In addition, according to the Institute for Peace Education (based in Tel Aviv), which has monitored every broadcast of the Palestinian Authority's television and radio networks and scrutinized every statement released in Arabic by their Ministry of Information since the signing of the Oslo Accord in 1993, they have never found in any Arabic speech or publication to the Arab people any words of peace![13]

The prophets Jeremiah and Ezekiel warned Israel on the eve of the destruction of its monarchy with these words: "They have healed the brokenness of My people superficially, saying, 'Peace, peace,' but there is no peace" (Jeremiah 6:14; see also 8:11); "they have misled My people by saying, 'Peace!' when there is no peace" (Ezekiel 13:10).

Israel had made unwise and unworthy alliances with enemies who had the potential to fight for Israel, but whose plan was to fight against her. The nation had moved away from trusting in God because of the fear of man (see Isaiah 7:1-9). As we have seen, a similar situation will occur when the Day of the Lord commences with the Tribulation period. Israel will seek security with the help of the Antichrist's governmental system (Revelation 13:4,7,16-17). At that time people will be saying: "Peace and safety!" then "destruction will come upon them suddenly like birth pangs upon a woman with child; and they shall not escape" (1 Thessalonians 5:3). The deception and disappointment of pseudopeace is that those who believe they have prevented future trouble only end up making it difficult for themselves to escape from it. ENGLAND's PRIME minister CHAMBERLAIN

The Consequences of Pseudopeace MuN ILH PAct 1938

Pseudopeace seems to offer the possibility of peace, but in fact only makes more probable the necessity of war. The Israeli agreement with the Palestinians has effectively turned back the calendar to 1947 when Israel was contained within its least-defensible boundaries, only nine miles in width in some places (see map on page 143). The agreement has removed the necessary buffer zone between Israel and its hostile Arab neighbors, and has made possible the establishment of an enemy army in the territories under Palestinian authority, which could cut off access to vital water resources and invade Israel. While the world hopes for peace in the Middle East, more seasoned analysts are now forecasting just the opposite. They see the peace process as part of a phased program devised to weaken Israel as its enemies prepare for the next and perhaps final Arab-Israeli war. It is probable that the failed peace process—due

to Israel's refusal to redivide Jerusalem—will force an invasion of the country. This invasion most likely would begin
from the Palestinian-controlled areas and then would be
joined by all the bordering Arab countries and supported
by neighboring Arab nations and their foreign allies. The
result will be the greatest war Israel has ever fought, and it is
possible that the international community, fearing in
Israel's desperation the threat of a nuclear holocaust, will
be forced to intervene and concede Israel's sovereignty over
Jerusalem, since that will be the issue that precipitated the
war. The peace pact offered, with its inclusion of control
over the Temple Mount, will be accepted by Israeli leaders
who believe this internationally brokered treaty will finally
guarantee the security they have long sought.

Jerusalem and the Future

The enemies of Jerusalem have arisen and are moving
decisively toward the day of final conflict. The darkness is
rapidly descending and the night will seem long, but the
Light of the world is returning to Jerusalem, and the dawn
is about to break. However, Jerusalem must first come to
the very brink of ruin . . .

SENTIENT

~~AWARNESS~~

BEINGS

1. MATTER
2. SENSATION
3. PERCEPTION
4. MENTAL THOUGHT (DREAMS)
5. CONSCIOUSNESS

RECOGNIZE
ONE'S
SELF

SELF-AWARE

O God, the nations have invaded Thine inheritance; They have defiled Thy holy temple; They have laid Jerusalem in ruins.

—Psalm 79:1

I will gather all the nations against Jerusalem to battle, and the city will be captured, the houses plundered, the women ravished, and half of the city exiled.

—Zechariah 14:2

In that hour there was a great earthquake, and a tenth of the city fell; and seven thousand people were killed in the earthquake.

—Revelation 11:13

8

DESTINED FOR DISASTER:
The Ruin of Jerusalem

It will be a miracle if Israel survives another twenty years. But then, it has been a miracle that it has survived the first twenty years.

—J. Robert Moski, Foreign Editor,
Look magazine, 1968

This was a chapter that I did not want to write. Like the wish of a woman in labor, it would be far more pleasant to skip past the birth pangs and go directly to the delivery. But life is not like that. The blessing of birth has to follow a period of pain. It is the same in prophecy. The glorious announcements of Jerusalem's return and restoration follow the grim admonitions of its ravage and ruin. Therefore, difficult though it may be, we cannot bypass the Tribulation and proceed into the kingdom, for it is the sufferings of the one that bring the Savior to the other. Jerusalem is predicted to have one more dark hour ahead before the times of the Gentiles come to an end and the dawn of Jewish redemption begins. After all, the nations will not relinquish their dominion without force, and the force required to make a world release its two-millennia hold on this world can be nothing short of Armageddon. From Jerusalem the Jews are destined to rule the world (under God). Therefore, the world (under Satan) is determined to ruin Jerusalem and the Jews. Satan's plan of the hour is to destroy the Jews. But as we shall see, God has other plans.

"How to Destroy the Jews"

In a metropolitan city with a sizeable Jewish community, the title of the coming Sunday sermon of a prominent pastor was posted on the church marquee in front of the building. In plain sight of a busy main street, the words read: "How to Destroy the Jews." When Sunday morning came, the pastor noticed a number of new visitors in the congregation—officials from the B'Nai Brith, the Jewish Congress, the Jewish Defense League, and scores of rabbis and Yeshiva students—all waiting to hear what this Christian minister would tell his flock about "how to destroy the Jews." The atmosphere was tense as the pastor rose to the pulpit and opened his Bible. He then read the text from which he would speak:

> Thus says the LORD, who gives the sun for light by day, and the fixed order of the moon and the stars for light by night, who stirs up the sea so that its waves roar; the LORD of hosts is His name: "If this fixed order departs from before Me," declares the LORD, "then the offspring of Israel also shall cease from being a nation before Me forever." Thus says the LORD, "If the heavens above can be measured, and the foundations of the earth searched out

below, then I will also cast off all the offspring of
Israel for all that they have done," declares the LORD
(Jeremiah 31:35-37).

The Jewish members of the audience were silent for a
moment. Then one of the rabbis leaned over and said to
another, "I think it's going to be all right!"

Can Israel be destroyed? Yes, there is a way: simply stop
the sun and stars from shining, move away the moon, calculate the cosmos, and investigate the insides of the earth.

Now it goes without saying that if Jerusalem is at the
very center of Israel's future fulfillment, and Israel cannot
be destroyed, then neither can Jerusalem. Yet the attacks
upon Jerusalem have been—and will be—so severe that
God has had to and will continue to give it a double assurance of security. In language similar to that which Jeremiah
used when he spoke of God's care for Israel, the prophet
Isaiah writes of Jerusalem, "The moon will be abashed and
the sun ashamed, for the LORD of hosts will reign on Mount
Zion and in Jerusalem, and His glory will be before His
elders" (Isaiah 24:23). If only Jerusalem's enemies would
read these texts—they would save themselves a lot of
trouble! But Jerusalem's enemies do not concern themselves with its future—only their present. And judging
from the city's past history it appears that the presently
powerful enemies believe the city to be easy prey.

In order to better understand the unprecedented
nature of the present attacks on Jerusalem, let's look briefly
at the horrible history of ruin that the city has suffered.

Jerusalem's Legacy of Ruin

No city has a greater rival for ruin than Jerusalem. In its
33 centuries of existence, it has been ravaged by frequent

earthquakes and sacked by numerous invaders, including the armies of the Egyptians, Assyrians, Babylonians, Macedonians, Ptolemies, Seleucids, Romans, Byzantines, Persians, Arabs, Seljuks, Crusaders, Mongols, Mamlukes, Turks, British, and Jordanians. Jerusalem has been the stage for 36 wars and has endured over 20 sieges and blockades. Its hills have been leveled, its valleys filled, its buildings and Temple burned, its priests and people slain in the streets, sold into slavery, and exiled. The entire city has been reduced to rubble 17 times, rebuilt 18 times, and has suffered through two periods of desolation and Diaspora. No wonder the prophet Jeremiah, filled with sorrow over the loss of the city in 586 B.C. yet filled with visions of still future destructions, cried out, "To what shall I compare you, O daughter of Jerusalem? To what shall I liken you as I comfort you, O virgin daughter of Zion? For your ruin is as vast as the sea" (Lamentations 2:13).

However, after the 70-year captivity, ruin was turned to restoration. The exile ended, and Judah and Jerusalem were rebuilt and resettled. But the restoration was only partial. Jewish people had returned to the Land, but not wholly to the Lord. Eventually Christ came, but God's city refused to receive Him (John 1:11). Therefore, God brought down His beloved Jerusalem. The Romans first besieged it, then destroyed it—Temple and all—in A.D. 70.

The Jews who survived the Roman conquest could not have imagined a more horrible holocaust, but an even greater one was yet to come. The Nazi genocide of the 1930s and 1940s horribly murdered more Jews than had inhabited all of Jerusalem, Israel, and the Diaspora of the first century combined. Today's Jews continue to think nothing worse could ever happen to the Jewish people. Yet half a century later, the seeds of anti-Semitism and anti-Judaism that sowed the *Shoah* (Holocaust) have sprouted anew in even larger numbers with more deadly potential to destroy.

Troubles in the Tribulation

The Old Testament book of Zechariah and the New Testament book of Revelation depict the purpose of the future Armageddon campaign as the world's "final solution" to "the Jewish problem." Like the Nazi Holocaust, it will be nothing less than a satanic attempt to annihilate the Jewish remnant in a last-ditch effort to thwart God's future plans, which depend on the Jewish people for their fulfillment. This battle for Jerusalem follows the gathering of the armies of Antichrist at "Har-Magedon" in the Valley of Jezreel (Revelation 16:12-16), as well as the destruction of Babylon, the Antichrist's commercial center (Jeremiah 50:9-42; 51:7-64; Revelation 18:1-24). This destruction, like Antichrist's desecration of the Temple, is a signal event, in this case heralding the soon coming of the Messiah. Apparently when the Antichrist receives the troubling report about Babylon's fall, Satan will recognize that the end is near and move the Antichrist to turn his armies south to attack the last vestige of a holy hope on earth—the Jewish remnant (Daniel 11:44-45; Zechariah 12:3; 14:2). Some people suggest that the realization that the end is near will come as "the sign of the Son of Man" appears in the sky (Matthew 24:30).[1] The Gentile armies under Antichrist will attack Jerusalem, but God will supernaturally empower the meager Jewish forces to fight against overwhelming odds (Zechariah 12:4-8), demonstrating to Antichrist and the Gentile powers that their dominion is nearly at an end (Zechariah 12:9).

Even though God will protect Jerusalem, the attack will greatly ruin much of the city. Zechariah said that "the city

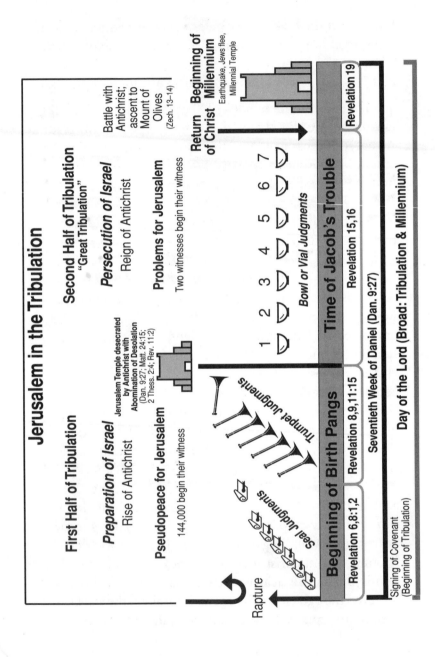

Jerusalem in the Tribulation

First Half of Tribulation

Preparation of Israel
Rise of Antichrist

Jerusalem Temple desecrated by Antichrist with Abomination of Desolation (Dan. 9:27; Matt. 24:15; 2 Thess. 2:4; Rev. 11:2)

Pseudopeace for Jerusalem

144,000 begin their witness

Second Half of Tribulation
"Great Tribulation"

Persecution of Israel
Reign of Antichrist

Problems for Jerusalem

Two witnesses begin their witness

Battle with Antichrist; ascent to Mount of Olives (Zech. 13–14)

Return of Christ

Beginning of Millennium
Earthquake, Jews flee, Millennial Temple

Rapture

Seal Judgments
Revelation 6,8;1,2

Trumpet Judgments
Revelation 8,9,11:15

Bowl or Vial Judgments
1 2 3 4 5 6 7
Revelation 15,16

Revelation 19

Beginning of Birth Pangs

Time of Jacob's Trouble

Seventieth Week of Daniel (Dan. 9:27)

Signing of Covenant (Beginning of Tribulation)

Day of the Lord (Broad: Tribulation & Millennium)

will be captured, the houses plundered, the women ravished, and half of the city exiled" (Zechariah 14:2; see also Joel 3:2-6). If it is in this attack that the two witnesses are killed (Revelation 11:7-10), then the great earthquake that follows and destroys a tenth of the city (Revelation 11:13) also contributes to the ruination during this siege. What distinguishes this siege against Jerusalem from other sieges is that it is by "all nations," and thus it will be greater in scope than any previous attack made on the city. Thus, it will be a fitting climax to the history of Jerusalem's ruin.

This final scene is being staged today as the world sets itself against a Jewish Jerusalem. The international position on Jerusalem, as represented by the United Nations, is that "Israel's occupation is illegal and its actions invalid under international law. . . ."[2] Israel's "violation" of this international law will soon force the world court to make its judgment and support the alignment of nations that will "punish" Israel's continued "occupation" of Jerusalem through conquest.

The Key to the Conquest of Jerusalem

In order to conquer Jerusalem, strategic places in other areas of Israel must first be possessed or controlled. So elementary is this fact that it has been included in a textbook on Jerusalem prepared by the Board of Jewish Education for use in Jewish schools. In a statement instructing students on the tactics of the Romans in their invasion of Jerusalem in A.D. 70, the following is noted:

> The Romans did not proceed directly to the conquest of Jerusalem. On the contrary, they left Jerusalem to the last. First they fought for Galilee and Judea, and only after they had conquered the

country was Jerusalem invested. *For it is impossible to hold Jerusalem unless the whole of the country is held.*[3]

The pattern of conquest in Jerusalem's past is being repeated in the present. When the PLO and Israel signed the Oslo Accord in 1994, Benjamin Netanyahu, then the Likud party leader, explained that PLO leader Yasser Arafat could have negotiated with the Israelis only as part of the PLO's "phased plan," first devised in 1974. This document proposed that "any portion of land liberated from the Zionist occupiers, whether by peaceful or military means, will be used as a staging ground for the complete destruction of Israel." These intentions of Yasser Arafat, especially concerning his promised conquest of Jerusalem, were revealed in speeches made in Arabic to his fellow Muslims. In one secretly recorded speech made in a mosque in Johannesburg, South Africa, Arafat called for faithful Muslims to "come and to fight and start the Jihad [holy war] to liberate Jerusalem," comparing the agreement signed with Israel to Muhammad's peace pact with the Quraysh tribe. This ten-year pact was made because the Quraysh tribe was too strong for Muhammad to defeat. But after only two years, when Muhammad's forces had increased, he broke the pact and and wiped out the entire tribe.

Later in the same speech, Arafat asked his Arab audience to join him "to continue our way to Jerusalem" as "*Mujaheddin* [warriors of Jihad]."[4] Such a war launched against Jerusalem (and Israel) by forces in the region has been predicted by God's prophets.

The Battle of Gog and Magog

Somewhere along the prophetic path will come a war called "the Battle of Gog and Magog" (Ezekiel 38–39). In the context of Ezekiel, this war is placed between the chapters dealing with Israel's return to the Land and spiritual restoration (chapters 33–37) and the building of the Millennial Temple (chapters 40–48). Therefore, the battle could occur prior to the Tribulation, during the Tribulation, or at its end.[5] The repeated description of the time period given in the text is of an Israel living "securely... without walls, and having no bars or gates" (Ezekiel 38:11). At present the only walled city in Israel with bars and gates is the Old City of Jerusalem, but the majority of Jewish Jerusalemites live in the new city outside these walls. Jerusalem and its environs also agree with Ezekiel's identification of cities as "inhabited waste places" predicted for this time (Ezekiel 38:12).

In the end-time battle of Gog and Magog, Gog is depicted as a military leader that arises from "the northern region" (from Israel's vantage point) of Magog (ancient Scythia). Today this area is comprised of the former Soviet republics of Kazakhstan, Kirghiza, Uzbekistan, Turkmenistan, and Tajikistan. According to Ezekiel, the other nations that will align themselves with Magog to invade Israel are Meshech and Tubal (territories in Turkey), Gomer (Germany), Togarmah (Turkey), Persia (Iran), Cush/Ethiopia (Sudan), Put (Libya), and Egypt (according to Daniel 11:40-42). While there is a difference of opinion as to the precise timing of this war, most premillennial scholars place it sometime before or during the Tribulation period (see Ezekiel 37:8,16; 39:9).[6]

Can it be only coincidental that the balance of power in this part of the world has for decades been concentrated in Russia and the Arab countries? Since the dissolution of the Soviet Union, six of the former southern republics have become independent *Islamic* nations: Azerbaijan, Kazakhstan, Uzbekistan,

Kirghiza, Turkmenistan, and Tajikistan. All of these new nations, which are today in the region of Ezekiel's prediction, have militant Islamic movements and are virulently anti-Semitic. Also they all have experienced economic hardships and political instability that have forced them to make alliances with other nations that have been able to supply them with nuclear technology.

In mother Russia there is also a strong anti-Semitism among nationalists and ultranationalists. One of Russia's prominent ultranationalists, Vladimir Zhirinovsky, in a book entitled *The Final March to the South,* proposed a military strategy for world domination that is remarkably similar to the prophetic sketch of the end-time one-world government that will be divided into ten national entities (Daniel 7:24; Revelation 17:12-13). He has voiced a new radical desire for a restoration of Russia's primacy and has threatened to use nuclear weapons to achieve his ends. He argues that it is Russia's destiny to capture the lands to the south, including Israel. Interestingly, his plan does not call for the destruction of Israel, but control over it.

If Russia is allied with the Arab countries, it might be in a position to negotiate with Israel. Russia could also invade Israel and gain control of it by guaranteeing security for the Jewish people by a covenant of peace. This is similar to what's described in Daniel 11:41 and Ezekiel 38:8, where we see a non-destructive invasion of Israel from the north. It appears that the groundwork for such an invasion has been laid as a result of the political and economic circumstances in Russia. Because Russia cannot produce sufficient industry to survive economically, its only course has been to align itself with Third World countries. An axis is thought to have been formed among the Middle Eastern countries of Iraq, Iran, Syria, Sudan, and Ethiopia to overthrow the United States and its allies. (The only ally the United States has in the Middle East is Israel.) Russia has already forged alliances with some of these countries and others: Iran, Syria, Pakistan, Libya, and Turkey. In addition, the Central Asian Republics of Kazakhstan, Turkmenistan, Tadzhikistan, Uzbekistan, and Krygzstan have signed a military assistance pact with the Russian Federation. These countries are all Islamic and have been confirmed to possess nuclear weapons.

As the twenty-first century neared, the international community expected that the nuclear armaments issue was a thing of the past. However, that dream is now dead. Iran and Iraq have been arming themselves with weapons supplied by Russia and China as never before—an act which in itself calls for international involvement. Iraq has again threatened the West and Middle East, causing Yasser Arafat to believe that "a Palestinian victory over Israel and Iraqi victory over the U.S. are mutually dependent."[7] The Islamic country of Pakistan has tested nuclear weapons and declared that it has long-range missiles able to deliver a nuclear payload in Southeast Asia. The global implications of renewed nuclear proliferation threatens the stability of the Middle East and is today causing the international community to take greater steps of intervention (sanctions, at the time of this writing).

These developments, combined with the foundering of the peace process, led Gershon Salomon, leader of Israel's Temple Mount Faithful, to announce in his newsletter that he expects the next Arab-Israeli war to be the prophetic battle of Gog and Magog:

> I consider it my duty to warn my people and all the friends of Israel that a terrible war, the most terrible war of all the seven wars of Israel, is going to be perpetrated in this land against the people of Israel as a

direct result of these terrible agreements and the giving away to the enemies of G-d our Holy Temple Mount and the most holy and important Biblical areas of Israel. . . . According to the prophetic plans of G-d these areas must be, and will be, even more so than in the past, the land of G-d and the people of Israel to carry the great mission in the end-times. . . . We read in the prophetic Scriptures of Ezekiel and Zechariah about the terrible Gog and Magog war which is going to come on the people of Israel in the end-times, in the time of the redemption. When we see these terrible, critical events in Israel we can understand why, in this time of redemption, this terrible war of Gog and Magog is going to take place. . . . This war will not be an easy time for Israel . . . but it will be the last war of redemption of the people of Israel. This will be the war when the Messiah, Mashiach ben David, will appear and again be the eternal King of Israel. This war will also open a new moral and spiritual page in the history of Israel. After this war the people of Israel will not be the same people. . . . [8]

If this expected coming war is that of Gog and Magog, or some other war involving similar peoples, and it neutralizes the pervasive political clout of Islam, Israel will emerge as a major player in the end-time scenario and a force with which to be reckoned by all nations (see Zechariah 12:3,9; 14:2).

On the Edge of Disaster

In my library I discovered a book I had forgotten about until recently. It is the type of book that we might pick up at a garage sale because we think it might be interesting to read someday. Someday had arrived for me, so I opened the book *The Greatest Disasters of the 20th Century*, and read these words on the first page:

> Disaster is unlike anything else in human experience. It strikes quickly, it changes the lives of all it touches, and its effects are felt long after the event. And, perhaps more important, its forces are largely outside the control of the people whom it most affects.[9]

The disasters of the Gog and Magog war, the Tribulation, and Armageddon are coming, and with them the final threat of ruin for Jerusalem. It will, as this book's definition of disaster goes, come rapidly upon a world unawares, with life-changing effects beyond anything we can humanly control. If the events taking place today in preparation of the future wars are not interrupted, they will soon lead to this predicted disaster for Jerusalem.

The Perspective for Disaster

Terrorism and Controversy

The Palestinians, along with most all of the Arab and Islamic world, continue to deny official recognition of the existence of the State of Israel and constantly call for its destruction. The PLO has not changed its charter and recognized Israel's *right* to exist. They have simply recognized the *reality* that Israel exists and left the charter as it was, still calling for the elimination of the Jewish State. And what of the renunciation of terrorism? Following the day of the handshake on the White House lawn, the United States removed the PLO from its list of terrorist organizations. However, since the beginning of the "peace" process, statistics reveal that PLO terrorism has actually increased. Between September 1993 and April 1997 there have been 32 Israeli civilians murdered, 438 Israeli civilians injured, 21 Israeli soldiers murdered, 527 Israeli soldiers injured, 239 Israelis stabbed, 88 bombings, 1,220 petrol bombs thrown, 210 shootings, and 51 hand grenade attacks.[10] There were 286 attacks in 1996 (from firebombs to suicide bombings), and 521 attacks in 1997. In 1998 (at the time of this writing) there have already been extensive and intensive attacks such as the suicide bombings at a Tel Aviv restaurant and at Jerusalem's crowded outdoor market, Mahane Yehuda.[11] In addition, Israeli officials have been able to prevent over 100 planned attacks on such places as Jerusalem's largest mall, its amphitheater, railroads, and a bypass road in the West Bank, as well as kidnapping attempts on Jerusalem's mayors and a car bomb planned for Tel Aviv's Diamond Exchange.

Even with all these attacks against Israel, the Rabin-Perez government made dramatic concessions to the enemies of Jerusalem, stopping short only of negotiating away Jewish sovereignty over the city. Yasser Arafat claimed that there had been a secret meeting in which East Jerusalem had been promised to him; however, Rabin had also stated publicly and privately (to Jerusalem's mayor), only 3 days before his assassination, that the city would never again be divided.[12]

Since 1996, the spectre of Har Homa, a region of East Jerusalem, has haunted the peace process. Termed "a new Berlin Wall," it has precipitated every nation taking sides against Israel on the question of its right to retain sovereignty within its borders (see photos #18 and #19). For this reason it has been called the "cornerstone of the next war" by peace activists.

For Israel, Har Homa is within the municipal boundaries of Jerusalem (since East Jerusalem was annexed in 1980) and is simply a necessary use of legitimate land for planned construction. For the Palestinians, it is an expansionist appropriation of Arab property[13] (Abu Ghuneim) for new Israeli settlements on land that will be part of their capital. The European Union, not recognizing Israel's annexation of East Jerusalem, also rejects any Israeli settlement in so-called "occupied" territory. In response to criticism from the world press, Prime Minister Netanyahu stated, "We will build in Jerusalem, without conditions, without concessions, without restrictions. We will build throughout the city. . . . "[14]

This stance has led to a polarization between Israel and the world over the issue of a Jewish-controlled Jerusalem. Israel's intractable attitude today is much the same as that demonstrated by one of the early church fathers in his refusal to recant, in the face of hierarchical threats, what he understood to be the truths of Scripture. A friend came to this church father in his prison cell and appealed to him to compromise, saying, "Don't you know the world is against you?" The reasonable but resolute saint responded, "Well, then, I am against the world!"

This posture was adopted by Prime Minister Benjamin Netanyahu and his coalition in the government when the United States and Great Britain demanded the Har Homa construction be stopped—a direct challenge to Israeli sovereignty over Jerusalem. On that occasion Netanyahu cautioned, "One thing is clear; it is Israel who will decide its security needs—and only Israel can do this."[15] Where but to the predicted confrontation can such attitudes be leading? This is the contemporary question that has but one prophetic conclusion. This was noted by one recent observer who, assessing the international vise closing hard upon Israel, concluded: "Weakening Israel territorially or spiritually, Washington will soon force it to face the choice Chamberlain faced when appeasement failed and Hitler invaded Poland: fight a desperate war or perish."[16] This is not an acceptable option for those whose cherished goal is peace. Unable to deter it they have now chosen to deny it in the vain hope that everything will work out because it must. This helps explain the bewildered recognition that "the blindness of American, and even Israeli leaders . . . academics and media to the 'jihad' peril to world order and peace is appalling; for an intelligence figure to be so blind is incredible."[17]

One explanation could be that which authors John Loftus and Mark Aarons assert when they warn that a secret war against the Jewish people has been orchestrated by Western leaders for many decades: "The major powers of the world have repeatedly planned covert operations to bring about the partial or total destruction of Israel. Long before there was even a Jewish State in Palestine, Western spies already were out to wreck the Zionist dream."[18] However, if we are not willing to entertain the idea of a Western anti-Semitic conspiracy, we may find an answer in people's ignorance of the future as predicted by the prophet Daniel: " . . . none of the wicked will understand, but those who have insight will understand" (Daniel 12:10). The wicked will not understand even though the outcome of their policies and pressures are clear, because the "insight" needed to understand the future with respect to the Jews is a practical knowledge of the end-time prophecies, which only the righteous possess (Daniel 12:3). More specifically, the context of the passage in Daniel tells us this "insight" has to do with the timing of the promised deliverance of the Jews living during the last half of the Tribulation (Daniel 12:11-12).

The Weapons of War

The prophetic predictions concerning Jerusalem's future invasion seem closer to fulfillment as the Arab nations and their allies and suppliers in the former Soviet Union and Red China progressively plan for war against Israel. Israel's Arab enemies are known to have weapons of mass destruction—nuclear, chemical, and biological—all of which are aimed at Israel. It has also been made public that Israel's much-rumored nuclear program has at least 100 nuclear devices in storage.[19] Furthermore, neither the Arab countries nor Israel have signed the Nuclear Nonproliferation Treaty. And finally, the former Soviet Union, which was thought to have dismantled their chemical weapons program at the end of the cold war, has actually been continuing the production of bacteriological arsenal and has supplied technology and training to Syria, Iran, and Iraq.[20]

However, in the event of a full-scale guerilla war within the small boundaries of Israel and the West Bank (Judea and Samaria), only conventional weapons could be employed. Knowing this, the Palestinians have been making military preparations for some time. According to several sources, the Palestinians have smuggled from Egypt (via Sinai tunnels) and Jordan hundreds of mortars, armor-piercing heavy machine guns, rocket-propelled grenades, Stinger shoulder-fired anti-tank missiles, rocket launchers, anti-aircraft missiles (SAM-7), and Katyusha rockets.[21] They have created their own factories for manufacturing Uzi submachine guns, trained an army of some 50,000 soldiers (currently called "police," a large number of whom have a history as terrorists), and practiced war drills (such as the digging of ditches and building of obstacles to slow an Israeli advance).[22] All of these activities, of course, are forbidden in the agreements the PLO have signed, and there can be only one purpose for such preparations—a war, the possibility of which has often been stated by Yasser Arafat: "We still have the option of *Jihad* [Holy War]."²³

With the failure of the peace process this has been seen as the only option not for a new militant generation of Palestinians alone, but also for Bedouin and Israeli-Arabs who have become increasingly polarized from the Jewish State and adopted an activist response to the Israeli authorities.²⁴ In March of 1998 the chairman of Yasser Arafat's Fatah faction of the PLO in Jenin announced the reestablishment of the Black Panther military units, stating: "We are ready for a military confrontation. . . . The bullets of the Black Panthers will strike at Netanyahu's soldiers."²⁵ With this modern Arab solidarity forming the basis for a guerilla army, the Palestinians will take up Arafat's foremost objective: "We will enter Jerusalem victorious and will raise the [Palestinian] flag on its walls."²⁶

The Laughing Rabbi and Redeeming Lion

According to the Talmud, "everyone who mourns for Jerusalem merits to share in her joy" (Ta'anit). However, the famous Rabbi Akiba once presented an exception to this saying. When he and a group of his students were walking among the ruins of the Temple, his students began to mourn, but Rabbi Akiba began to laugh. Startled, his students asked him why he was laughing. The rabbi replied, "Because if the prophecies of its destruction have come to pass, we are certain to see the prophecies of its restoration fulfilled!" Just as this rabbi laughed, so God who sits in the heavens will laugh as the nations fall over themselves in defenseless defiance of His will (Psalm 2:4). In seeking to conquer His plans they will instead confirm them, and overthrow themselves. For with the same prophetic certitude that they have been destined for disaster, Israel has also been destined for deliverance. These were but the birth-pangs; the new birth is at hand.

Despite disasters, destructions, exiles, pogroms, holo-causts, and enemies on every side for over 20 centuries, the Jews have returned to live in Jerusalem because, however ruined, it holds the promise of restoration. No wonder Benjamin Netanyahu, when talking of the threats to Israel's sovereignty over Jerusalem, said, "We will confront any-one!" That confrontation will come, and with it another ruin of the city. Yet its end this time will not be in a ruin, but a rescue. That rescue is embodied today in one of Jerusa-lem's most visible symbols—the Lion of Judah, the protec-tor of Jerusalem who keeps watch over the apple of God's eye. This symbol is seen throughout the city wherever the emblem of the Jerusalem municipality is displayed—on building plaques, statuary, banners, posters, and flags (see photo #2). This Lion of Judah is the same One who is pre-dicted to return and overcome for the sake of Zion: "Behold, the Lion that is from the tribe of Judah, the Root of David, has overcome" (Revelation 5:5).

Jerusalem—destined for disaster, but also deliverance! In the next chapter we will explore the prophecy of Jerusalem's deliverance and the Redeemer's promise to rescue it from ruin.

PART THREE

The Days
of
Deliverance

"A Redeemer will come to Zion,
and to those who turn from
transgression in Jacob,"
declares the LORD.

—Isaiah 59:20

In that day His feet will stand on
the Mount of Olives, which is
in front of Jerusalem on the east.

—Zechariah 14:4

He who testifies to these things
says, "Yes, I am coming quickly."
Amen. Come, Lord Jesus.

—Revelation 22:20

9

REDEEMER TO THE RESCUE:

The Return of Jerusalem's Messiah

I believe with perfect faith in the coming of the Messiah, and though he should delay his coming, I wait daily for his coming.

—Twelfth of the *Thirteen Principles of Faith* in the *Siddur*

The Yom Kippur War began at 2:00 P.M. on October 6, 1973. It was a surprise attack on Israel from the Arab nations of Egypt and Syria, which were intent on the destruction of the Jewish State. Overwhelming evidence of large-scale Arab military preparations on the morning of October 6 had compelled Chief of Staff David Elazar to ask the United States to help restrain the Arabs. U.S. Secretary of State Henry Kissinger urged Prime Minister Golda Meir to not issue a preemptive strike, but to trust international guarantees for Israel's security. To which Mrs. Meir, in her characteristic upfront manner, retorted, "By the time they come to save Israel, there won't be an Israel!"[1] When international intervention finally came in calling for cease-fire negotiations, Israeli casualties had mounted to 2,552 dead and over 3,000 wounded. It would have been much worse had Israel waited upon her allies. For that reason, Israel has come to rely upon their own defenses for their security. That attack is just a foretaste of what Israel can expect in the future, when the worst attack in its history will come and will be centered on Jerusalem. In that day there will be no allies, not even reluctant ones. Just as in 1973, Jerusalemites will surely fear that were there anyone to attempt to save them, they would arrive too late! But Scripture has prophesied otherwise. At the right time, Jerusalem's Savior will return.

Where Will the Messiah Return?

Zechariah 8:3 tells us where the Lord will return: "I will return to Zion and dwell in the midst of Jerusalem." From the days of the prophets onward, the Jews have believed that the Messiah would be revealed only in Jerusalem. This belief was evident in Jesus' disciples; when Jesus predicted the destruction of the Jerusalem Temple, they responded, "What will be the sign of Your coming, and of the end of the age?" (Matthew 24:3). This question reveals that they believed that the future of the city was connected with the coming of the Messiah in the end times. In like manner, after Jesus' resurrection, when He again gathered the disciples to the Mount of Olives, they asked, "Lord, is it at this time You are restoring the kingdom to Israel?" (Acts 1:6).

This question implies that they understood that Jesus' return to Jerusalem and to the Mount of Olives was connected with the prophesied restoration of Israel. Jesus appears to confirm their understanding in His answer: "It is not for you to know times or epochs which the Father has fixed by His own authority" (Acts 1:7). In other words, their theology was right, but the time was wrong. Jesus would return in His resurrected state to Jerusalem, and from the Mount of Olives, initiate the process of restoration (Zechariah 14:4-8), but the end of the age for Israel had not yet come. God's plan was to show mercy to the Gentiles as well as a Jewish remnant (Romans 11:5,11,25,31). His plan was for the church age to come first (Acts 1:8).

As for the location of Jesus' return, some people might point to Acts 1:11, which says "This Jesus, who has been taken up from you into heaven, will come in just the same way as you have watched Him go into heaven" (Acts 1:11). This statement, however, does not indicate the *place* of the return, only the *procedure*—to the earth in a visible, glorified state. Yet, when we wonder *where* on earth this return will take place, no other answer can be given than Jerusalem. This does not require that the return be *initially* to Jerusalem; however, all the passages dealing with the return indicate that the reason for the return revolves around Jerusalem.

However, some Christians do not interpret these passages of Christ's return to Jerusalem as literal. They say Israel has been replaced by the church because they believe only *spiritual* Israel, not physical Israel, was relevant in the prophetic program. But in Old Testament times there was no such thing as a spiritual Israel that was distinct from the physical Israel. There have always been both believing and unbelieving Jews within the physical nation, just as there are also believing and unbelieving Gentiles within the professing church. This is what Paul meant when he said: "For he is not a Jew who is one outwardly. . . . But he is a Jew who is one inwardly" (Romans 2:28). Since in the context Paul is addressing only Jews (Romans 2:17), his distinction is between unbelieving and believing *physical* Jews. Therefore, when Zechariah says of the Lord, "I will return to Zion and dwell in Jerusalem," he means literal Zion and literal Jerusalem. Furthermore, this future Jerusalem is to be a *Jewish* Jerusalem. As CBS radio correspondent Dave Dolan observes:

> In praying about how to end my prophetic novel *The End of the Age,* I came to the conclusion that it could end in no other place but with the Mount of Olives. The spot where the Bible says the Lord Yeshua, Jesus, will return to. And it's so exciting for me to look out in this area today and see that it is so full of Jews. This whole city is so full of Jews. Not just Jewish graves, which are also back here on the Mount of Olives and 100 years ago were the main Jewish presence in the area, but a living Jewish city as Jesus implied we would see in the last days when He came back.[2]

This same city of Jerusalem must be the place the Jewish Messiah will return. According to biblical history, Jesus has never been anywhere else. How then could He ever be understood to return to somewhere else? Neither can this return be interpreted as a return to the New Jerusalem in heaven. In Acts 1:11 the angels do say that Jesus returned to heaven. But their point is that the same Jesus who was taken up into heaven will also return to earth! Furthermore, the heavenly Jerusalem itself may someday appear on earth (more on this in chapter 14).

If we discern the distinction between the first and second comings of the Messiah in the prophetic texts of the Old Testament, we can observe that a return to a literal Jerusalem is required for both sets of texts to be fulfilled. For example, Zechariah 9:9-10 predicted:

> Rejoice greatly, O daughter of Zion! Shout in triumph, O daughter of Jerusalem! Behold, your king is coming to you; He is just and endowed with salvation [triumphant], humble and mounted on a donkey, even on a colt, the foal of a donkey (verse 9).
>
> And I will cut off the chariot from Ephraim, and the horse from Jerusalem; and the bow of war will be cut off. And He will speak peace to the nations; and His dominion will be from sea [Gulf of Aqaba] to sea [Mediterranean], and from the River [Euphrates] to the ends of the earth [everywhere else] (verse 10).

The New Testament interprets Jesus' "triumphal entry" into Jerusalem riding on a donkey as fulfilling only the first portion of this prophecy (Matthew 21:2-5; John 12:13-16). Both Matthew and John understood Jesus to be the triumphant king and cite verse 9 (Matthew 21:5; John 12:15), but neither of them cite verse 10. They seem to be aware that it was improper to view all of Zechariah 9:9-10 as finding fulfillment in the gospel era. The contrasts in the descriptions of the Messiah in these two verses from Zechariah reveal the reason why. Jesus triumphed spiritually, but He died within days after His triumphal entry, and was not established as a king with a reign on earth—much less a universal king with dominion over all the nations of the earth. In verse 9 the Messiah is a humble and peaceful Savior, in verse 10 He is a sovereign and warring conqueror.

Every Christian accepts the fact that the prophecy in Zechariah 9:9 was fulfilled *literally*. Why, then, should not the remainder of this passage, which must be understood in reference to Messiah's future return and reign to Jerusalem, also be accepted as literal?[3] And, if Messiah is going to fulfill Zechariah 9:10 literally, then we know He will also literally fulfill the prophecies related to the restoration of Jerusalem, the rebuilding of the Temple, and His rule from the city as His throne. For these things to happen, He must return to Jerusalem.

When Will the Messiah Return?

The Jewish people have had a number of disappointments in their long wait for the Redeemer. History has offered several opportunities for the Redeemer to rescue His people. For example, in 586 B.C., when King Zedekiah stood bound by Babylonian fetters in the smoldering ashes of his conquered kingdom, the people of Jerusalem most likely were hoping that their prophets' predictions of God's intervention would be fulfilled upon the city's fall. But no help appeared, and the king's last sight on earth was the slaughter of his sons—the last heirs to the Davidic throne, and symbols of the Messianic hope (2 Kings 25:6-7). In A.D. 70, a Jerusalem that had rejected the Messianic claims of Jesus watched in disbelief as the Romans set their city and its inviolable Temple ablaze. Priests stood high on top of the burning Temple with arms outstretched, believing until the end that the Messiah would come. It is reported that some priests even hurled themselves into the flames to provoke God's pity and hasten His help. But no help came, and priest and people alike perished without redemption.

However, the New Testament indicates that Israel's Messiah will come when the full number of Gentiles have received God's mercy. Not until then will the period of Gentile rule end:

> I do not want you, brethren, to be uninformed of this mystery . . . that a partial hardening has happened to Israel until the fulness of the Gentiles has come in; and thus all Israel will be saved; just as it is written, "The Deliverer will come from Zion, He will remove ungodliness from Jacob" (Romans 11:25-26).

This passage makes it clear that when the times of the Gentiles is over, an end will come to the present period of Jewish rejection. God's mercy upon the Gentiles has come as a result of Jewish disobedience (Romans 11:12,15,30-31), but once Jewish obedience is obtained, God's mercy will again be returned to them. This, however, applies to Jews and Gentiles in a national, rather than individual, sense. This is the understanding of the phrase "all Israel" in Romans 11:26. There are individual Jews who have received mercy and believed in Jesus as Messiah since the first-century: "a remnant according to God's gracious choice" (Romans 11:5). Likewise, individual Gentiles will continue to receive mercy and believe throughout the period of Israel's restoration (Revelation 7:9-17).

By contrast, Israel's *national* salvation, spiritually (and physically), will occur when "the Deliverer will come." This Deliverer will come *from Zion,* emphasizing His identity as a Jewish Messiah for the Jewish nation.[4] The word here translated "Deliverer" is in the Old Testament text from which is cited the Hebrew term *go'el,* "Redeemer." It is the word used in the book of Ruth to speak of Boaz as the kinsman-redeemer. The qualifications for this position was threefold: 1) He had to be physically related; 2) he had to be able to redeem (that is, free from obligation himself and able to pay the required price); and 3) he had to be willing to redeem. Jesus, as the Messiah who is coming to save Israel, met these qualifications at His first advent: He was born of the seed of Abraham and belonged to the lineage of David (Matthew 1:1); He was sinless (John 8:46); and He was willing to redeem (Matthew 26:42; Mark 14:36; Luke 22:42; John 6:38; 10:15,18; Hebrews 10:9). While this redemption was accomplished for Israel at Messiah's first coming (Matthew 1:21; 15:24), it will not be applied nationally until His second coming. The precise timing for this redemption coincides with the regeneration of Israel prior to the judgment of the nations at the end of the Tribulation.

The Circumstances at Messiah's Return

According to the prophetic scenario revealed in both the Old and New Testaments, Jesus will return to Jerusalem at the time of its greatest need to bring its greatest deliverance. In the previous chapter we examined the passages that detailed the Gentile armies' attack upon Jerusalem at the end of the Tribulation period. Much destruction and devastation will occur. However, because the Jerusalemites will be supernaturally assisted and empowered in their defense of the city (Zechariah 12:5-9), Jerusalem's ruin will not be complete: "half of the city [will be] exiled, but the rest of the people will not be cut off from the city" (Zechariah 14:2).

Meanwhile, another Jewish remnant will take refuge in southern Jordan at the city of Bozrah. This remnant is comprised of Jews from Judah who will understand the significance of the Antichrist's desecration of the Temple and breaking of the covenant and flee to this mountainous region at the mid-point of the Tribulation (Matthew 24:16). The Antichrist's armies will turn their attention away from Jerusalem in order to destroy these Jews (Jeremiah 49:13-14; see also Isaiah 34:1-7; 63:1-6; Micah 2:12-13; Habakkuk 3:3). As a result of this seemingly invincible invasion coming against them, these Judean Jews will repent of their sin of rejecting Jesus as Messiah and cry out for Him to return. The preparation for this repentance will be through the 144,000 witnesses and then the two witnesses, who will preach the gospel during the Tribulation (Revelation 7:1-8; 11:1-11; see also Acts 2:19-21). It appears that the Jews in Jerusalem will also join in this moment of national repentance (Zechariah 12:10-14).

In response, their Messiah and His heavenly armies[5] will come to rescue these Judean Jews by direct divine and personal intervention (Revelation 19:11-14) and to begin the destruction of the Gentile invaders (Zechariah 14:12-13; Revelation 19:15-21). This will fulfill the passage in Zechariah that says "The LORD also will save the tents of Judah first in order that the glory of the house of David and the glory of the inhabitants of Jerusalem may not be magnified above Judah (Zechariah 12:7).[6] The returning Redeemer will be visible to all (Revelation 1:7)—both the repentant Jewish remnant and the attacking Antichrist and his armies (Matthew 24:27,30; Luke 21:27). This will be a sign to the Jews of their redemption (Luke 21:28), but to their attackers it's a sign of their doom (Luke 21:26). The New Testament describes this judgment on the nations in dramatic fashion:

> ... when the Lord Jesus shall be revealed from heaven with His mighty angels in flaming fire, dealing out retribution to those who do not know God ... (2 Thessalonians 1:7-9).

> I saw heaven opened; and behold, a white horse, and He who sat upon it is called Faithful and True; and in righteousness He judges and wages war. And His eyes are a flame of fire. . . . and He is clothed with a robe dipped in blood. . . . And from His mouth comes a sharp sword, so that with it He may smite the nations (Revelation 19:11-12,13,15).

The Old Testament prophets also predicted this cataclysmic battle in Bozrah in similar language: "The sword of the Lord is filled with blood. . . . For the Lord has a sacrifice in Bozrah, and a great slaughter in the land of Edom" (Isaiah 34:6-7). The casualties that the armies of the Antichrist will suffer in this engagement (Revelation 19:15-18) will force him, in satanic desperation, to turn back toward Jerusalem to finish off its inhabitants (Zechariah 14:2). But the Messiah and His armies will follow after them and finish the battle in Jerusalem's Kidron Valley, known also as the valley of Jehoshaphat: "I will gather all the nations, and bring them down to the Valley of Jehoshaphat. Then I will enter into judgment with them there on behalf of My people and My inheritance, Israel" (Joel 3:2).

It is at this point that the divine intervention is predicted for Jerusalem: "Then the LORD will go forth and fight against those nations, as when He fights on a day of battle" (Zechariah 14:3). In this battle both the False Prophet and the Antichrist, who once held the empires of the world in his hand and sought to rally them against heaven (Revelation 19:19), will be slain in a moment (2 Thessalonians 2:8; Revelation 19:15,20). In addition, the armies of Antichrist will suffer from a horrible heaven-sent plague (Zechariah 14:12-15).

The Messiah will then victoriously ascend Jerusalem's Mount of Olives:

> In that day His feet will stand on the Mount of Olives, which is in front of Jerusalem on the east; and the Mount of Olives will be split in its middle from east to west by a very large valley, so that half of the mountain will move toward the north and the other half toward the south (Zechariah 14:4).

This splitting of Jerusalem into three divisions (apparently through the great earthquake described in Zechariah 14:5) will be in preparation for the building of Messiah's Temple and His Millennial reign (Zechariah 14:4-8; Ezekiel 47:1-12; Revelation 20:4).[7] As we've noted earlier, earthquakes happen frequently in the Jerusalem area, and evidence indicates that the Mount of Olives is set to split should an earthquake of sufficient size strike the region. The evidence for this was first presented by Professor Bailey Willis, a seismological expert at Leland Stanford University. He is said to have made the following statement in a report to the British Association for the Advancement of Science: "The region around Jerusalem is a region of potential earthquake danger. A 'fault line,' along which an earth slippage may occur at any time, passes directly through the Mount of Olives."[8] The valley that is created by the earthquake will provide an escape route for the Jews in Jerusalem who seek protection from its devastating aftershock as well as the blackout and meteor shower that accompany it (Joel 3:14-16; Matthew 24:29). By this time the glorious second coming of Christ to judge the world and restore Jerusalem will have been completed.

The Conditions Prior to Messiah's Coming

Clearly, the Scriptures have much to say about what will happen at the time of Messiah's return. That brings us to an important question: How do Jewish people today understand these events for themselves and interpret the present-day preparations that are taking place in light of their Messiah's expected advent to Jerusalem?

Jews today who look for a literal appearance of the Messiah believe that social and spiritual conditions in Israel will eventually become so wicked that only God's sending of the Messiah can bring deliverance. This expectation is based on the teaching of the earliest rabbinic scholars, the Tanaim, who put together a detailed description of the pre-Messianic era based on their interpretation of the prophetic texts of the Old Testament. These predictions, as they have been recorded in tractate *Sota* (49) of the Talmud, foretell that:

> In the days prior to the Messiah's coming, insolence will increase, the man of virtue will become perverse; the vine will grow its fruit, yet wine will be expensive; the government will turn to apostasy; there will be no admonition; the house of the wise will serve prostitution; the Galilee will be destroyed and Israel's borders will become desolate; the border inhabitants will roam from one city to another and no one will pity them; the wisdom of the Torah scholars will become odious and those who fear God will be despised; the men of truth will be forced to flee; youths will insult elders, and the aged will have to stand up before young boys; the son will dishonor the father, the daughter will rise up against her mother, the daughter-in-law against her mother-in-law; a man's enemies will be the men of his own family; the generation will have the appearance of a dog [no shame]; the son will not be embarrassed before the father—on whom shall we rely and lean upon if not our heavenly father!

The impossibility of the reversal of such conditions, apart from divine intervention, has been understood by Jewish rabbis up through today. For example, in giving commentary on these predictions, the late Jerusalem Rabbi Rafael Eisenberg remarks:

> The wickedness which will prevail during the period before the Messiah's coming cannot be overcome until God's Redemption of Yisrael will be actualized. At that time, Yisrael, together with all the nations, will repent and mend their ways. As Micah describes: " . . . I will look to the Lord; I will wait for the God of my salvation. . . . "[9]

These views are held by Orthodox Jews, who have always believed that it is necessary to wait for their Messiah to identify himself by a self-revelation of some sort—most usually by appearing in Jerusalem at a time of national crisis, overcoming the enemies of the Jewish people, restoring the Jewish State, and rebuilding the Temple. These same Orthodox Jews believe that it is not only dangerous but heretical for individual Jews to attempt to identify the Messiah. The reason for this concern by the ancient Jewish sages was not only from a fear that prophecy might be misapplied, but because past erroneous identifications in Jewish history have led to unfounded confidence in messianic claimants, inciting revolutionary movements.[10] Of course, from the Jewish viewpoint, a prime example would be the identification of Jesus as the Messiah, which resulted in Christianity and a long history of persecution of the Jewish people in the name of Christ. But the Jewish people themselves have had their own history of misidentified messiahs. Rabbi Akiba proclaimed Bar Kokhba as Messiah in A.D. 132; the whole Jewish community of Crete followed a messiah named Moses in the fifth century; Abu Issa of Isfahan raised an army of 10,000 men; and European Jewry crowned Shabbetai Zvi messiah in the seventeenth century, although he later converted to Islam!

Yet beyond the political humiliation and sometimes military disaster that accompanied these messianic misidentifications, there was also a basic spiritual concern. The Jewish scholar Rambam explained this by saying that the sages were troubled that a predicted time of Messiah's return could come and go without the expected fulfillment. If that were to happen, people of insufficient faith could end up believing that Messiah would never come. As a result, strict prohibitions against efforts to calculate or predict the end were included in the Talmud and Jewish writings. For example, *Sefer Hasidim* warns: "If you see that a man has prophesied the advent of the Messiah, know that he is engaged either in sorcery or in dealings with devils. . . . One has to say to such a man: 'Do not talk in this manner.'. . . Eventually he will be the laughingstock of the whole world."[11]

The Expectation of Messiah's Return

Despite such warnings, a Messianic movement developed within ultra-Orthodox Jewish circles toward the end of the twentieth century. It developed first in Israel as a response to the almost-disastrous 1973 Yom Kippur War. In this war Israel was surprised by an Egyptian attack and would have seen the Soviet Union join with Arab allies had the fighting not been turned by U.S. intervention in favor of the Israelis. In the aftermath of this conflict an Orthodox Jew within the settlement group *Gush Emunim* ("Bloc of the Faithful") said:

> We [Jewish messianists[12]] were born out of the Yom
> Kippur War. . . . Our Bibles told us that before
> Messiah comes, Israel will experience great dis-
> tress. So while other Jews were depressed over the
> outcome of the war, we were encouraged. We
> believed this was the beginning of the redemption
> of Israel. Our belief is quite simple, really; when we
> possess all of the land historically held by the Jewish
> people, the Messiah will come.[13]

As an example of the prophetic fervor surrounding the
Yom Kippur aftermath, a Rabbi Stein published a 125-page
book in Hebrew entitled *Magog: The War of Russia with
Israel.*[14] This book documented a widely held belief among
many Jewish rabbis at that time (and many more since) that
the end-time battle between Israel and an allied Russian-
Arab League (Ezekiel 38–39) was predicted to occur in our
days. Rabbi Stein even went so far as to suggest the date of
the attack as 1994!

In 1992 a more aggressive Messianic movement sur-
faced through the Lubavitch Chasidic group known as
Chabad[15] "in order to recapture the faith in a Messiah from
the Gentiles (Christians)."[16] Claiming 250,000 followers
worldwide, the group propelled the Messianic revival to
international status with their colorful banners, billboards
(on highways, taxis, street signs), and bumper stickers in
Hebrew and English saying, "Prepare for the Coming of
Messiah," and "We Want Moshiah Now!" Soon this multi-
million-dollar advertising campaign was supplemented by
books on the Jewish doctrine of the Messiah,[17] "prophetic"
newsletters,[18] international newspaper advertisements,[19]
banners, posters, electric signs atop cars, and national Messianic information hotlines.[20] The explosive growth of the

campaign was highlighted in articles in *Time* and *Newsweek* magazines.[21]

The basis for this new Messianism was the teaching of the movement's leader, Rabbi Menachem Mendel Schneerson. He taught that the "pinnacle" of history has now been reached: "Not only is *Moshiach* [Yiddish for "Messiah"] among us, but the 'revelation of *Moshiach Tzidkeinu*' [Messiah our righteousness] has already occurred, and 'we can already see a semblance and beginning of *Melech Hamoshiach's* [King Messiah's] influence on the nations.'"[22] As this statement reveals, Lubavitch Chasidism is convinced that this generation has been the first to realize the fulfillment of Messianic prophecies. The founding of the State of Israel is considered to be one such sign, although Rabbi Schneerson refused to come to Israel until the Messiah had appeared to legitimize the state. Yet he achieved his messianic status primarily because he had taught that the Messiah would appear with the seventh rebbe in the Lubavitcher succession of rebbes, which happened to be Schneerson himself! Because the number seven is considered the number of completion to Chasidic Jews, no other candidate could be considered.

Rabbi Schneerson declared that the present world conditions are an exact fit with the description of what the world will be like at the coming of the Messiah as predicted in *Sanhedrin* 97-98. Schneerson's followers identified him as the Messiah when the Gulf War hostilities were threatening Israel, and he predicted that "Israel would be the safest place in the world." Although only a few Israelis died as a result of the Scud attacks, most died from heart problems. Therefore, it did indeed appear that Israel had been spared by God as Schneerson predicted. However, before Schneerson could confirm his Messiahship, he suffered a stroke that left him partially paralyzed and unable to speak.

But, according to Lubavitcher literature, their children first recognized him as Messiah, thus making the identification certain.[23]

When Schneerson had another stroke in 1994 on the same day as his previous stroke, many took this as a sign that the rebbe would be restored to perfect health, travel to Israel, and rebuild the Temple. In my own discussions with rabbis at a local Chabad House, as well as at Kfar Chasidim (near Tel Aviv), where a duplicate of the Rabbi Mansion in Crown Heights, Brooklyn (Messiah Headquarters) had been specially built for Schneerson's move to Israel, I was told by followers they believed Schneerson was fulfilling the Messianic afflictions of Isaiah 53. Nevertheless, the rabbi died that same year at age 91, having never publicly proclaimed his Messianic status nor having ever visited Israel.[24] Even so, Lubavitchers cited the Messiah's death in Isaiah 53 as further proof of Schneerson's messiahship! Today most of his followers continue to believe that he will be resurrected as the Messiah before the general resurrection of the dead (Daniel 12:2) and fulfill his predicted role (although a significant number believe he never really died!). As Lubavitcher Rabbi Kupchick declares: "Most at Mount Sinai thought Moses died and so they built a golden calf. They did not have faith. The Rebbe promised to redeem us, and we have faith."[25] In June of 1997 over 7,500 of Schneerson's followers assembled in a Tel Aviv stadium under the banner "Behold, the Messiah Comes!"

Many thousands of Schneerson's followers continue to listen to his tape recordings and talk about him guiding them in a greater way from his disembodied state (in language similar to the Christian understanding of the Holy Spirit). In prominent places throughout Jerusalem (especially the Jewish Quarter) and Tel Aviv are displayed photos of

Schneerson with the words: "Blessed is he who comes, King Messiah," and "Long live our rabbi, our teacher, and master, King Messiah forever and ever." These posters proclaim a theological dogmatism that disturbs a minority in Chabad. For example, Rabbi Shaul Shimon Deutsch of New York left the movement to form his own, contending: "Ninety-eight percent of Habad believe that the rebbe is either alive, or has died and will be resurrected as the Messiah. . . . This is not Judaism, but the beginning of a new religion."[26]

Such desperate expectation and unwillingness to accept disappointment, even at the cost of abandoning Judaism, reveals that massive Messianic deception exists today and seems only to be preparing Jews worldwide for the Tribulation's counterfeit messiah. One bright note, however, is that Chabad's desire for the Messiah, and its belief that the Messiah can die and be resurrected, have brought some disillusioned followers to consider the claims of Jewish believers in Jesus (Yeshua), who have had a resurrected Messiah for 2,000 years. While only a small number of former Schneerson followers have become believers, notable rabbis are among this number, joining that truly redeemed remnant reserved for Israel in the last days (Romans 11:5).

Jerusalem's Promised Redemption

Just as we can be certain that God's judgment will come upon Jewish people for propagating deceptive claims about the Messiah, so can we also be certain that one day, the Messiah will come to redeem His people. The degree to which that judgment came in the past has determined the extent of the salvation coming in the future. In regard to the wrath Jerusalem has experienced in the past, the prophet Daniel stated: ". . . for under the whole heaven there has not been done anything like what was done to Jerusalem" (Daniel 9:12). In like manner, there will be nothing comparable to the great salvation that the nation will someday enjoy:

> "Sing for joy and be glad, O Daughter of Zion; for behold I am coming and will dwell in your midst," declares the LORD. . . . "the LORD will possess Judah as His portion in the holy land, and will again choose Jerusalem" (Zechariah 2:10).

With the return of the Redeemer, Jerusalem will finally be rescued and begin to realize the purpose for which she was chosen. In the next chapter we will move on into the millennium and look at the role of restored Jerusalem under the reign of King Messiah.

The LORD builds up Jerusalem; He gathers the outcasts of Israel.

—Psalm 147:2

Thus says the LORD of hosts, "Behold, I am going to save My people from the land of the east and from the land of the west; and I will bring them back, and they will live in the midst of Jerusalem."

—Zechariah 8:7-8

So the ransomed of the LORD will return, and come with joyful shouting to Zion; and everlasting joy will be on their heads.

—Isaiah 51:11

10

REGATHERING THE REMNANT:
The Revival of Jerusalem's Population

"Jerusalem above" and "Jerusalem below." For three thousand years the very existence of the Jewish people has been bound up with this. . . . Jews are re-entering Yerushalayim [Jerusalem] with the most profound wonder. . . . this of all times is the beginning of the ingathering in Jerusalem.[1]

—Prof. Emil Fackenheim

For centuries it was said that old people came to Jerusalem to die. Today young people come to Jerusalem to live! Israel has been called "the miracle on the Mediterranean," but the miracle of Jerusalem goes beyond regained ground and a reestablished government. When Mark Twain visited

the city in 1869 its despicable state under Muslim rule was
that of a backwater town, confined to the Old City, with a
population of only 14,000. In his satirical travelogue *The
Innocents Abroad* he complained:

> We pressed on toward the goal of our crusade,
> renowned Jerusalem. The further we went, the
> hotter the sun got, and the more rocky and bare,
> repulsive and dreary the landscape became. There
> could not have been more fragments of stone
> strewn broadcast over this part of the world. . . .
> There was hardly a tree or shrub anywhere. Even
> the olive and the cactus, those fast friends of a
> worthless soil, had almost deserted the country. No
> landscape exists that is more tiresome to the eyes
> than that which bounds the approaches to Jeru-
> salem. . . . Jerusalem . . . so small! . . . A fast walker
> could go outside the walls of Jerusalem and walk
> entirely around the city in an hour. . . . The appear-
> ance of the city is peculiar. . . . To reproduce a Jeru-
> salem street, it would only be necessary to upend a
> chicken coop and hang it before each window in an
> alley of American houses. . . . how narrow the
> streets are. . . . a cat can jump across them without
> the least inconvenience. . . . Rags, wretchedness,
> poverty, and dirt, those signs and symbols that
> indicate the presence of Muslim rule. . . . Lepers,
> cripples, the blind, and the idiotic assail you on
> every hand . . . Jerusalem is mournful and dreary
> and lifeless. I would not desire to live here.[2]

Compare that assessment with today's modern city of
government buildings, businesses, skyscraper hotels,
world-class museums, parks, and more than a half-million
people, which, despite wars, terrorist bombings, and Palestinian riots has arisen in only 30 years, and we cannot help

but sense the supernatural at work! To what else can this be attributed? God's intention is to make Jerusalem again "beautiful in its loftiness" (Psalm 48:2 NIV), and change its condition from a "dreary and lifeless" place where one of earth's great authors did "not desire to live" to "the joy of the whole earth" (Psalm 48:2). The hope of realizing this restored Jerusalem has been at the heart of the Jewish hope since the destruction of the city and the exile of its Jewish population in A.D. 70, as well as the reason why a Jewish presence was maintained in the city from that time onward.

Jews Always in Jerusalem

Many people worldwide have assumed that over the past 2,000 years, Jerusalem has been bereft of Jews. They hold to the misconception that after Jerusalem's destruction and the scattering of its people among the nations, Jewish people did not inhabit the city again until the Zionist movement at the beginning of the twentieth century. This view has been promoted by those who seek to justify their own occupation of the city; they claim they have the rights to it based on the absence of the Jews. For instance, in an article released by the Palestinian Authority's "Palestine Ministry of Information," it is asserted that Jerusalem has had no Jewish connection at all:

> Outside of what is written in the Old and New Testaments [which Muslims believe have been corrupted], there is no tangible evidence of any Jewish remains in the Old City of Jerusalem and its immediate area. What is more, after 30 years of excavations by Jewish archaeologists and others in Jerusalem since 1967, nothing tangible of theirs was found.[3]

One reason for such a contention is that the Arabs sought to erase every trace of a Jewish presence in the Old City during the two decades they occupied the site between 1948 and 1967. When Israeli troops recaptured the Old City in 1967, they found all of its ages-old synagogues razed to the ground. The Jewish Quarter had been looted, burned, and bombed by the Jordanians. Every vestige of Hebrew on street signs and buildings was plastered or painted over. Furthermore, Arab houses were found to have been built with ancient Jewish stones and Jewish tombstones used for steps and latrines. Nevertheless, despite this systematic destruction of all signs of Jewish life in the Old City, which had constituted the majority before the middle of the last century, the Arab claim is patently absurd. Anyone who has seen the monumental finds of Jewish Jerusalem from 1000 B.C. through the Roman period, as well as later inscriptions[4] and synagogue[5] remains from the Byzantine through Turkish occupations can attest that the evidence of a past Jewish presence is overwhelming.[6] A Jewish presence in Jerusalem can be verified for the past 2,000 years. From the time of the Roman destruction, when it was forbidden for Jews to enter Jerusalem (during the Hadrianic era), Jews still came, though under derision and threats, even paying exorbitant sums to purchase permits that merely permitted them to weep over the destruction of their city.[7] This fervent devotion to Jerusalem above earthly comforts and securities continued undisturbed throughout the millennia despite the conquerors who controlled the city. Dan Bahat, former district archaeologist of Jerusalem, explains:

> Although the Temple was destroyed, the physical and spiritual nexus between the Jewish people and the Land of Israel was not broken. Throughout the succeeding centuries, even if a large part of the

nation was driven from exile to another, many
stayed on, reinforced from time to time by
returning exiles, maintaining their communities
and settlements in the face of all manner of persecutions, natural disasters and alien conquests. For
nearly two thousand years, they provided the
nucleus around which the aspirations of the dispersed nation crystallized and, through them, the
nation clung to the dream of returning to its Land.[8]

This nucleus, or remnant of Jews in Jerusalem, although
under oppressive rule, were a minority of the resident population and at times wielded a formidable influence, with certain individuals going so far as to hold important places of
service. By the nineteenth century, prior to the immigration
of the majority of modern Palestinian Arabs in the twentieth
century, the Jews appeared to have constituted the majority
of the population at intermittent periods.[9] But as we have
seen, under the Muslim occupation of the Land the conditions were poor, and the Jewish remnant's only hope for the
future rested in the many prophetic passages that promised a
revival of the Jewish population. Let us look at this expectation as it has been preserved for us in Scripture.

Prophecy and the Regathering

In the end-time texts of the Bible, the return of the
Jewish people to their promised Land of Israel is the most
frequently prophesied event. In biblical terms, the event of
regathering is the evidence of redemption: "I will restore
them because I have compassion on them. They will be as
though I had not rejected them, for I am the LORD their God
and I will answer them. . . . I will signal for them and gather
them in. Surely I will redeem them; they will be as
numerous as before" (Zechariah 10:6,8 NIV). This event is

also prophesied by Jeremiah, who also connects the regath-ering with restoration: "Return, faithless people," declares the LORD, "for I am your husband. I will choose you—one from a town and two from a clan—and bring you to Zion" (Jeremiah 3:14).

However, some Christians believe that God's plan today and for the future should not be interpreted with respect to the physical land, but to spiritual salvation. For them the New Testament has taken precedence over the Old Testament and the ascension of Christ has shifted the focus from earth to heaven. This viewpoint removes forever any significance that might be connected to a return of Jews to the Land and a repossession and restoration of Jerusalem. Walter C. Kaiser, president of Gordon-Conwell Theolog-ical Seminary, counters that view with this reply:

> While many Christians find it difficult to see how God's work of salvation should have any attach-ments to geography, the fact remains that God Himself linked the two from the very beginning with the call of Abraham in Genesis 12. This is simply another way of affirming that God's activi-ties do not take place in an abstract vacuum but in the midst of the concrete space and time of human history. The events of our salvation have strong attachments to Canaan, Bethlehem, Jerusalem, Nazareth, the Mount of Olives, and Golgotha. If the dispersion was a mark of God's judgment, according to the prophets, then Israel's return to the land is the mark of God's grace.[10]

Therefore, if God's grace to Israel is to be demonstrated in future history, it must come, in part, as a reversal of the Jewish people being scattered into exile. The fulfillment of God's plan for Israel, then, will be a homecoming that

brings an end to the geographical and spiritual estrange-
ment suffered throughout the times of the Gentiles.

Four facts concerning the prophetic Jewish homecoming must be kept in mind as we consider both the
present and future regathering to the Land. First, *the Bible
predicts that Israel would return to the Land in unbelief.* Since
the Jewish people will repent (Zechariah 12:10; Matthew
24:30) and be regenerated (Ezekiel 36:25) *in* the Land, it is
obvious they are already in the Land in a state of unbelief.
The majority of Israelis today are secular Jews, and of
course even though religious Jews believe in God they reject
Jesus (Yeshua) as their Messiah. This state of unbelief will
continue through the Tribulation period for the Jewish
nation (Isaiah 6:9-13) despite the fact that then, as now,
God has preserved a remnant of Jewish believers to bear
witness to the Messiah (Romans 11:1-6; Revelation 7:1-8).

Second, *the Bible predicts that Israel would return to the
Land in stages.* The prophetic texts indicate that the restoration is a process, and such a process would take time to
achieve. While spiritual regeneration for the majority takes
place as a culminative event, physical regathering assumes
time to transport and resettle a population. Waves of immigration (beginning in 1882) and continuing today with the
transplantation of Ethiopian Jewry (1984, 1991) and the
massive exodus of Soviet Jewry (1989 and on) have been a
part of the early stages of this return. We will deal with the
prophecies that reveal this and the final stage of restoration
in just a moment.

Third, *the Bible predicts that Israel would return to the
Land through persecution.* Jeremiah 16:15-16 says:

> . . . as surely as the Lord lives, who brought the Israel-
> ites up out of the land of the north, and out of all the
> countries where He had banished them. For I will

> restore them to the Land I gave to their forefathers.
> But now I will send for many fishermen . . . and they
> will catch them. After that I will send for many
> hunters, and they will hunt them down . . ." (NIV).

These verses include both the persecution that will force world Jewry to the Land during the latter half of the Tribulation (Deuteronomy 4:30; Revelation 12:13,17) as well as the modern reality of the establishment of the Jewish State as a result of the previous century of pogroms and holocaust, and the present threat of anti-Semitism in the international community.

Fourth, *the Bible predicts that Israel would return to the Land to set the stage for end-time events.* The prophetic texts assume a partially regathered people functioning as a Jewish State with religious laws and institutions entact (Matthew 24:15-20). Every prophetic scholar who understood these prophecies to be fulfilled literally expected the Jews to return to Israel and for Jerusalem to again become its holy city in order for the future to be fulfilled. Today this has, and is, becoming a reality.

Now let us consider the prophetic texts that support these conclusions.

A Homecoming in Stages

I have always enjoyed going to homecomings. Depending on the occasion, it is a time when family, friends, or acquaintances travel to a designated place to relive the past and rejoice in the present. The regathering of Israel will be the greatest homecoming the world will ever witness.

When we examine what the biblical prophets said about the regathering of the Jewish people, we can discern two phases or stages, each separated by an indeterminable period of time. The first stage of the homecoming will be to the *Land* (geographical), and the second stage will be to the *Lord* (spiritual). This pattern was established by the previous exile and return, as Rabbi Nisan Aryeh Novick explains:

> Hashem [God] never said that both forms of *Galus* [exile] have to end together at the same exact moment—they certainly do not even begin in the same instant. Isn't it true that *first* the Jews acted inappropriately and then some time later they were exiled from the Land; this phenomenon has occurred twice. . . . Isn't it also true that there were two forms of *Galus* [exile] in Egypt which were cast off at two different points of time? *The geographical Galus [exile] ended* the moment the Jews left Egypt. The estrangement, *the spiritual Galus [exile] ended* in a very slow and deliberate fashion. . . . But both *Galuyot* [exiles] did not end at the same moment. Both ended in a serial fashion—first the physcial *Galus* [exile] and later the spiritual.[11]

This Zionist teaching of a two-stage return can be traced back to Rabbi Zvi Hirsch Kalischer (1795–1874), who on the basis of Isaiah 27:6 argued that the return would be constituted by the "bud and blossom"—an initial pioneering stage that would progressively prepare the Land for occupation, and the "fruit"—a final massive ingathering.[12] Many Bible commentators have also noted that prophecies about the regathering include both a declaration of divine intervention: "Thus says the LORD, I will bring them back . . ." as well as a statement of human accomplishment: "and they will return. . . ." So a two-stage operation has been observed: the first by man, the second by God. This corresponds to the Zionist efforts to revive the barren land

and reduce population and build a secular state, which would be followed by God's revival of all Israel, reversal of nature's curse, and building of a spiritual state. The fact that the physical Land of Israel is currently under independent Jewish control makes possible the end of physical exile for all of the Jewish people, which is the first step of the homecoming process. Let's look at a sampling of Scripture texts in which the prophets testify to this two-stage fulfillment.

Ezekiel's Prophecy of the Return

Ezekiel's famous prophecy of the "valley of dry bones" coming to life illustrates the two phases of Israel's restoration. In Ezekiel 37:1-14 the vision of a graveyard resurrection depicts the national return and regeneration of "the whole house of Israel" (verse 11). The vision first shows Israel restored physically ("bones," "sinews," "skin"), but left in a spiritually lifeless condition (verse 8). Then "winds from the four quarters of the globe" (indicative of the Spirit, see John 3:8) breathe on Israel's physical form and bring it to new life (verses 9-10).

Many Jewish and Christian interpreters have observed that the modern state of Israel literally arose out of the death camps of the Nazi holocaust. The people came to their Land, made barren and unproductive through millennia of neglect and abuse, and transformed it agriculturally, architecturally, and politically into the only Western democracy in the Middle East. While the "whole house of Israel" has yet to be fully regathered and the spiritual regeneration will not occur until the advent of Messiah, what was once—in the world's estimation—a pile of bones has come together and taken shape as a formidable nation among the nations.

Three additional prophecies in Ezekiel reveal the two-stage process of Jewish redemption. These appear next, with the labels *Stage I*: Physical Regathering to the Land; and *Stage II*: Spiritual Restoration to the Lord.

Ezekiel 11:17-19

Stage I: I will gather you from the nations and bring you back from the countries where you have been scattered, and I will give you back the land of Israel again (verse 17 NIV).

Stage II: They will return to it and remove all its vile images and detestable idols. I will give them an undivided heart and put a new spirit in them; I will remove from them their heart of stone and give them a heart of flesh (verses 18-19 NIV).

Ezekiel 36:24-27

Stage I: I will take you out of the nations; I will gather you from all the countries and bring you back into your own land (verse 24 NIV).

Stage II: I will sprinkle clean water on you, and you will be clean; I will cleanse you from all your impurities and from all your idols. I will give you a new heart and put a new spirit in you; I will remove from you your heart of stone and give you a heart of flesh. And I will put my Spirit in you and move you to follow my decrees and be careful to keep my laws (verses 25-27 NIV).

Ezekiel 37:21, 23

Stage I: I will take the sons of Israel from among the nations where they have gone, and I will gather them from every side and bring them into their own land (verse 21).

Stage II: And they will no longer defile themselves with their idols, or with their detestable things, or with any of their transgresions and [I] will cleanse them . . . (verse 23).

Each of these prophecies states that God will first gather His people from the nations and bring them to their own Land. Ezekiel 37:25 makes it clear that this Land is "the land that I [God] gave to Jacob My servant, in which your fathers lived." Then, after the Jewish people are again in the Land, the Lord will bring spiritual redemption and renewal. It should be evident from these texts that since the spiritual return occurs *after* the Jews have been gathered to the Land, the first stage of the regathering is in *unbelief.* Some Christians have taught that the Jews have no right to the Land while they remain in unbelief. This is also the position adopted by ultra-Orthodox Jews, who refuse to recognize the legitimacy of a Jewish State until the whole of Jewry adopts an observant lifestyle. However, Scripture makes it clear that God will regather His people while they are yet in unbelief, and that is exactly the condition of the Jewish nation during the present preparatory period of regathering.

In Ezekiel 37:26-27 Jerusalem is the focus of this regathering, and we read of a rebuilt Temple at which the presence of the Lord will return, never to depart. Like the process of regathering, a physical Temple will be rebuilt in the Land with the Jewish people in a state of unbelief (Matthew 24:15,30) prior to the spiritual return of God's glory (Ezekiel 43:1-7).

Jeremiah's Prophecy of the Return

Like Ezekiel, Jeremiah also distinguishes between the physical and spiritual work accomplished in two separate regatherings:

Jeremiah 23:3-4

Stage I: I Myself shall gather the remnant of My flock out of all the countries where I have driven them and shall bring them back to their pasture; and they will be fruitful and multiply (verse 3).

Stage II: I shall also raise up shepherds over them and they will tend them; and they will not be afraid any longer, nor be terrified, nor will any be missing (verse 4).

Jerusalem is included in this prophecy as the place where the Messianic-Shepherd, called here both the righteous Branch of David (verse 5) and "the LORD our Righteousness" (verse 6), will "reign as king and act wisely and do justice and righteousness in the land" (verse 5). As with other regathering prophecies, Jerusalem's restoration is vital proof that true restoration has finally occurred.

While the prophecies of Ezekiel and Jeremiah reveal the two stages of regathering, and indicate that the first will occur *before* the second coming of Messiah and the second *at* the second coming of Messiah, they do not necessarily establish that the modern-day regathering is to be equated with the first stage. However, such an equation can be supported in one of Isaiah's prophecies of the return.

Isaiah's Prophecy of the Return

The Timing of the Regathering

The prophet Isaiah announced a specific time that the Jews would be regathered from all the nations of the earth:

> On that day the Lord will again recover the *second time* with His hand the remnant of His people who will remain, from Assyria, Egypt, Pathros, Cush, Elam, Shinar, Hamath, and from the islands of the sea. He will lift up a standard for the nations, and will assemble the banished ones of Israel and will gather the dispersed of Judah from the four corners of the earth (Isaiah 11:11-12, emphasis added).

The time period indicated by this prophecy is more precise than might be discerned at a first reading. The term "that day" (Hebrew *yom hahu*) is used as a prophetic expression of the future "Day of the Lord," a period which includes both the Tribulation and Millennium. In the immediate context of verses 6-9 the time period being spoken of is the Millennium; however, since the regathering takes place in preparation for the blessings of the Millennium, the time frame must be at the end of the Tribulation. Comparative regathering texts also indicate this (see Matthew 24:29-31; Mark 13:24-27).

This event is further defined as the final fulfillment of regathering by the term "the second time," which is also the *last* time. This "second" regathering is clearly an international event, from "the four corners of the earth," specified by the reference to the Middle Eastern countries plus the

Gentile nations ("islands of the sea"). But if this second regathering is international, so must be the implied first regathering. With what time period should this first regathering be identified? The period of regathering closest to Isaiah's time of writing was that from Babylon under the priest Zerubbabel in 537 B.C. But this was a "local" regathering of only a small portion of the Jewish remnant in Babylon. There is no way we can possibly interpret this as a worldwide regathering as described in Isaiah 11:11-12. Since the context of Isaiah's words concerns a future "second" regathering in preparation for blessing, this "first" regathering must also be future to the time of the prophet, and have a preparatory purpose. Therefore, the best identification for this "first" regathering must be the present one, which—since May 8, 1948, when the modern state became a reality—has been preparing the nation for the judgment to come during the Tribulation. This is confirmed by Zephaniah 2:1-2:

> Gather yourselves together. . . . O nation without shame, before the decree takes effect—the day passes like the chaff—before the burning anger of the LORD comes upon you, before the day of the LORD's anger comes upon you.

The "day of the LORD's anger" is one of several Hebrew expressions used to refer to the Tribulation.[13] Although the context deals with the immediate judgment of Israel by the Babylonians, as in similar passages by other prophets, Zephaniah's language prophetically illustrates the ultimate judgment for Israel typified by any great judgment of God. Here the nation is gathered *before* that day comes, pinpointing the first regathering as preparatory to the Tribulation. Therefore, Isaiah predicted a regathering of Jews in unbelief as a nation before the Tribulation in order to be regathered for belief and blessing at its end.

Some Christians say that the modern state of Israel could collapse at any time, the Jews be scattered yet again among the nations, and then sometime in the future they could return again to fulfill the prophecies. But, in light of the Bible passages we just considered, how many dispersions and regatherings could we fit in between the first and the second? As my friend Arnold Fruchtenbaum noted when commenting on this question, "Even with new math, *not one!*" Thus the regathering taking place during our generation is the "first" regathering that will bring a remnant of the Jewish people into the Tribulation, which will be followed by a second regathering that will rescue them from the persecutions of the Antichrist (Matthew 24:16-21; Mark 13:14-19; Revelation 12:6,13-17).

The Location of the Regathering

The prophecy in Isaiah chapter 11 centers the Jewish regathering in Jerusalem. In verse 10 it is predicted that "it will come about in that day that the nations will resort to the root of Jesse, who will stand as a signal for the peoples; and His resting place will be glorious." The "root of Jesse" [father of King David] is a title of the Messiah, around whom as a "signal" (banner) the Gentile "peoples" will rally in the Millennium. His "resting place" is a reference to Jerusalem, the site for Messiah's glorious reign. When the last regathering occurs, the nation, as well as all nations, will be brought together to worship the Messiah enthroned on the Temple Mount in the Holy City. There is no question this prophecy will be fulfilled, for as Isaiah said, it will be the Lord's hand that will bring about this final recovery of the nation.

Zechariah's Prophecy of the Return

One of the most vivid depictions of Jewish regathering in the last days is Zechariah's prophecy of a return to Jerusalem by both God and His people:

> Thus says the LORD, "I will return to Zion and will dwell in Jerusalem. . . . Old men and old women will again sit in the streets of Jerusalem. . . . and the streets of the city will be filled with boys and girls playing in its streets. . . . I am going to save my people from the land of the east and from the land of the west. And I will bring them back, and they will live in the midst of Jerusalem . . . " (Zechariah 8:3-5,8).

This prophecy describes an ingathering from the lands east and west of Israel, while other prophecies include the lands north and south (see Isaiah 43:5-6; Jeremiah 23:7-8; 31:8). In either case the thought is of an international exodus to the Land, and especially to its center, Jerusalem. The quaint picture of the renewal of daily life in the streets is one that can be witnessed today in the modern city. Even so, the prophecy here is of the restored and secure conditions of the millennial age when Jerusalem will become "the City of Truth, and the mountain of the LORD of hosts . . . the Holy Mountain" (verse 3). God will be their "God in truth and righteousness" (verse 8), and the united "house of Judah and house of Israel" will experience "peace" in the Land and "become a blessing" to the nations (verses 12-13). So great, in fact, will be the blessing in that day that "many peoples and mighty nations will come to seek the LORD of hosts in Jerusalem and . . . grasp the garment of a Jew saying, 'Let us go with you, for we have heard that God is with you'" (verses 22-23). Whereas today the physically regathered nation is alone among the nations, and considered more of a burden than a blessing, the final spiritual regathering will attract believing Gentiles to the special favor Jerusalem has experienced and can extend.

Let us now consider the preparation for this special favor—preparation that is being experienced in Jerusalem today—for in the history and progress of the modern regathering are sown the seeds of God's plan to bring His promises to full flower.

The Modern-Day Regathering

A Firm Determination

Immigration to the Land, known in Hebrew as *aliyah* ("ascent"), has been one of the foremost commandments for the Jewish people. Jerusalem for most of the past 2,000 years has been impoverished, diseased, desolate, and even hazardous to habitation. However, because Jerusalem is the Holy City it could not be abandoned by its Jewish caretakers. Therefore, the inhabitants of the city have often been dependent upon the charity of Jews from outside the city to maintain their continued existence. Both living in Jerusalem and giving to Jerusalem have been considered meritorious acts by the Jewish people.

Various waves of immigration have taken place during the twentieth century, each one contributing to the growing population of Ashkenazi, Sephardic, American, Russian, and Ethiopian Jews. At the beginning of the twentieth century the population of Jerusalem only numbered about 15,000—a fraction of whom were Jews, along with a large number of Europeans and Christians. At the beginning of the twenty-first century that number stands at some 600,000 people, 75% of whom are native Israeli Jews.

A Rapid Increase in Population

According to the latest statistics published by the Institute of the World Jewish Congress, Israel's Jewish population is dramatically increasing. At the beginning of the 1998 Jewish year (September), the population of Israel was 5,863,000, of which 80% (4,700,000) were Jewish; 61.6% being born in the Land and 71,000 arriving as immigrants. Of this last category, 59,000 came from Russia, making the total for these immigrants 845,000 (the largest single group in Israel). Based on such figures, it is predicted that by the year 2003 Israel will have the largest Jewish population in the world (today only the United States has a slightly larger Jewish population). Jerusalem is currently Israel's largest city, both in area and population, and since its reunification in 1967 has experienced a growth unprecedented since the time of Jesus. In addition, of the more than 550,000 people who live in Jerusalem, more than 320,000 now live on land that was not under Israeli control until 1967. The majority of these people are Jewish and will never concede to international opinion that they are "occupiers of greater Jerusalem" or to pressure to relocate outside of the holy site they prayed for and fought for over the last 2,000 years. In fact, Jerusalem's Jewish population in East Jerusalem already exceeds the Arab population, and will continue to increase, even in the Old City, despite the problems East Jerusalem now faces and the threat of future confrontation. This resolve was affirmed by Prime Minister Benjamin Netanyahu when he declared: "I will not return to the May 1967 borders. Those were war borders, which almost led to the annihilation of the State of Israel. . . . This is our Land, our homeland."[14] What other option can there be for the one site on earth that is

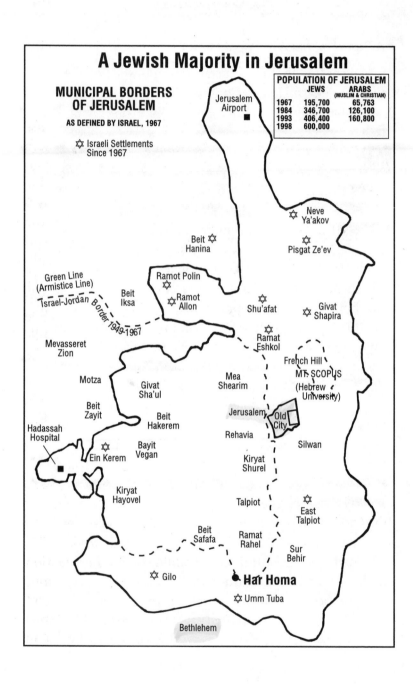

A Jewish Majority in Jerusalem

MUNICIPAL BORDERS OF JERUSALEM

AS DEFINED BY ISRAEL, 1967

✡ Israeli Settlements Since 1967

POPULATION OF JERUSALEM		
	JEWS	ARABS (MUSLIM & CHRISTIAN)
1967	195,700	65,763
1984	346,700	126,100
1993	406,400	160,800
1998	600,000	

Jerusalem Airport

✡ Neve Ya'akov

Beit ✡ Hanina

✡ Pisgat Ze'ev

Green Line (Armistice Line)

Israel-Jordan Border 1949-1967

Beit Iksa

Ramot Polin ✡

✡ Ramot Allon

✡ Shu'afat

✡ Givat Shapira

Mevasseret Zion

✡ Ramat Eshkol

Motza

Givat Sha'ul

Mea Shearim

French Hill

MT. SCOPUS

(Hebrew University)

Beit Zayit

Beit Hakerem

Jerusalem Old City

Hadassah Hospital

Rehavia

Silwan

✡ Ein Kerem

Bayit Vegan

Kiryat Shurel

Kiryat Hayovel

Talpiot

✡ East Talpiot

Beit Safafa

Ramat Rahel

Sur Behir

✡ Gilo

● **Har Homa**

✡ Umm Tuba

Bethlehem

regarded as the place of Messiah's future revelation and the beginning point for the era of redemption?

The Permanence of the Regathering

While the present regathering and restoration are merely the preparatory stage of God's plan for Israel's future, the prophecies that speak of this regathering emphasize the *permanent* state of this event, an irreversible condition based on God's covenant with the Land: "'I will bring back my exiled people Israel; they will rebuild the ruined cities and live in them. They will plant vineyards and drink their wine; they will make gardens and eat their fruit. I will plant Israel in their own land, *never again to be uprooted from the land* I have given them,' says the LORD your God" (Amos 9:14-15 NIV, emphasis added). While both stages of the regathering prophecies will find fulfillment, the permanent stage may be contrasted with the present preparation.

Present Regathering	Permanent Regathering
• Worldwide in its scope	• Worldwide in its extent
• Return to a part of the Land	• Return to all of the Land
• Restoration is to the Land	• Restoration is to the Lord
• The work of man (secular)	• The work of God (spiritual)

These contrasts are the natural effect of preparation and fulfillment. However, if the present revival of the population does not presage the permanent ingathering of Israel, then we must assume that the prophets envisioned all the world's Jews immigrating at the same time to an unclaimed Land in unbelief in order to be simultaneously revived and restored spiritually. This, however, is not supported by the prophetic texts, nor is it possible by reason of human and geographical limitations. Therefore, we should expect, according to the prophets, a preparatory period that gradually places the Jewish people in the Land, forcing the nations to deal with their independent status and creating the conditions for the fulfillment of God's future plans.

Welcome to the Land

Everyone arriving into Israel by plane from foreign destinations must enter the country through the Ben-Gurion Airport. Once they have passed through passport control and are about to exit, they are greeted by a huge and colorful tapestry welcoming them to the Land. On it is depicted masses of peoples streaming into the gates of the City of Jerusalem. On the tapestry, in Hebrew, is a prophetic text from Jeremiah that speaks about the ingathering of the exiles: "'So there is hope for your future,' declares the LORD. 'Your children will return to their own Land'" (Jeremiah 31:10 NIV). Whether or not the incoming Jewish people can yet read the words, the lesson is understood, for they who are coming home are part of God's present purpose in regathering His people for the fulfillment of His promise.

"Behold, days are coming," declares
the LORD, "when the city [Jerusalem]
shall be rebuilt for the LORD. . . . it
shall not be plucked up, or overthrown
anymore forever."

—Jeremiah 31:38,40

"Jerusalem will be inhabited without walls,
because of the multitude of men and
cattle within it. For I," declares the LORD,
"will be a wall of fire around her."

—Zechariah 2:4-5

At that time they shall call Jerusalem
"The Throne of the LORD," and all the
nations will be gathered to it, to Jerusalem,
for the name of the LORD. . . ."

—Jeremiah 3:17

11

WATCH OUT, WORLD!
The Restoration of Jerusalem's Status

*Now if their transgression be riches for the world
and their failure be riches for the Gentiles, how
much more will their fulfillment be!*

—Romans 11:12

*Jerusalem is destined to become a beacon light-
ing the way for all nations.*

—Yalkut Shimoni, Isaiah 499, Midrash

As I walked through a shop in Jerusalem an interesting poster caught my attention. The picture was a photographic montage of an ancient pottery vessel from which protruded a modern chemical beaker filled with colorful chemicals (see photo #5). The caption underneath read "Our future is where our past is." This makes the striking point that the future status of the Jewish people, who for 3,000 years have claimed Jerusalem as their eternal capital, can be found only in this place. The poster also reflects one of the greatest miracles of our age: the transformation of Jerusalem from an archaeological site to a technological city. That fact was impressed on me one Sabbath in Jerusalem when I took an Arab taxi across the city. As we passed one of many sections of the city where new construction and landscaping were taking place, the driver, a lifelong resident of East Jerusalem, remarked: "In 100 years we would never have done this!" His admission was that the Arab population in Jerusalem preferred the status quo, a city that had not changed radically since the Islamic conquest 1,300 years earlier. It was the Israelis who, though at that time had only had access to the city for 30 years, had amazingly transformed Jerusalem by rebuilding its structure and restoring its status.

Prime Minister Benjamin Netanyahu set Jerusalem's present revitalization in the context of the greater restoration of the Land when he said, "Let us not forget that the State of Israel is one of the most amazing success stories of the twentieth century. And I am convinced that this is only the beginning."[1] Indeed it is only the beginning, for the biblical prophets paint a resplendent picture of the days to come after Messiah returns to Zion and makes it glorious (Isaiah 11:10).

The Age to Come

The Jewish concept of the Messianic era was formed in an attempt to understand the many Old Testament prophecies that speak of Israel and Jerusalem's redemption in the future age. It is roughly equivalent to the period understood by many Christian interpreters as the Millennial age or Millennial kingdom spoken of by John in the last prophetic book of the New Testament (Revelation 20:1-15). Jewish rabbinic sages made a broad distinction between our present age—"this age" (*ha-'olam hazeh*), and the future age—"the age to come" (*ha-'olam habba*). They also made a more specific distinction between "the days of the Messiah" (*Yemot ha-Mashiach*), the time of "the Redemption" (*Ge'ulah*), and "the resurrection of the dead" (*techiyyat ha-metim*).

These prophetic distinctions were discussed by the Jewish rabbis in the earliest centuries after the destruction of the Temple. An example of this was the Amoraic sage Rabbi Aha, who sought deeper insight as to why the seventh benediction in the *Eighteen Benedictions* concerned "the redemption of Israel." His answer came from Rabbi Rava, who said that it was "to teach that Israel will be redeemed in the seventh year of Messiah's advent" (Babylonian Talmud, *Megilla* 17b; compare *Tosefta Sanhedrin* 13.1; *Rosh Hashana* 16b). A prophetic sidenote to this interpretation explains that the present age is ". . . the *septennium* (seven 1,000 year periods), at the end of which the son of David will come. . . ." It went on to elaborate that "in the first year" the following verse will be fulfilled:

> "I will cause it to rain upon one city and cause it not to rain upon another city"; in the second, the arrows of famine will be sent forth; in the third, there will be a great famine and men, women, and children, men of piety, and miracle workers will die, and the Torah will be forgotten by its students; in the fourth, there will be plenty; in the fifth, there will be great plenty, and people will eat and drink and rejoice, and the Torah will be restored to its students; in the sixth

there will be (heavenly) sounds; in the seventh, wars;
and at the end of the septennium the son of David
(Messiah) will come (*Sanhedrin* 97a; *'Avoda Zara* 9a).

The *Gemara* (commentary) to this notes that "war is
also the beginning of redemption," indicating that the messianic era would also be throughout the seventh millennium.

Another account is that of a Tannaitic sage of the School
of Elijah. According to his interpretation, "The world will
exist for 6,000 years, for 2,000 there will be desolation, for
2,000, Torah, and for 2,000 the Days of the Messiah" (*Sanhedrin* 97a-b; *'Avodah Zarah* 9a; cf. *TRosh Hashana* 31a).
After this, the 7,000th year will be a year of renewal (*Sanhedrin* 97b). This "Great Sabbath Week" of 7,000 years is patterned after the six days of creation (6 days = 6,000 years)
and the rest on the seventh day (the last day = last 1,000
years). God is said to hide behind "this present world"
(*'olam ha-zeh*) of the 6,000 years, for the three Hebrew root
letters that make up the word "world" (*'olam*)—*ayin*,
lamed, mem—indicate a "vanishing" of God from the
world. In the last 1,000 years, "the World to Come" (*'olam
ha-ba*), God will not be in the background, but will appear
and transform the natural order into one that is spiritual.

A Thread of Hope

This theology of the Messianic era, formulated by the
Jewish sages based on their interpretation of the biblical
prophets' teachings, has supported the Jewish people
through the long dark days of the Diaspora by providing
the hope that the prophetic promises would come true, the
world would change, and the Jews would fulfill their destiny. This destiny particularly depended on Jerusalem

becoming the glorious center of God's revelation which would shine throughout the earth—or, as the Jewish Midrash stated, "Jerusalem is destined to become a beacon lighting the way for all nations" (*Yalkut Shimoni*, Isaiah 499). With the establishment of the Jewish State, this destiny seemed once again assured, as Jerusalem's status is now being restored in line with the predictions made by the prophets. Such belief led Israel's first Prime Minister, David Ben-Gurion, to proclaim:

> The Jewish people, after 2,000 years and tribulation in every part of the globe, having arrived at the first step of renewed sovereignty in the Land of their origin, will not abandon their historic vision and great spiritual heritage—the aspiration to combine their national redemption with universal redemption for all the people of the world. Even the greatest tragedy ever wrought by man against a people did not dim the profound faith of the Jews, including those who went to their death in the ovens of Europe, in their national redemption and in that of mankind. Unlike other ancient people ours did not look backward to a legendary Golden Age in the past, which has gone never to return, but turn their gaze to the future—to the latter days, in which the earth will be filled with the knowledge [of the Lord] as the waters cover the sea, when nations will "beat their swords into plowshares, and nation will not lift up sword against nation, or learn war anymore."[2]

Although Jewish communists and socialists, along with most Reform Jews, have sought to make the political State of Israel the fulfillment of the "symbolic vision" of the prophets, most Orthodox and all ultra-Orthodox Jews have clung tenaciously to the hope of a literal fulfillment of a restored and glorified Israel, with Jerusalem at its center, in the latter days.

From Promise to Fulfillment

After Israel's spiritual redemption is accomplished, the hope of restoration for which they long will be realized on earth. In Christian eschatology the Messianic era is often referred to as the Millennium or the Millennial kingdom. The magnitude of this glorious age is implied in the New Testament when it considers the superlative condition of Israel once its sins have been forgiven and its fulness restored: "Now if their [the Jews collectively] transgression be riches for the world [Gentiles collectively] and their failure be riches for the Gentiles, how much more will their fulfillment be! . . . For if their rejection be the reconciliation of the world, what will their acceptance be but life from the dead?" (Romans 11:12,15). Paul here contrasts the Jewish nation's failure and fulfillment—rejection and reception—in terms of the prophetic language of restoration. When the time of Gentile inclusion is complete (Romans 11:25), the world had better watch out, for Israel is coming back into her own! The Jewish people as a national entity will be returned to the Land and to life (Ezekiel 36:24-28; 37:1-14,25-26), and the whole world will be transformed as a result (Habakkuk 2:14).

This age will be the time when all of the covenants of the past find final fulfillment. The *Abrahamic Covenant* will be realized with Israel's full occupation of its promised boundaries and the Gentile nations of the world being blessed through God's spiritually restored people (Isaiah 10:21-22; 19:25; 43:1; 65:8-9; Jeremiah 30:22; 32:38; Ezekiel

34:24,30-31; Micah 7:19-20; Zechariah 13:9; Malachi 3:16-18). The *Davidic Covenant* will be realized with David's greatest descendant reigning in Jerusalem (Isaiah 11:1-2; 55:3,11; Jeremiah 23:5-8; 33:20-26; Micah 4:7-8), if not also a resurrected David as an undershepherd over Israel (Ezekiel 37:23-25; Hosea 3:5). The *Deuteronomic* (or "Palestinian") *Covenant* will find its fulfillment in Israel's permanent and unrestricted possession of the Promised Land (Isaiah 11:11-12; 65:9; Ezekiel 16:60-63; 36:28-29; 37:25; 39:28; Hosea 1:10–2:1; Micah 2:12; Zechariah 10:6). The *New Covenant*, which includes the spiritual blessings now shared by Jew and Gentile in the church age and the Land promised to Israel, will be enjoyed by the entire nation (Jeremiah 31:31-34; 32:35-39; Ezekiel 11:18-20; 16:60-63; 36:25-28; 37:26; Romans 11:26).

A View of the Restored Jerusalem

When the Millennium begins, topographical changes will occur that will cause the city itself to be elevated above the surrounding land, which will be flattened into a vast plain (Zechariah 14:10). This will be done so that the Temple Mount will occupy the highest elevation in the region, making Jerusalem the new center of the Land (Isaiah 2:2; Micah 4:1). The city will also be greatly enlarged (Jeremiah 31:38-40). According to Ezekiel 48:15-20,30-35, the city will be increased to a size of approximately 36 square miles, with its suburbs more than one-third of a mile in each direction (Ezekiel 48:17). The Temple Mount itself will hold a Temple at least 30 times larger than the former Temple (Ezekiel 40:48–41:26). Adding up the total for the sacred portion of land—which includes the city and the area within which the priests, Levites, and the prince (city administrator) function and forage for food—we come up with 182 square miles (Ezekiel 45:1-17; 48:16-21). Furthermore, the city will be without walls, for the Lord will be a wall of fire around it (Zechariah 2:4-5), and its gates will be open day and night (Isaiah 60:11). Jerusalem will be a secure city that, unlike former times, no longer requires protection:

> The King of Israel, the LORD, is in your midst; you will fear disaster no more. In that day it will be said to Jerusalem: "Do not be afraid, O Zion. . . . At that time I will gather you; at that time I will bring you home. I will give you renown and praise among all the peoples of the earth, when I restore your fortunes before your eyes," declares the Lord (Zephaniah 3:15-16,20).

In addition to protection there will be prosperity. One of the topographical changes guarantees this by creating a river that will flow from beneath the throne area on the Temple Mount toward both the Dead Sea and the Mediterranean Sea (Ezekiel 47:1-2; Joel 3:18; Zechariah 14:8). As a result of the fresh water flowing into it, the Dead Sea will also be restored to yield new life (Ezekiel 47:8-12). Finally, the Millennial Jerusalem will have an independent light source, which will illuminate the city both day and night (Isaiah 24:23; 60:19-20). This light apparently will be the Shekinah glory of God, which will return to the Millennial Temple (Ezekiel 43:1-7), constituting the whole city "The Throne of the LORD" (Jeremiah 3:17). No wonder as the psalmist looked ahead to this time of Jerusalem's glory he could say, "Beautiful in elevation, the joy of the whole earth, is Mount Zion in the far north, the city of the great King" (Psalm 48:2).

This future restoration will clearly be the *final* restoration since the Lord declares, "I will also plant [Israel] on their land and they will *not again* be rooted out from their land which I have given them" (Amos 9:15). This is also evident from the promise of an inviolable security that will be realized by the nation: "... they will *no longer* be afraid or terrified, nor will any be missing"; "Jacob will again have peace and security, and no one will make him afraid"; "they will live there in safety and will build houses and plant vineyards; they will live in safety" (Jeremiah 23:4; 30:10b; Ezekiel 28:26 NIV).

According to the book of Ezekiel, this future restoration will also include social and economic changes. In Ezekiel chapter 36 we find one of the greatest of the Old Testament prophecies regarding Israel's national restoration. In verse 28 we read, "You will live in the land that I gave to your forefathers; so you will be my people and I will be your God." Here God promises geographical resettlement rather than regathering (which is mentioned in verse 24). The new, purified obedience ("new heart ... new spirit") described in verses 26-27 will assure permanent residence in the Land because disobedience to the covenant—which guaranteed secure possession—will be impossible (see Genesis 17:8; Deuteronomy 11:19,21; 18:35; Jeremiah 7:7; 11:5; Ezekiel 20:28,42; 47:14). The words "My people ... your God" describes this relationship of obedience between God and the Jewish people by use of an ancient wedding metaphor. It depicts an intimacy and fidelity that will be unique to this New Covenant. This promise is of perpetual relationship with God and is a fitting complement to permanent resettlement in which the people are also wedded to the Land. It restores the original union of God-people-Land previously disrupted by sin.

In Ezekiel 36 we are told that the Land will also be restored to productivity: "Moreover, I will save you from all your uncleanness; and I will call for the grain and multiply it. . . . And I will multiply the fruit of the tree and the produce of the field, that you may not receive again the disgrace of famine among the nations" (see verses 29-30). The word "uncleanness" at the beginning of this verse must include the desecrated Land (see verse 17). What follows is a divine command to restore the Land to prosperous conditions. The effects of the new inward creation is extended to the outward creation—the Land. To Israel, who saw a lack of productivity as a curse on the Land (Deuteronomy 28:38-42), the renewed fertility of the Land was assurance of restoration. The condition before the nations at the time this passage is fulfilled will be one of apparent rejection, resulting in national shame. But Israel's change in fortune—from an unproductive Land to a productive one—will witness to the nations of Israel's return to divine favor. God's program of agricultural restoration is seen in His promise to fertilize the land and free His people from the penalty of being unproductive. This renewal is described in a specific order, going from the lower vegetative order, "grain" (verse 29), to the next higher order, "fruit of the tree" and "the field" (verse 30), to reproduce the order found in Genesis 1:11-12. In this way God demonstrates that there is a restoration to the pre-fall conditions enjoyed in the Garden of Eden.[3]

A similar description is found in the familiar texts of Isaiah 11:6-9 and 65:25, where the wolf and lamb, leopard and kid, and calf and lion lie down peaceably together. It has been observed more than once that the only time today that the lamb lies down with the wolf is when the lamb lies down *within* the wolf! The future world described by

Ezekiel and Isaiah will obviously be a different world than what we have today, and for that reason many Christian interpreters of the Bible have concluded that these descriptions are too good to be true. They prefer these descriptions to be symbolic of heavenly realities rather than an earthly restoration.

Symbolic Restoration or Literal?

The Symbolic Viewpoint

As strongly as Jews have held to the concept of an earthly restoration of their kingdom, much of Christendom has opposed it. That Jerusalem would return to Jewish control was once thought by the church to be not only blasphemous, but impossible. This was because, as Jewish historian Shmuel Katz observes, "Jewish rule over the Christian holy places constitutes a direct challenge to the almost preternatural assertion that (because of the Jews' rejection of Jesus) no Jewish polity would or could ever arise again in Jerusalem." For many centuries the ruin of Jerusalem and its control by foreign nations (and especially those under the auspices of the Catholic Church), was held as an apologetic for the Christian faith, a proof of Christ's prophecy regarding the city's desolation, and a witness to the divine inspiration of the New Testament. To believe that Jerusalem would be reunited with the Jewish people as their capital was unthinkable, for it would appear to counter the very claims of Christianity. It is for this reason that, despite the obvious political realities, a segment of Christianity today continues to deny that the status of Jerusalem has changed. They consider the Jewish return and restoration of the city as a temporary achievement of secular Jews who, having been severed from the spiritual promises, are no different than any other people. They argue that the earthly Jerusalem has been superseded by the heavenly Jerusalem and, like the Jewish people, has no significance other than serving as a historical reminder of the past.

Catholicism—whether Roman, Russian, or Greek Orthodox—has for centuries been built on the belief that the promises made to Israel concerning its future blessings have been inherited by the church. Known as Supercessionism or Replacement Theology, the view is shared by a significant percentage of Protestant Christianity as well. While evangelical Protestants may be able to separate politics and theology, most of Christendom cannot. This has led to a theological bias toward Zionism and especially toward Jerusalem, which symbolizes the pivotal events which caused replacement: Christ cursing the fig tree, being rejected and crucified by the leadership of Jerusalem, and prophesying the fall of the city. For example, when the Zionist movement began over 100 years ago, Pope Pius X staunchly opposed immigration to Jerusalem:

> We [the Roman Catholic Church] are unable to favor this movement [Zionism]. We cannot prevent the Jews from going to Jerusalem—but we could never sanction it. As the head of the Church I cannot answer you otherwise.[4]

Given such an attitude and the history of the Inquisition, pogroms, and complicity in the Nazi Holocaust, when recent diplomatic Vatican-Israeli relations were achieved, Orthodox Jews protested with signs and graffiti reading "No Pope" in places throughout Jerusalem (see photo #21).

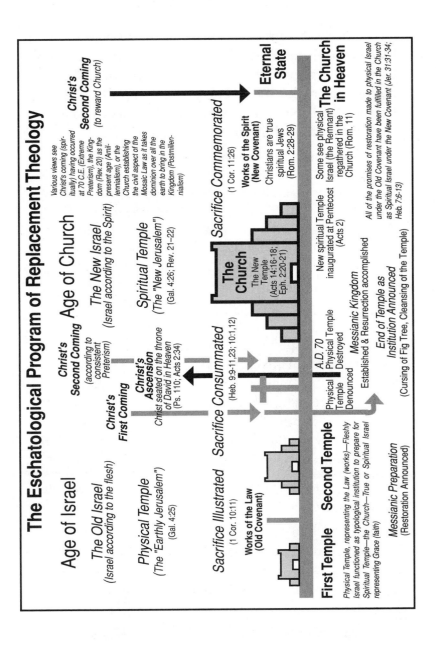

The Eschatological Program of Replacement Theology

Age of Israel

The Old Israel
(Israel according to the flesh)

Physical Temple
(The "Earthly Jerusalem")
(Gal. 4:25)

Age of Church

Christ's Second Coming
(according to consistent Preterism)

The New Israel
(Israel according to the Spirit)

Spiritual Temple
(The "New Jerusalem")
(Gal. 4:26; Rev. 21–22)

Christ's Second Coming
(to reward Church)

Eternal State

Various views see Christ's coming (spiritually having occurred at 70 C.E. [Extreme Preterism], the Kingdom (Rev. 20) as the present age (Amillennialism), or the Church establishing the civil aspect of the Mosaic Law as it takes dominion over all the earth to bring in the Kingdom (Postmillennialism)

Christ's First Coming

Christ's Ascension
Christ seated on the throne of David in Heaven
(Ps. 110; Acts 2:34)

Sacrifice Commemorated
(1 Cor. 11:26)

Works of the Spirit
(New Covenant)
Christians are true spiritual Jews
(Rom. 2:28-29)

Sacrifice Illustrated
(1 Cor. 10:11)

Works of the Law
(Old Covenant)

Sacrifice Consummated
(Heb. 9:9-11,23; 10:1,12)

The Church
The New Temple
(Acts 14:16-18;
Eph. 2:20-21)

Some see physical Israel (the Remnant) regathered in the Church (Rom. 11)

The Church in Heaven

First Temple   Second Temple

Physical Temple Denounced

A.D. 70
Physical Temple Destroyed

Messianic Kingdom
Established & Resurrection accomplished

End of Temple as Institution Announced
(Cursing of Fig Tree, Cleansing of the Temple)

New spiritual Temple inaugurated at Pentecost (Acts 2)

Messianic Preparation
(Restoration Announced)

Physical Temple, representing the Law (works)—Fleshly Israel functioned as typological institution to prepare for Spiritual Temple—the Church—True or Spiritual Israel representing Grace faith)

All of the promises of restoration made to physical Israel under the Old Covenant have been fulfilled in the Church as Spiritual Israel under the New Covenant (Jer. 31:31-34; Heb. 7:6-13)

Evangelical Christians of Preterist and Historicist (Amillennial and Postmillennial) prophetic persuasion have for the most part also adopted the same theological position of replacement. For example, in 1961 Baptist author Russell Jones, in his book *The Latter Days,* wrote this concerning the establishment of the State of Israel:

> Many accept this as proof that the Jews are still God's Chosen People with a definite mission to be performed in the future. This cannot be true. . . . The new Jewish state may or may not succeed politically. But to restore them to a primary place in the future outworking of God's redemptive purpose is to ignore the clear teaching of the New Testament and do violence to the cross of the Lord Jesus Christ. . . . Jews collectively can have no such hope.[5]

The "clear teaching" Jones refers to is presented especially in one chapter of his book, entitled "The people of God's Future."[6] In this chapter he outlines the typical evangelical Christian replacement position on the question of Israel's future status. Each of his main points below have supporting Scripture and arguments, but I have provided the data only for the first point because the other points logically follow from the first:[7]

1. *Those who were once God's people are no longer His people.*

   a) The end of the peculiar mission of the Jews is definitely indicated (Matthew 23:33-36; Luke 21:20,22-24).

   b) As a people, the Jews are under a curse and rejected by Jehovah because of their rejection of the Messiah (Matthew 23:37-38; 1 Thessalonians 2:14-16).

c) Their kingdom and inheritance are given to another, the true seed, composed of an elect remnant of Jews and believing Gentiles (Matthew 8:11-12; 21:43; 1 Peter 2:7-10; Galatians 3:15-29).

d) The Jews are no longer called God's people (Romans 3:21-23; Galatians 3:28-29).

e) The New Testament does not contain a word promising the restoration of the Jews to Palestine.

2. *Those who are Christ's, and those only, are God's people now and forever.*

3. *The New Testament writers explain fully this new departure in God's plan.*

The Literal Viewpoint

Writers who accept the viewpoint that the collective Jewish "mission" was ended and the Jews removed as the Chosen people forget that the national rejection of the Messiah had been predicted long before His birth (Isaiah 6:9-10; John 12:37-40; Isaiah 53:4), but promises of national restoration had also been made by the same prophet. In addition, it also seems to have been forgotten that those Jews who believed the prophetic promise concerning the Messiah before the birth of Jesus—as well as those who accepted Jesus as the Messiah before the birth of the church—were still part of collective Israel (national Israel) *as individual believers.* As such, they legitimately maintained a national restoration hope based on the promises of the prophets (Luke 24:21). This is why the disciples, numbered in this group, could ask Jesus in Acts 1:6 if the time of the promised restoration was at hand. Since they were present when Jesus pronounced "the curses" and denounced "the Jews," why did they not ask Jesus what this would mean for the future of their people? Furthermore, when Jesus spoke to them about the coming judgment on their nation, why did He not explain that their Jewish leaders' rejection of His messiahship had disqualified them *as Jews* from being God's chosen people and had abrogated any promise of future restoration to them as a nation? Since this was at the heart of the Messianic hope in the Old Testament, why was Jesus so silent about the unexpected replacement of promise that had supposedly occurred?

Yet the disciples *did* ask about the restoration of the kingdom to Israel while on the Mount of Olives in Acts 1:6. And Jesus gave them a reply in Acts 1:7. If there was ever an appropriate moment for the Messiah to correct any erroneous theological expectations concerning Israel's restoration, this would have been that moment. Why did Jesus, in His answer, leave the disciples with the understanding that their expectations were correct? More puzzling is this: How could the disciples have asked this question in the first place, knowing Jesus' own statements about judgment upon the Jews (Matthew 23:37-38); having being instructed concerning Jewish blindness and hardness (John 12:37-40); hearing personally the rejection by the Jewish leaders (Matthew 26:65-66; 27:41-43) and the Jewish people in Jerusalem during the Passover (Matthew 27:22,25); and finally, having witnessed the Jews crucifying their Messiah (Matthew 27:26; Luke 24:20; Acts 2:23; 3:14-15; 7:51-52; 1 Thessalonians 2:15)?

The reason the disciples could ask this is that *they also* had departed from Him (Matthew 26:31,33,56), lost faith in Him (Luke 24:21,25; John 20:27), and even betrayed Him (Matthew 26:21-22,70-75). With the resurrection, all of their sins of rejection had been forgiven (Luke 24:38,49; John 21:15-23) and they had been restored as His apostles

(Acts 1:2,4-5,8). Their experience matched the Old Testament pattern of restoration after judgment, so if their nation likewise repented, could they not expect Jesus to restore it (corporately) as He had them (individually)? This is, in fact, the very message they preached at Pentecost:

> And now, [Jewish] brethren, I know that you [individuals] acted in ignorance, just as your rulers [corporate nation] did also. . . . Repent therefore and return, that your sins may be wiped away [individual restoration], in order that times of refreshing may come from the presence of the Lord; and that He may send Jesus, the Christ appointed for you [Jewish nation], whom heaven must receive until the period of restoration of all things [corporate/ national restoration] about which God spoke by the mouth of His holy prophets from ancient time (Acts 3:17,19-21).

In this context, the word "restoration" immediately draws our thoughts back to Acts 1:6, where the same word was used of national Israel. Furthermore, this restoration is said to be that spoken from ancient time by the prophets and is connected with the second coming of Christ, after Jewish [national] repentance. The descriptive terms "times of refreshing" and "restoration *of all things*," as understood in an Old Testament prophetic context, further define this "period of restoration" as the original Jewish national hope. How can we interpret this as the promise of "the present spiritual kingdom of God" or of "individual regeneration" with no connection to the Old Testament prophetic context of Israel's restoration?

Notice too that Peter, who gives this message and was an eyewitness of Jesus' sufferings and crucifixion under the Jewish authorities (1 Peter 5:1; 2 Peter 1:15; see also 1 John

1:1-2), says that *both* the people of Israel and their rulers acted in "ignorance" (Acts 3:17). This emphasis on "ignorance" reminds us of Jesus' prayer of forgiveness from the cross for those who crucified Him because "they do not know what they are doing" (Luke 23:34). Paul also conveys a similar attitude (Acts 13:27; 17:30; Romans 10:2; 1 Timothy 1:13). Peter further mitigates the people's guilt by attributing their rejection to God's plan to fulfill the prophet's predictions (Acts 3:18). All this requires replacement theologians to reassess their conclusion that God rejected the Jewish nation based on the people's and leaders' rejection of Jesus.[8]

Misunderstandings about the Term *Palestinian*

Christian Replacement Theology took a more literal form with Arab and Islamic Revisionist theology. This has brought the Jewish hope of Jerusalem's restoration under attack by supplanting the interpretation of Jerusalem's Jewish past in order to obliterate its future. The current use of revisionist history seeks to make Jerusalem the capital of a Palestinian state whose people's origin is claimed to have been rooted in the country and city's past. Some of this revisionism revolves around the understanding of the name *Palestine*.

Until the Arab-Palestinian refugee situation was created in 1948, the term *Palestinian* applied to both Arabs and Jews living in the Land of Israel, then called *Palestine*. For instance, the English-language newspaper originating from Jerusalem and today called *The Jerusalem Post* was at one time known as *The Palestine Post*. Similarly, the famous Israeli Philharmonic Orchestra was formerly the Palestine Philharmonic Orchestra. When postage stamps were issued during the

early period of the British Mandate, they bore the appella-
tion "Palestine—(E-I)," the abbreviation meaning "Eretz-
Israel" (Land of Israel). Once the State of Israel was declared,
Jewish and Arab "Palestinians" became "Israelis" and
"Israeli-Arabs," leaving the Arab population outside the
boundaries of Israel to keep the name "Palestinians."

However, it can be shown that the term *Palestinian* was
once eschewed by Arabs because it was considered to refer
predominately to Jews. In 1917, when the Balfour Declaration referred to the historic land of Palestine as the place for
a "national home for the Jewish people," Arabs rejected this
application with the explanation that there was no such
thing as Palestine except as the southern part of Greater
Syria. During this period, too, the Arab political representatives, headed by the Mufti of Jerusalem, were not called
"The Palestinian Committee," as today, but merely "The
Arab Higher Committee." And finally, when the Anglo-
American Committee of Inquiry convened in Jerusalem in
1946, the distinguished Arab historian Professor Philip
Hitti testified, "There is no such thing as Palestine in [Arab]
history, absolutely not."[9]

The term *Palestinian* was not even used in the founda-
tional 1967 Security Council Resolution 242 or the 1973
Resolution 338. It only appeared in the mid-1970s when it
became politically expedient for the PLO to use the term
Palestinian to refer to the Arab population in exclusion of
the Jews. From the time that the Palestinian Authority was
created in 1993, the Israeli-Arabs, in a show of solidarity,
began calling themselves "Palestinians." So today, we hear
the PLO state that the Arabs as "Palestinians" were in the
Land for more than 5,000 years, being the relatives of the
Philistines, from which the word *Philistia,* or in Latin (via
the Romans) *Palestinea* is derived. They have also claimed

descendancy from the Jebusites who had control of Jerusalem until the time of King David 3,000 years ago. Today
we also hear, as in Yasser Arafat's comments to more than
300 journalists in Europe, that "Jesus was a Palestinian
freedom fighter," or as in his speech at the Israeli withdrawal from Bethlehem, that Bethlehem was the "home of
the Palestinian, Jesus."

However, the Jebusites have been traced to a Hurrian
(Horite) origin, one of the pagan Canaanite peoples of
ancient Canaan, and there is no such Islamic heritage trace-
able in the Koran. In fact, the Arabs originated as nomadic
tribes in the Arabian peninsula and emerged in "Palestine"
only after the Islamic invasion of the Land and Jerusalem in
the seventh century A.D. However, even after this conquest,
most of Jerusalem's Muslim rulers—during the 1,174 years
they held dominance—were not even Arab. Saladin, who
defeated the Crusaders and retook the city, was a Kurd; Suleiman the Magnificant, who rebuilt the walls of the Old City
to their modern appearance, was an Ottoman Turk; the Seljuks were Turkish mercenaries; and the Mamluks were from
the Caucasus. Furthermore, the majority of "Palestinian"
Arabs immigrated to the Land on the heels of the Zionist
Jews in the twentieth century. Nevertheless, many of the
United States' most prestigious and authoritative international news, political, and geographical journals, as well as
popular encyclopedias, have adopted and promoted the
revised Arab history of Israel and Jerusalem.[10]

The World Against Jerusalem

The United Nations has embraced the Palestinian
cause, generally adopting Arab revisionism concerning
Jerusalem as a matter of course in its dictates to Israel. As

such, this organization no longer simply represents "The United Nations," but "The Nations United Against Jerusalem." In the spring of 1998 when U.N. Secretary-General Kofi Annan listed the world community's grievances against Israel, he noted:

> Here is what the great majority of the member states of the United Nations say: They regard Israel as having been responsible, directly or indirectly, for provocative acts that undermine goodwill and spark hostilities. . . . They see that you have expanded settlements, and started new ones. . . . land for peace is the only principle that has a chance of bringing peace to this land.

Kofi Annan's statements reflect the international attitude toward Israeli sovereignty over Jerusalem, focused for the moment on the building activity going on at Har Homa. Annan referred to Har Homa as an "illegal Israeli activity" and reported that the project posed a serious threat to Arab-Israeli peace and was "seen as the final step toward the isolation of Jerusalem from the West Bank."[11] Annan's verdict followed the U.N.'s condemnation of Israel over Har Homa at an emergency session that convened in the spring of 1997—at the request of the 22-member Arab group—to deal with the situation created by the building project. The seriousness with which the U.N. regards this issue of Jewish sovereignty over Jerusalem may be seen by the fact that this was the first emergency session called in the past 15 years. In fact, between 1956 to 1997, there have only been nine emergency sessions,[12] and four dealt with Israel: the Suez crisis of 1956, after the Six-Day War of 1967, the question of "Palestine" in 1980, and the situation regarding the occupation of the West Bank and Golan Heights in 1982. While the outcome of an emergency session cannot impose legal obligations, it can affect international opinion and increase international pressure on Israel.

What Secretary-General Annan's statement fails to disclose is the U.N.'s unbalanced condemnations of Israel. When in 1997 the United Nations condemned Israel over Har Homa, out of the then 321 U.N. General Assembly resolutions and 49 U.N. Security Council resolutions condemning Israel (a total of 370 condemnations), Israel was condemned 370 times and the Arab nations not once![13] This means that despite the PLO's history of terrorism, its public instigation against Israel and Jerusalem, its statements of *jihad*, its vows to eradicate Israel, its open support of Hamas leadership and Saddam Hussein, and its "police" illegally shooting Jewish soldiers and civilians (such as in the 1996 Western Wall tunnel riots), no condemnations have been made against it. Such a biased posture against Israel led Israeli ambassador to the United Nations, Dore Gold, to call Annan's report "hostile" and "one-sided," and Knesset Speaker Dan Tichon to warn the Secretary-General:

> Israel is a long-standing member of the U.N., but only on rare occasions is it treated in a friendly way. Our country has seen attacks and unbalanced condemnations. The strategy of isolating and delegitimizing [Israel] will only go sour. . . . If there is no dramatic turnaround in the U.N.'s attitude towards Israel, the organization will continue to be distanced. . . . [14]

As we've already seen, before Jerusalem's status is restored in the future, it will face enormous destruction from an international attack. It appears that the present breach in relations between Israel and the United Nations will increase, further isolating Israel from the international community and perhaps opening the way for, as one writer speculates, "the coming invasion of Israel by the United Nations army bent on evicting Israel from Jerusalem."[15]

No Place Like Jerusalem

As the world prepares to oust the Jews from a united Jerusalem, the prophetic day of its restoration draws ever closer. Jerusalem's future is to be where it has been in the past—firmly planted in the promises of God to Israel. Indeed, Jerusalem's promised restoration has always held a distinct place within the hearts and borders of the modern State. Its uniqueness in this regard was noted by Menachem Mendel Ussishkin in 1947 when the status of the city was in debate:

> The Land of Israel without Jerusalem is merely "Palestine." Down the generations the Jews have been saying not, "Next year in the Land of Israel," but "Next year in Jerusalem.". . . One can create Tel Aviv out of a Jaffa but one cannot create a second Jerusalem. Zion lies within the walls, not outside them.[16]

Within the walls, as Ussishkin observes, lies "Zion," or as he understands it, the Temple Mount. It is to this place that the glory of God is predicted to return. It is from here that the future restoration is predicted to erupt and spread throughout all the earth. If, then, Jerusalem is to be restored, its restoration depends upon the Temple also being restored. It is to this prophetic hope that we now turn.

God is known in Judah; His name is great
in Israel. And His tabernacle is in Salem;
His dwelling place also is in Zion.

—Psalm 76:1-2

Thus says the LORD, "I will return to Zion
and dwell in the midst of Jerusalem. Then
Jerusalem will be called the City of Truth,
and the mountain of the LORD of hosts
will be called the Holy Mountain."

—Zechariah 8:3

Thus says the LORD of hosts, "Behold, a
man whose name is Branch, for He will
branch out from where He is; and He will
build the temple of the LORD."

—Zechariah 6:12

12

GOD COMES HOME:
The Rebuilding of Jerusalem's Temple

Only on the soil of Israel, in the place chosen by God (Mount Moriah in Jerusalem), could the permanent Sanctuary of the Jewish people be built; only there would the Jews be able to fully realize their potential as a people; only there could they make good their promise to God.

—National Conference of Brazilian Bishops,
Rio de Janeiro

I was taking a risk, but I had to explore and photograph the region adjacent to the Eastern Wall of the Temple Mount. This area is closely guarded by the Muslims because of the remains from the Second Temple period within the inner portion of the Eastern Gate and within the corridor behind the southeastern wall leading to the Al-Aksa mosque. Although people are normally unable to approach these areas, I went ahead and climbed the backside of the Eastern Gate and made my way along the wall to the south, which overlooked the monumental staircase from the Second Temple—a staircase uncovered years earlier by Israeli archaeologists. Never before, and never since, have I been able to make this distance without being forced from the site. Even so, I was being watched all during my explorations, and as I was leaving the enclosure near the Al-Aksa mosque I was approached by a well-dressed Arab who questioned me about what I had been doing. Seeing no reason to conceal my purpose, I explained that I was doing research on the ancient Temple that had once occupied that place. To which the Arab, with an ominous tone, replied, "You'd do better to forget the past and think about your future!"

I've thought about that advice and how it relates to the Temple Mount many times since. But I can't do what he suggested and hold true to my hope for the future, for my future—indeed, that of the world and even the Arabs—depends on *not* forgetting the Temple that stood there. It was there that "the LORD commanded the blessing—life forever" (Psalm 133:3), and from there that "the law will go forth" and "the word of the LORD from Jerusalem" (Isaiah 2:3). Jerusalem's uniqueness with respect to the Temple is a matter of past history: "In Judah God is known; His name is great in Israel. His tent is in Salem, His dwelling place in Zion" (Psalm 76:1-2 NIV). Where else on earth could it be said, "Great is the LORD, and greatly to be praised, in the city of our God, His holy mountain. Beautiful in elevation, the joy of the whole earth, is Mount Zion in the far north, the city of the great King"? (Psalm 48:1-2).

The Pattern of Prophecy

From the beginning, the city of Jerusalem was tied to the Temple in prophecy: "Then it shall come about that the

The Jerusalem Temple in History & Prophecy

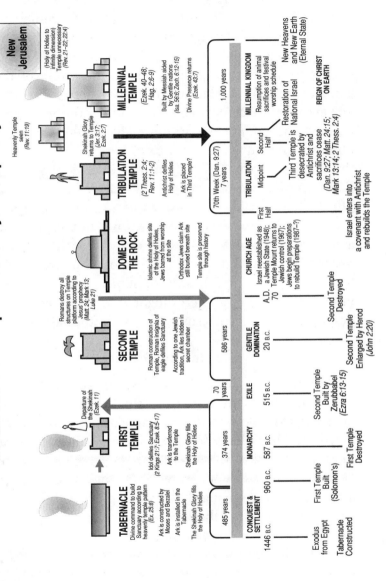

New Jerusalem
(Holy of Holies to infinite dimension) Temple unnecessary (Rev. 21-22; 22:4)

Heavenly Temple seen (Rev. 11:19)

MILLENNIAL TEMPLE (Ezek. 40–48; Hag. 2:6-9)
Built by Messiah aided by Gentile nations (Isa. 56:6; Zech. 6:12-15)
Divine Presence returns (Ezek. 43:7)

Shekinah Glory returns to Temple (Ezek. 2:7)

TRIBULATION TEMPLE (2 Thess. 2:4; Rev. 11:1-2)
Antichrist defiles Holy of Holies
Ark is placed in Third Temple?

DOME OF THE ROCK
Islamic shrine defiles site of the Holy of Holies, Jews barred from worship at the site
Orthodox Jews claim Ark still buried beneath site
Temple site is preserved through history

Romans destroy all structures on Temple platform according to Jesus' prophecy (Matt. 24; Mark 13; Luke 21)

SECOND TEMPLE
Roman construction of Temple, Roman insignia of eagle defiles Sanctuary
According to one Jewish tradition, Ark lies hidden in secret chamber

FIRST TEMPLE
Idol defiles Sanctuary (2 Kings 21:7; Ezek. 8:5-17)
Ark is transferred to the Temple
Shekinah Glory fills the Holy of Holies

Departure of the Shekinah (Ezek. 11)

TABERNACLE
Divine command to build Sanctuary according to heavenly temple pattern (Ex. 25:8)
Ark is constructed by Moses and Bezalel
Ark is installed in the Tabernacle
The Shekinah Glory fills the Holy of Holies

---

	485 years	374 years	70 years	586 years		70th Week (Dan. 9:27) 7 years	1,000 years	
	CONQUEST & SETTLEMENT	MONARCHY	EXILE	GENTILE DOMINATION	CHURCH AGE	TRIBULATION	MILLENNIAL KINGDOM	New Heavens and New Earth (Eternal State)

1446 B.C.   960 B.C.   587 B.C.   515 B.C.   20 B.C.   A.D. 70

Exodus from Egypt
Tabernacle Constructed

First Temple Built (Solomon's)

First Temple Destroyed

Second Temple Built by Zerubbabel (Ezra 6:13-15)

Second Temple Enlarged by Herod (John 2:20)

Second Temple Destroyed

Israel reestablished as a Jewish State (1948); Temple Mount returns to Jewish control (1967); Jews begin preparations to rebuild Temple (1987–?)

Israel enters into a covenant with Antichrist and rebuilds the Temple

First Half

Midpoint

Second Half

Third Temple is desecrated by Antichrist and sacrifices cease (Dan. 9:27; Matt. 24:15; Mark 13:14; 2 Thess. 2:4)

Restoration of National Israel

REIGN OF CHRIST ON EARTH

place in which the LORD your God shall choose for His name to dwell, there you shall bring all that I command you: your burnt offerings and your sacrifices" (Deuteronomy 12:11). When the glorious prophecies of Jerusalem's future restoration were given, the future of the Temple was mentioned as well. These prophecies were usually given in the context of judgment; the prophets proclaimed the comforting promise that after a time of punishment God would restore prosperity. An example is this prediction from Isaiah: "It is I [the Lord] who says of Jerusalem, 'She shall be inhabited!' and of the cities of Judah, 'They shall be built.' And I will raise up her ruins again. . . . and he declares of Jerusalem, 'She will be built,' and of the Temple, 'Your foundation will be laid'" (Isaiah 44:26,28). Such Old Testament restoration prophecies form a pattern for future fulfillment that remains unchanged in expectation throughout the New Testament despite the rejection of Jesus as Messiah by the nation.[1]

Jesus and the Temple

For this reason, even though Jesus announces to Jerusalem that "your house [the Temple] is being left to you desolate" (Matthew 23:38), He immediately adds, "For I say to you [Jerusalem], from now on you shall not see Me until you say, 'Blessed is He who comes in the name of the LORD'" (Matthew 23:39). Jesus' citation is from Psalm 118, a psalm of thanksgiving that was sung when the people were in procession to the Temple. Note that Jesus put His words in the future tense by the use of the word "until." In other words, when the people of Jerusalem next see Jesus (and they will), it will be at the time they have turned to Him as Messiah (Zechariah 12:10). After that, the Temple will no longer be desolate—with the return of the Lord will come the return of His house. The very next verses in Matthew 24, and Jesus' response to His disciples' questions, confirm this.

Matthew 24 is part of what is known as the Olivet Discourse (because its prophecies were delivered from the Mount of Olives in Jerusalem). It begins with Jesus and His disciples viewing recent architectural additions to the Herodian Temple (verse 1). As they are leaving, Jesus uses the setting to announce the coming destruction of the Temple (verse 2). This provokes the disciples to ask Jesus about this prediction, an event so earthshaking to their way of thinking that they assume it would usher in the end of the age and be attended by Jesus' advent as the Messianic King (verse 3). This is because the Temple stood as a symbol of the nation's relationship to God and served as the spiritual cement holding their often divisive people together. Without the Temple, they thought, Israel would be devastated.

The Gospel of Luke alone records Jesus' answer to the disciples' question as to when the destruction of the Temple ("these things") would occur. In Luke 21:20-24 He makes it clear that this disaster will not end the age nor bring the Messiah. Because it will be the "days of vengeance" (verse 22) it will begin the period of the Temple's desolation and Messiah's absence—a time more specifically referred to in this passage as "the times of the Gentiles" (verse 24). Jesus again uses the word "until" here to assure them that *after* this time has run its determined course, Messiah will come and the age of Israel's national redemption will arrive (verses 27-28). The details of the progression of these latter-day events are given to us in the Gospels of Matthew and Mark. It is evident from Jesus' description of the times of

Jerusalem's Future According to the Olivet Discourse

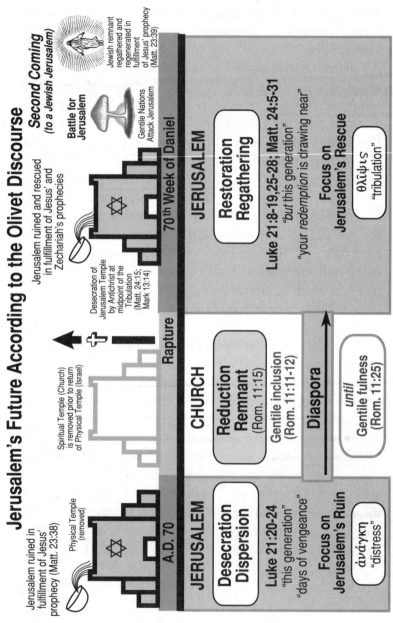

Second Coming
(to a Jewish Jerusalem)

Jewish remnant regathered and regenerated in fulfillment of Jesus' prophecy (Matt. 23:39)

Jerusalem ruined in fulfillment of Jesus' prophecy (Matt. 23:38)

Jerusalem ruined and rescued in fulfillment of Jesus' and Zechariah's prophecies

Battle for Jerusalem

Gentile Nations Attack Jerusalem

Physical Temple (removed)

Spiritual Temple (Church) is removed prior to return of Physical Temple (Israel)

Desecration of Jerusalem Temple by Antichrist at midpoint of the Tribulation (Matt. 24:15; Mark 13:14)

Rapture

70th Week of Daniel

A.D. 70

JERUSALEM

Desecration Dispersion

Luke 21:20-24 "this generation" "days of vengeance"

Focus on Jerusalem's Ruin

ἀνάγκη "distress"

CHURCH

Reduction Remnant (Rom. 11:15)

Gentile inclusion (Rom. 11:11-12)

Diaspora

until Gentile fulness (Rom. 11:25)

JERUSALEM

Restoration Regathering

Luke 21:8-19,25-28; Matt. 24:5-31 *but this generation* "your redemption is drawing near"

Focus on Jerusalem's Rescue

θλῖψις "tribulation"

Note: "This generation" is understood as the generation that would experience the particular events during the time described in the prophetic context.

the Gentiles in Matthew 24 and Mark 13 that things will go from bad to worse for Israel, culminating in a time of unparalleled tribulation (Matthew 24:21; Mark 13:19). During this time Jesus speaks of a signal event connected with the Temple—its desecration by an abomination which was prophesied by the prophet Daniel (Matthew 24:15; Mark 13:14). What Temple is being spoken of here by Jesus? Was the Temple that was to be desecrated the same Temple as the one He predicted would be destroyed? There are a number of contrasts within this text that indicate that Jesus was talking about *two different* Temples:

1. The Temple described in Matthew 24:15 is not said to be destroyed, only desecrated (see Revelation 11:2). By contrast, the Temple in Jesus' day (or Matthew 24:2) was to be completely leveled: "not one stone would be left standing on another" (Matthew 24:2; Mark 13:2; Luke 19:44).

2. The Temple's desecration would be a signal for Jews to *escape* destruction (Matthew 24:16-18), "be saved" (Matthew 24:22), and experience the promised "redemption" (Luke 21:28). By contrast the destruction of the Temple in Matthew 24:2 was a judgment "because you did not recognize the time of your visitation [Messiah's first advent]" (Luke 19:44b) and resulted in the Temple being "level[ed] to the ground and your children [the Jews] within you" (Luke 19:44a).

3. The generation of Jews that are alive at the time that the Temple is desecrated will expect Messiah's coming "immediately after" (Matthew 24:29), and are predicted to not pass away until they have experienced it

(Matthew 24:34). By contrast, the generation of Jews who saw the Temple destroyed would pass away and 2,000 years (to date) would pass without redemption.

4. The text Jesus cited concerning the Temple's desecration, Daniel 9:27, predicts that the one who desecrates this Temple will himself be destroyed. By contrast, those who destroyed the Temple in A.D. 70 (in fulfillment of Jesus' prediction)—the Roman emperor Vespasian and his son Titus—were not destroyed but returned to Rome in triumph carrying vessels from the destroyed Temple.

5. The time "immediately after" (Matthew 24:29) the time of the Temple's desecration will see Israel's repentance (Matthew 24:30), followed by, as Matthew 23:29 implies, a restoration of the Temple. By contrast, the time following the destruction of the Temple only saw a "hardening" happen "to Israel," which is to last "until the fulness of the Gentiles has come in" (Romans 11:25)—still 2,000 years and counting.

6. For the Temple that is desecrated, the scope is of a worldwide tribulation "coming upon the world" (Luke 21:26; compare Matthew 24:21-22; Mark 13:19-20), a global regathering of the Jewish people "from one end of the sky to the other" (Matthew 24:31; Mark 13:27), and a universal revelation of the Messiah at Israel's rescue (Matthew 24:30-31; Mark 13:26; Luke 21:26-27). This scope accords with the prophesied end-time battle for Jerusalem recorded in Zechariah 12–14, where "all nations of the earth will be gathered against it" (Zechariah 12:3). By contrast the A.D. 70 assault on Jerusalem predicted in Luke 21:20 is by the armies of

one empire (Rome). Therefore, if there are two different attacks on Jerusalem, separated by more than 2,000 years, then two distinct Temples are considered in Matthew 24:1-2 and Matthew 24:15.

Therefore, one of the Temples prophesied here was that destroyed by the Romans (Matthew 24:1-2) and the other is prophesied to be desecrated in the future (Matthew 24:15). This desecrated Temple, and one final Temple, are the subject of several end-time texts.

Two Temples to Come

Two Temples have been built and destroyed in Israel's past. According to prophecy, two more will yet be built in the future. The next in order will be a "third" Temple that will be built sometime before or during the first half of Daniel's seventieth week and continue through this period. For this reason it is referred to by many Christians as the "Tribulation Temple." The last in order will be a "fourth" Temple that will be built by the Messiah after His return—a Temple that will stand throughout the Millennial kingdom. Therefore, it is often called "Messiah's Temple" or "the Temple of Messiah's Glory."

The Temple of the Tribulation

The Third Temple is the Temple that will be desecrated, as recorded in Daniel's prophecy of the seventy weeks (Daniel 9:24-27). According to the chronology of this text, *before* the seventieth week Messiah comes and is "cut off" (put to death) and the city of Jerusalem and its Temple are destroyed in a war (verse 26). Then during the seventieth week (the final one), the Temple is desecrated by an abomination brought by "the prince who is to come" (verses 26-27), who himself will be completely destroyed (verse 27).[2]

In part, because the events of verse 27 were interpreted by Jesus in the Olivet Discourse as part of the future time of Tribulation (which, as we have seen, cannot fit the A.D. 70 Roman destruction of the Temple), the Temple destroyed *before* the seventieth week was the Second Temple (of Jesus' day), and the one desecrated at the midpoint of the seventieth week is the Third Temple (of the Tribulation period).

In the New Testament, the apostle Paul described in more detail this desecration and identified "the prince who is to come" as the Antichrist:

> ... and the man of lawlessness is revealed, the son of destruction, who opposes and exalts himself above every so-called god or object of worship, so that he takes his seat in the temple of God, displaying himself as being God (2 Thessalonians 2:3-4).

Paul's context is the future "day of the Lord" (2 Thessalonians 2:2), the period of time encompassing the Tribulation and Millennium. The events surrounding the Third Temple and its desecration take place in the time shortly before the revelation of Christ (to earth), since the "lawless one" is destroyed by the Lord at His coming (verse 8; see Daniel 9:27). According to 2 Thessalonians 2:3-4, it seems that the Antichrist will seek to deify himself by usurping the place of the only true God within the Temple's Holy of Holies.[3] Because of this action, some Christians have referred to this Temple as "Antichrist's Temple." That is improper, since this Temple must first be holy in order to be desecrated, and Paul still calls it "the Temple of God" even after its defilement (verse 4). This Temple is also called "the Temple of God" by the apostle John, who describes the Jewish worship taking place at the sacrificial altar as well as the Temple's desecration by the nations (Revelation 11:1-2). John is told that the

Jerusalem in Daniel's Prophecy of the Seventy Weeks

Jerusalem's Temple Mount serves as the focal point of the prophetic events

Daniel's "Seventy Weeks" (490 years) for the Holy City (Dan. 9:24a)

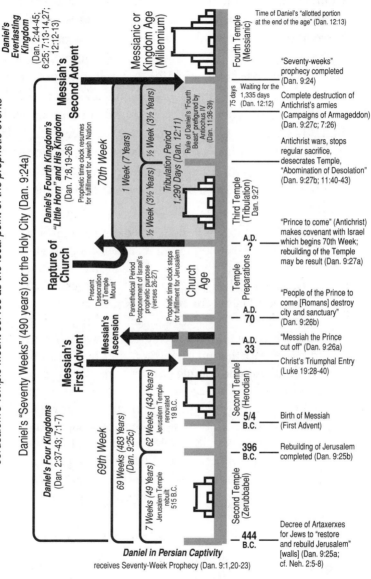

outside precinct of the Temple, known as the court of the Gentiles, will be included in the territory invaded by the nations (those under Antichrist) for 42 months (the last three-and-one-half years of the Tribulation period). This agrees with the time period given for the abomination of desolation as recorded in Daniel 12:11, as well as the prophecy of the international assault on Jerusalem in Zechariah 12–14 and the warning concerning the abomination of desolation in the Temple in the Olivet Discourse (Matthew 24:15; Mark 13:14). The remarkable events presently shaping Jerusalem politics and moving them toward the fulfillment of these texts has been noted by CBS radio correspondent and author David Dolan, who lives in Jerusalem. He states:

> The final status of Jerusalem is definitely the most difficult problem in the Arab-Israeli conflict. The Arab world means it when they say that they want Israel out of the Old City and out of East Jerusalem entirely. They want real sovereignty restored to Arab hands. The Israelis, of course, mean it when they say that this is our Temple Mount, our holiest place on earth. And we will not, after 2,000 years of wandering and coming back and capturing it, give it over to anybody else. How a real solution is going to be found by the parties is impossible for me to see. And, in fact, I anticipate that it will have to be imposed on both the Arabs and the Jews from the outside, which, of course, considering the prophecies, we can imagine who it might be that would impose such a solution on the parties here in the region.[4]

Based on the aforementioned texts, and especially Daniel 9:27, it appears that this future Third Temple may be rebuilt as a result of the covenant made between "the prince

who is to come" (the Antichrist) and the Israeli government (Hebrew *rabim:* "many") sometime in the future.
Harold Foos, Professor of Bible at Moody Bible Institute,
writing before the 1967 capture of the Temple Mount, came
to this conclusion:

> ... it is the conviction of this writer that the repos-
> session of the Temple site and the rebuilding of the
> Temple with its renewed worship will be in direct
> consequence of the covenant that the Antichrist
> makes with Israel for the "one week," the seven
> years of the Tribulation period.[5]

The following possibilities may be offered in support of
this conviction: 1) The Second Temple was rebuilt by the
permission and power of a Gentile ruler (Cyrus), setting
the precedence for the same to happen with the rebuilding
of the Third Temple. 2) If a political power or leader could
guarantee the rebuilding of the Temple, any covenant made
with Israel would be expected to include this. 3) When the
covenant moves from policy to persecution in the middle
of the seventieth week, the Antichrist takes the prerogative
to cause the sacrifices to cease (Daniel 9:27; 12:11) and to
occupy the Temple himself (Matthew 24:15; Mark 13:14;
2 Thessalonians 2:4). This could imply that he had been
involved in some prior relationship with it. 4) A pivotal
event marked both the beginning and end of the first 69
weeks and the interval between the end of the sixty-ninth
and the beginning of the seventieth (Daniel 9:25-26). Such
an event might be expected at the beginning of the seventieth week as well, especially if it marks a revival of God's
direct dealing with the nation. 5) Since the purpose of the
Tribulation is to prepare Israel for its fulfillment of God's
prophetic promises in the Millennium (where the Temple

is prominent), and the Temple suffers with the nation during the Tribulation, its rebuilding should be connected with the beginning of the Tribulation (the signing of the covenant, Daniel 9:27).

Having looked at the Third Temple, let's move on to the Fourth, which occupies significantly more passages in Scripture.

The Temple of the Millennium

God's plan when he established the nation of Israel was to be present with His people: "Let them construct a sanctuary for Me, that I may dwell among them" (Exodus 25:8). However, God's presence with Israel in this manner was provisional. His glory dwelt in the First Temple, but not in the Second. Nor will it return to the Third Temple during the Tribulation. Therefore, ever since the departure of God's presence before the destruction of the First Temple in 586 B.C., the prophetic fulfillment of Israel's complete restoration in the Land has centered on a final, inviolable Temple to which the divine presence would return: "Thus says the LORD, 'I will return to Zion and will dwell in the midst of Jerusalem. Then Jerusalem will be called the City of Truth, and the mountain of the LORD of hosts will be called the Holy Mountain'" (Zechariah 8:3). The prophet Ezekiel, who wrote the vivid account of the first departure of God's glory (Ezekiel 10–11), wrote of its return to the Millennial Temple in ten chapters of his book. One chapter (chapter 37) summarizes the permanency of this final Temple, of God's abiding presence with Israel through it, and of its relationship with the nations of the world (verses 26-28). The other nine chapters (chapters 40–48) offer a detailed description of the Temple's architecture, per-

sonnel, and performance. Here also we find mention of the
return of God's glory to the Temple. In the same manner as
God's glory departed, it will come from the east (from over
the Mount of Olives), through the Eastern Gate of the
Temple, and into the Holy of Holies (Ezekiel 43:1-5). But
this time God gave a promise not given before: ". . . this is
the place of My throne and the place of the soles of My feet,
where I will dwell among the sons of Israel *forever*" (Ezekiel
43:7).

Both Jewish and Christian commentators throughout
the centuries have sought to interpret that promise non-lit-
erally, making it either a visionary description of restoration, a spiritual preview of heaven, or a symbolic picture of
the church.[6] But these non-literal interpretations fail when
attempts are made to deal adequately with the precise
architectural measurements and geographical boundaries
that appear in the text. In addition, Ezekiel's prophecy was
written to comfort the Jews in exile in Babylon, who had
lost the physical Temple in the actual Land of Israel. Of
what consolation (or meaning) would a promise intended
for heaven or for other people (the church) have for those
who needed an earthly hope?

If this Temple is interpreted literally, it must be future
because such a Temple has never yet been realized in any
rebuilding in Israel's past history. Although some scholars
have tried to make this an idealist depiction of the Second
Temple—the Temple built after the return from Babylon—
this identification fails because the Second Temple was
woefully inferior to the First Temple, which it replaced. In
fact, the people's disappointed reaction to this Temple was
so pronounced (Ezra 3:12-13) that the prophet Haggai was
given another prophecy of the Temple's greater future just
to calm them (Haggai 2:3-9).

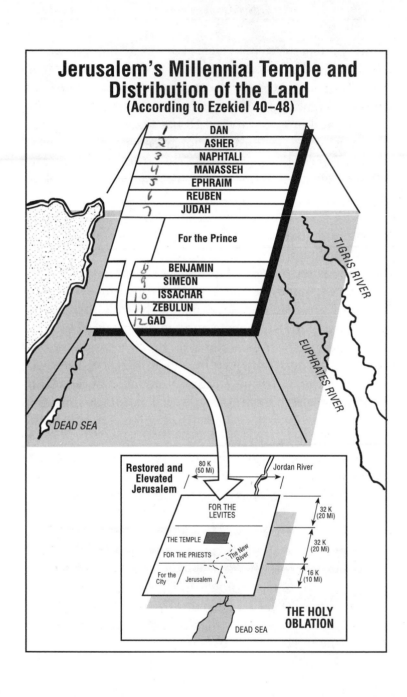

Jerusalem's Millennial Temple and Distribution of the Land
(According to Ezekiel 40–48)

1 DAN
2 ASHER
3 NAPHTALI
4 MANASSEH
5 EPHRAIM
6 REUBEN
7 JUDAH

For the Prince

8 BENJAMIN
9 SIMEON
10 ISSACHAR
11 ZEBULUN
12 GAD

TIGRIS RIVER

EUPHRATES RIVER

DEAD SEA

Restored and Elevated Jerusalem

80 K (50 Mi)

Jordan River

FOR THE LEVITES

32 K (20 Mi)

THE TEMPLE

32 K (20 Mi)

FOR THE PRIESTS

The New River

For the City

Jerusalem

16 K (10 Mi)

THE HOLY OBLATION

DEAD SEA

Taken literally, the Millennial Temple described in Ezekiel finally fulfills the holiness for the earth that previous Temples could only represent. Not only does the holiness surrounding this Temple reverse the condition of the defiled Tribulation Temple, but it also reverses the curse begun in the Garden of Eden, where man was first separated from God. This reversal is particularly evidenced by the fresh waters that flow from beneath the sanctuary, transforming even the Dead Sea into a body of water teeming with aquatic life (Ezekiel 47:1-12). What's more, God's presence dwells in this Temple in a more significant way than ever before, for the whole city of Jerusalem becomes holy (Zechariah 14:20-21) and will be called "The Throne of the LORD" (Jeremiah 3:17).

The Millennial Temple is built by the returned Messiah (Zechariah 6:12-14), but also by the Gentile nations who now recognize the blessing of Israel (verse 15; see also Haggai 2:7; Isaiah 60:10,14). These same believing nations, who survived the campaigns of Armageddon and passed through the "judgment of the nations" in the Valley of Jehoshaphat (Matthew 25:31-46) and have entered into the Millennial kingdom, will make annual pilgrimages to the Millennial Temple to worship (Zechariah 14:16-19; see also Isaiah 60:11). For this reason, Jesus, referring to Isaiah's prophecy of this restored Temple (Isaiah 56:6-7), said it would one day be called "a house of prayer for all the nations" (Mark 11:17). They will come to this Temple on the greatly enlarged Temple Mount in Jerusalem to learn the ways of the Lord and receive justice from the Righteous Judge enthroned there (Isaiah 2:2-4). It is at that time that the Jewish people will have received the means to fulfill the goal God established when He made the Abrahamic Covenant with them: to be a blessing to all the earth (Genesis 12:3).[7]

Why Rebuild the Temple Today?

For many Israelis, as well as Jews outside the Land today, the notion of building a literal Temple at any time in the future is considered ludicrous, fanatical, and dangerous. Two key reasons for this are their change in thinking about the Temple after its last destruction in A.D. 70 and the present-day desire to make peace with the followers of Islam, whose mosque and shrines have occupied the Temple Mount for over 1,300 years. After the loss of the Temple, and with no possibility of rebuilding, the rabbis were faced with the necessity of maintaining a Judaism that had previously depended on the Temple's existence. Most of the 613 biblical commandments, the festival calendar which regulated Jewish life, and the ritual prayers and performance were tied to the Temple. With no Temple available, changes had to be made; therefore, the synagogue became the place of teaching and worship, with certain aspects of ritual obligation and service becoming marginalized or reduced to their underlying spiritual principles. A similar transformation also occurred with the people's concept of a literal Messiah whose coming was expected to redeem and restore Israel and bring about a rebuilt Temple (Malachi 3:3-4; 4:5-6; Zechariah 6:12-13). Because this did not happen as expected, Jews of a more liberal persuasion came to think only in terms of a "Messianic age," which is now viewed as the quest and establishment of the Jewish State. In this interpretation, the past is past and the future has arrived in the modern State which can be preserved only if peace is attained with Israel's hostile neighbors.

Orthodox and Hasidic Judaism, by contrast, have strenuously held to a literal interpretation of the Bible, and believed that the prophetic promise of the revelation of the

Messiah and the Temple's rebuilding would be fulfilled when a generation of Jews came along who were worthy of redemption and the Temple's construction. While Hasidic Judaism came to believe that the final Temple would already be rebuilt in heaven and descend to the Temple Mount, Orthodox Judaism continued to look for a new Temple to be erected through human agency (although with the advent of the Messianic era). Many of these Orthodox Jews feel that this building effort should be carried out at any time it is possible to do so based on a command in the Torah: "Let them build a sanctuary for Me [God]" (Exodus 25:8), and the last command (in the Hebrew Bible) to "go up" and "build Him a house in Jerusalem" (2 Chronicles 36:23). One who shares this viewpoint is Gershon Salomon, who today heads a Temple activist organization based in Jerusalem:

> It is an act which must be done to complete the redemption of the people of Israel in this holy country, the Land of Israel, to fulfill the redemption of the people of the Bible in the Land of the Bible. I cannot imagine an Israeli State or Israeli life in this country without the Temple Mount in the center of this life, without Jerusalem in the center of this country, as a capital of national, spiritual, and moral life. The Temple Mount is for us the place of life, but also a symbol, a vision, the vision of the prophets. The Israeli people must renew their life as God chose for them to be, a people who have a biblical mission to fulfill the principles of God and the vision of the prophets, and the Temple Mount is the very big condition to fulfill this historical mission of the Israeli people. More than this, the Temple Mount, after its redemption, the rebuilding of the Third Temple, will be again as God

and the prophets decided it must be, not only a center for the Israeli people, but for all the world, a center of belief in God, of prayer to God. . . . So the redemption of all the world is connected, and the condition [for it], the first step, is the redemption of the Temple Mount, the coming of Israel back to the Temple Mount and the rebuilding of the Third Temple. Then the second step will be the redemption of all the world. We live now in a world which needs such a redemption, it is a materialistic world, and we must bring people close to the principles of the prophets, and then we will have a revolution in humankind. . . .[8]

Such hopes seemed close to realization when Israel became a nation in 1948. At that time former Prime Minister Menachem Begin, then a leader of an underground Israeli resistance movement, the Irgun, said with expectation, "The Third Temple as outlined by the prophet Ezekiel will assuredly be built in our generation." However, in that same year Jordan captured the eastern section of Jerusalem, with the Temple Mount, and 19 years would pass before the area was accessible to Israelis with its recapture in the 1967 Six-Day War. Yet even then, despite Israeli sovereignty over the Temple Mount, jurisdiction was returned to the Muslim authorities only one month later, ending a brief resurgence of Jewish hope for rebuilding. However, this hope, coupled with an unrgency to rebuild, revived with the beginning of the Palestinian *Intifada* when Orthodox groups determined that it was the last chance for this generation to realize the prophetic promise of a rebuilt Temple within a renewed Jewish State. They feared the possible rise of a Palestinian State, the loss of Israeli sovereignty, and an even greater Arab dominance over the Temple Mount.

These Orthodox groups are now part of what is known as the Temple Movement—diverse organizations working with different means to bring about the united goal of restored worship within a rebuilt Temple.[9]

A Growing Desire to Rebuild

Back in 1989, at the beginning of the Temple Movement, *Time* magazine reported that a 1983 newspaper poll had shown "that a surprising 18.3% of Israelis thought it was time to rebuild."[10] However, since that time Israel has suffered through the *Intifada*, the "peace process," and numerous riots and acts of terrorism provoked by the controversy surrounding the Temple Mount. The change in public opinion toward a rebuilt Temple was reflected in a poll conducted on February 11, 1996 by the international Gallup organization. The poll, commissioned by The Temple Mount and Land of Israel Faithful Movement, an Israeli activist organization that publicly demonstrates in favor of rebuilding the Temple, asked Israelis of all age groups the following question: "The Temple Mount and Land of Israel Faithful Movement, headed by Gershon Salomon, put forth its main ideology on the struggle for Israeli sovereignty and the Jewish future of the Temple Mount, Jerusalem, and Land of Israel, and the rebuilding of the Temple. How likely would you be to support the idea of this movement?" The results, according to the Temple Mount Faithful, were the largest show of support any organization in Israel had ever received (58.5%). Of the polled group, the highest percentage of favorable responses came from young Israelis. Depending on the usual variables in statistical surveys, this indicates a substantial increase in the readiness of Israelis to see Jewish sovereignty reasserted over the Temple Mount and a new Temple erected.

More recently, the question of Jewish access to the Temple Mount and sovereignty over the Temple Mount as a part of Jerusalem received an overwhelming response from Israelis in a survey done by the Guttman Institute of Applied Social Research. The results were that 99% of the total sample said that the Western Wall, as the last standing remnant of the Second Temple, was important as part of Jerusalem; 93% of Jerusalemites, 82% of Tel Aviv residents, and 65% of non-observant Jews affirmed that the Temple Mount was likewise vital. In addition, 84% of the total sample and 73% of non-observant Jews stated that it was important that Jews be able to pray on the Temple Mount.[11] These statistics support the many preparations by organizations within the Temple Movement to make rebuilding the Temple possible.

Preparations for Rebuilding the Temple

The Building and Its Furnishings

One of the most visible of Temple Movement organizations is the Temple Institute, which since 1987 has been comprised of a group of rabbinical researchers, designers, and craftsmen under the direction of Rabbi Yisrael Ariel. They have been creating in the Jewish Quarter of Jerusalem what they call a "Temple-in-waiting."[12] Their efforts have resulted in computerized visualizations of the Third Temple as well as the production of ritually qualified vessels, garments, and other items necessary for a restoration of the Temple services. Spokesman Rabbi Chaim Richman claims that detailed blueprints for the Third Temple, prepared by the Temple Institute, have existed since 1992. These plans were drawn according to the primary sources for this information: the Bible, Josephus, and the Mishnah tractate known as *Middot* ("Measurements"). Additions to these ancient specifications have included the use of electricity and other modern improvements that agree with *halakah* (Jewish law). Among the items that have been created—or are in the process of being created—are apparel for the high priest (his eight-layered woven robe, the golden crown worn on his head, and his jeweled breastplate bearing the names of the tribes of Israel), priestly garments and the blue-purple dye (*tchelet*) for the priestly *tsitsit*, the 11 sacrificial incense spices, urns, ewers, incense pans, forks, shovels, and carts (for burnt offerings), the gold and silver *mizrakot* (vessels used to dispense sacrificial blood on the altar), the golden laver, flasks, and measuring cups (used in the libation offerings), vessels for the meal offerings, the lottery boxes (for the Day of Atonement), the mortal and pestle, and the stone vessel (*kelal*) for grinding and holding the purifying ashes of the red heifer, the golden menorah (lampstand), cleaning instruments and oil pitchers for replenishing the oil for its light, silver trumpets (for assembling the people of Israel at the Temple), and the barley altar. They also expect the Ark of the Covenant, which is believed to still exist in a secret chamber located under the Temple Mount, to be recovered and take its place within the restored Temple.[13]

Some structures pertaining to the Temple's future function have also been planned or actually built. Under the auspices of the late Rabbi Shlomo Goren, the 70-seat supreme court building which housed the Sanhedrin in Temple times has been constructed in a building adjacent to the Temple Mount. Rabbi Goren told me in an interview shortly before his death that its present location is correct for the future Temple complex as envisioned by the prophet

Ezekiel, which is to be 30 times larger than that of previous Temples.[14] Since 1984, the legal stipulations that the Sanhedrin will use to govern Israel's relationship to the rebuilt Temple and its services have already been researched and progressively published by the Research Center for Jewish Thought under the direction of Rabbi Yoel Lerner.

The Priesthood

The priests who will make up the Sanhedrin and serve in the Temple priesthood are today being identified and trained. Many people have assumed it's not possible to determine descendants of the Temple priests because all the genealogical records of the Temple were lost in the destruction of A.D. 70. However, because of rabbinic tradition, those of the tribe of Levi who were scattered to foreign lands were forbidden to alter their names (which connoted their priestly heritage). Therefore to this day there remain those with the names of Levi, Cohen, and derivatives of these names. In 1997 a scientific test was devised that could actually verify those of priestly lineage. In studies of 188 male Jews claiming levitical descent it was found that as a group they uniquely carried a variation of the Y-chromosome that distinguished them from Jews who did not claim such a heritage.[15] Since each person's DNA is as individual as a fingerprint, this characteristic linked these men together as a separate and identifiable group that must be traced back to an original ancestor— Aaron, the first high priest. Yet even before such a test became available, Rabbi Nachman Kahane, head of the Young Israel Synagogue (the synagogue closest to the Western Wall, located in the Muslim Quarter) and The Institute for Talmudic Commentaries, began to create a computerized list of all Levitical candidates in Israel based simply upon their professed heritage.

There are also organizations in Israel that are attempting to train young Levites for the priesthood. A yeshiva (Jewish seminary) founded by Motti Dan Hacohen and known as Ateret Cohanim provides education for students in the order of priestly service. A sister organization, Atara Leyoshna, has worked to acquire numerous Arab properties in the Muslim Quarter next to the Temple Mount in order to establish a "Jewish presence" in preparation for the rebuilding of the Temple.

One major obstacle to the construction of a new Temple is that a priest must be ritually pure in order to perform certain holy tasks such as rebuilding and officiating in the Temple. Today, all Jews are ceremonially unclean because of contact with people or things that are dead (or with those who have had such contact, such as employees in hospitals). The only means to accomplishing a reversal of this condition and establishing a functioning priesthood is through the ashes of the red heifer (described in Numbers 19). A red heifer was born in Israel in 1997,[16] but due to the presence of several white hairs it became disqualified. Some red heifers were recently located in the American state of Mississippi and upon inspection, were found to be qualified. Plans are being made to transport them to Israel.[17]

Even with a qualified red heifer, a sacrifice cannot be made until there is an already-qualified priest available to sacrifice it. The solution for this is also underway. In 1998 Rabbi Elboim of the Movement for Establishing the Temple began searching for 20 couples who would be willing to dedicate their unborn male children to a special program designed to produce a purified priesthood. Four religious families in the Jerusalem area have been approached, and at least one mother has volunteered her yet-to-be-born baby. Rabbi Elboim claims that 95 percent of the observances performed in the Temple can't be carried out because of ritual impurity; this project will reverse that impediment. When the boys reach their thirteenth birthdays, they will be qualified to burn the red heifer and distribute its ashes.

The Movement for Establishing the Temple plans to raise newborn babies of levitical descent in isolation from contact with ritual defilement. This would be done by taking the chosen children to a secluded compound in the Jerusalem hills, where they would be brought up in a specially constructed building with a floor that has been elevated to prevent contact with the ground. The reason for that is because the ground could contain unmarked graves from ancient times, which could cause defilement. In addition, the strict seclusion would prevent the children from being ritually contaminated. The needed compound for this special project has already been donated by the ultra-Orthodox Jewish Idea Yeshiva. Members of Elboim's group were reported in the Israeli daily, *Ha-Aretz*, as saying, "The Temple is one of the central parts of our ideology; we view its rebuilding as part of Jewish experience, and that the restoration of the Temple is near at hand."

Efforts to Reclaim the Temple Mount

The Temple Mount and Land of Israel Faithful Movement (mentioned earlier, and headed by Gershon Salomon) has repeatedly demonstrated at the Temple Mount and around the gates of the Old City since 1989, when they first attempted to lay a cornerstone for the Third Temple at the Temple site. In 1990 plans for a similar attempt resulted in an Arab riot at the Western Wall and on the Temple Mount platform above. On that occasion 18 Arabs were killed, and Saddam Hussein used the situation to fire Scud missiles at Israel. During Passovers, the Temple Mount Faithful and another activist group, the Chai v'Kaiyam organization, have attempted to offer a *paschal* sacrifice on the Temple Mount on a specially prepared altar. This sacrifice was once offered annually during ancient Temple times, and these groups believe that reinstituting the sacrifice today will reestablish worship on the Temple Mount.

Before worship can be established as a first step toward rebuilding the Temple, the Jewish people need to regain access to the Temple Mount. The act of worship (which includes prayer, reading, reciting or teaching the Bible or Talmud) at the site of the Temple establishes the practical necessity for rebuilding, since the ceremonial service requires a functioning Temple to complete what has been started. However, aside from the Muslim fear of Jews regaining access to the area, any act of worship on the Temple Mount by a non-Muslim is strictly prohibited under Islamic law. Wakf administrator Adnan Husseini has stated that "the entire area is a mosque; and according to Islamic law, it is forbidden for non-Muslims to pray at a mosque. . . . If Israel intends to change its policy and begin allowing Jews to pray at Al-Aksa, it will find itself up against the entire Islamic world."[18] Nevertheless, Jewish groups now regularly ascend the Temple Mount to pray in carefully designated areas under armed guard after first going to the *miqveh* (Jewish ritual bath) to purify themselves.

This has not been without controversy; Police Chief Assaf Chafetz, Jerusalem District Commander Yitzchaki, and former Jerusalem Commander Aryeh Amit have referred to these Jewish worshipers as "those who were disturbing the still waters by their continued attempts to pray, on the Temple Mount." Yehuda Etzion, head of the Chai v'Kaiyam organization, and whose case secured the Israeli Supreme Court's recognition of rights of Jews to worship on the Temple Mount, considers this a reversal of previous promises made to the Jewish people. Before Prime Minister Benjamin Netanyahu came to office he sent Etzion a letter of support, pledging to permit Jewish worship at the Temple Mount. "Today," says Etzion, "Netanyahu has permitted the government to act to stop such prayers as was the case with previous governments."[19] Etzion contends that the Israeli police are working in unison with the Israeli General Security Service (GSS) to create a negative image of the Jews who are faithful to the Temple Mount. He says, "They want the world to believe that any Jew who yearns and attempts to pray on the Temple Mount, Judaism's holiest site, is mad and the idea should be considered taboo."[20] Etzion stated that it is not a tolerable situation when Jews in the State of Israel are the only religion banned from praying on the Mount.

As a result, some Orthodox activists have attempted to change the situation by provoking a battle with the Arabs for the Temple Mount. When in May 1998 the Temple Mount Faithful attempted to enter the Temple Mount and were prevented by the police, Gershon Salomon, founder and leader of the group, responded:

> We have lost the Temple Mount. Exactly 31 years after we heard, "The Temple Mount is in our hands," the situation is that it is not in our hands. Feisal Husseini [PA/PLO Minister of Jerusalem Affairs] orders the Israel Police to close off the Mount, and it is closed. We simply allow our sovereignty to disintegrate, and this is a terrible disgrace for the Jewish people.

To symbolize the situation, the group carried a replica Trojan horse, stating that the Palestinian Authority is a deceitful and dangerous presence in the midst of the Land of Israel. In addition, in the Israeli newspaper *Yediot Achronot,* one Jewish activist leader calculated that out of the approximately 100,000 Muslim worshipers who visit the Mount, at least 10,000 are likely to incite spontaneous violence that could lead to hundreds of deaths and perhaps even a world war.

The Israeli General Security Service has sought to arrest Jewish activists whom they believe have formed a conspiracy to sabotage the sanctity of the area used by the Muslim in an effort to disrupt their worship.[21] One rumored plot involved placing a pig's head on the Temple Mount during the month of Ramadan (the highest holy day in Islam). Such activities have been viewed as attempts to start a war with the entire Muslim nation ever since Tatiana Susskind was found guilty of offending the Muslim religion with her poster of the Muslim prophet Muhammad pictured as a pig. The poster was displayed in Hebron, and Susskind was arrested and sentenced to a jail term.

Yehuda Etzion stated that Susskind has become the scapegoat for the entire Temple Mount cause, and that the GSS is making Iskin out to be an extremist that no well-adjusted person would wish to identify with. This has been a setback to all the movements that are working within the framework of Jewish law to restore Jewish prayer on the Temple Mount. For such reasons the Palestinian security elements provide 24-hours-a-day "protection" at the Temple Mount and other sensitive areas in the Old City of Jerusalem.[22]

The Politics of the Temple Mount

For Judaism, the Temple Mount must be under Jewish control in order to fulfill the prophecies that "many peoples will come and say, 'Come, let us go up to the mountain of the LORD [the Temple Mount], to the house of the God of Jacob [the Temple]; that He may teach us concerning His ways, and that we may walk in His paths'" (Isaiah 2:3). According to this passage, the whole world will one day come to a rebuilt Jewish Temple situated on the Temple Mount in order to learn the truth of the Jewish God and follow His laws.

The Temple Mount has a different significance for the followers of Islam. For them, the great Day of Judgment will take place on Jerusalem's Mount Moriah before the seat of justice where today the *al-Mizan* (the Balances), pillars, and arches on the Temple Mount await the scales that will weigh the deeds of resurrected souls.[23] According to Islam, the whole world will be subjugated to Allah and the Koran will be universally revered as the final revelation of God. However, both Jews and Christians recognize that Allah is a pagan god—the moon god of Mecca chosen by Muhammad out of a pantheon of local gods—and therefore the presence of mosques dedicated to him on the Temple Mount is an abomination.

In Christianity, Christ's lordship demands that the whole world acknowledge and follow Him as King of kings and Lord of lords. Some Christians say Christ is the new spiritual temple that has replaced the old physical one, and others say that He will come again to reign over the world from a literal Jerusalem. Whatever the case, there can be no other god worshiped and no other allegiance outside of Him. While Muslims regard Jesus as a prophet, they and Judaism reject His deity.

These defining doctrines of the aforementioned religions are non-negotiables and, of course, at odds with one another. For this reason, each negotiation that has been made between Israel and its neighbors has included a specific statement concerning the status of the Temple Mount. When Anwar Sadat received the Sinai Peninsula in 1978 in exchange for Egypt's recognition of and peaceful co-existence with Israel, he made it clear to Israeli Prime Minister Menachem Begin that the Arab demands for full sovereignty over East Jerusalem and the Temple Mount would never be compromised. The same terms were on the agenda on October 26, 1994 when Jordan made its formal peace accord with Israel. In this agreement Israel officially made Jordan the custodian of the Islamic holy shrines on the Temple Mount. King Hussein of Jordan then installed his own Mufti to regulate Islamic worship at these sites and donated $8,249,000 to replace the leaking aluminum dome atop the Dome of the Rock with one plated with a gold-nickel alloy.[24] At the same time, an autonomy agreement between the PLO and Israel, known as the Oslo Accord (signed at the White House with a ceremonial handshake on September 13, 1994), included demands for East Jerusalem to be completely under Palestinian control and serve as the capital of the proposed Palestinian State. Because Israel hoped that the experience of peaceful relations with the Palestinians might make negotiations easier at future talks, the negotiations over Jerusalem's status were scheduled for the middle of 1997—after Israel had completed its military withdrawal from the areas inhabited by Palestinians, including part of Hebron. Most of these withdrawals took place, but instead of peace, more panic invaded Israel as a result of unrest over Jerusalem and the Temple Mount. That same year, the Palestinians contested Israel's right to build a settlement on a mountaintop area in Jerusalem known as Har Homa, which the Palestinians want as part of "their Jerusalem." At the close of 1998, conflict continued over Israel's further withdrawal from the West Bank.

The Palestinians demanded 16 percent withdrawal and the U.S. pressured Israel for 13 percent, but Ariel Sharon argued that more than 9 percent would fatally affect Israel's security. These "negotiations" have postponed the final stage in which Jerusalem's status would be considered. Nevertheless, Israel has said Jerusalem is nonnegotiable and the Palestinians have declared a Palestinian State by 1999. (Arafat's original proposal was to do this by May 4, 1999.) Each side views the current tensions as a prelude to future battles for the city and control of its holy sites on the Temple Mount.

The Coming Battle for the Temple Mount

We can be sure that when it comes time to determine who has sovereignty over the Temple Mount, a major battle will ensue. The question of the Temple Mount and the rebuilding of the Temple has always been at the forefront of the Arab-Israeli conflict centered in Jerusalem. For example, the Islamic Authority, which maintains rigid control of the Temple Mount, blamed the Israeli government for starting a fire in the Al-Aksa mosque in 1969. Israel was accused of wanting to destroy the structure so they could rebuild the Temple—despite the fact that the blaze was actually set by a mentally unstable member of a Christian cult! Ever since, the Muslims have assumed that every incursion in or near the area, whether for archaeological or religious reasons, has been for the same purpose. That's why riots followed an excavation effort designed to uncover the subterranean Western Wall Tunnel in 1982, a demonstration by the Temple Mount Faithful in 1990 (in which 17 people were killed), excavations to reveal the Herodian street next to the Western Wall in 1995, and the opening of an exit tunnel to the Hasmonean Tunnel in 1996 (in which 58 people were killed). In

March of 1997 Yasser Arafat was shown in a photograph—distributed internationally by the Associated Press—holding up an artist's rendering of a restored Jewish Temple and telling his people to "get ready for the next battle" (for Jerusalem). Similar calls for conflict were also issued from loudspeakers on the Temple Mount to Arabs in East Jerusalem during each of the aforementioned riots.

The day will soon be at hand in which a resolution must be sought for the Palestinian claims over the Temple Mount. The Temple Movement organizations, and perhaps a significant percentage of Jerusalemites, will violently oppose any Arab action that seeks to prevent Jews from gaining at least equal access to the area for religious purposes. And the Islamic Authority has sworn that it will fight any attempts by Jews to claim the 35-acre platform that now holds their mosque and shrines. However the battle may begin or be resolved, we know that events must lead to the building of a Third Temple at the beginning of the Tribulation, and then, beyond that, to the final resolution of every problem for the Temple when the Lord returns from heaven, restores Israel on earth, and rebuilds the Temple in Jerusalem.

So, as I again reflect on the Arab who encountered me on the Temple Mount and said that I should forget the past and look to the future, my response is yes, I will think about my future. It is a glorious future promised by the God of this universe, whose Temple will one day receive the sanctified worship of Jerusalem's past and present enemies (Isaiah 19:19-25). Such will be the future family awaiting on the Temple Mount when finally God comes home.

The LORD of hosts will reign on
Mount Zion and in Jerusalem,
and His glory will be before His elders.

—Isaiah 24:23

The LORD will reign over them in
Mount Zion from now on and forever.

—Micah 4:7

When the Son of Man comes in His
glory, and all the angels with Him,
then He will sit on His glorious throne.

—Matthew 25:31

The kingdom of the world has
become the kingdom of our Lord,
and of His Christ;
and He will reign forever and ever.

—Revelation 11:15

13

GOD ON THE THRONE:
The Reign of Jerusalem's King

In the end of time, Jerusalem will spread over the whole of the Land of Israel. And the Land of Israel will spread over the whole world.

—Aggadic Tradition

There is a rabbinical saying about Jerusalem that states, "If the nations understood, they would mourn the destruction of Jerusalem more than the Jews." The rabbis who stated this had in mind the blessing God has promised for the world when Israel is restored and the Lord has returned to His chosen city: "Thus says the Lord, 'I will return to Zion and will dwell in the midst of Jerusalem. . . . so I will save you that you may become a blessing'" (Zechariah 8:3,13). In recognition of this promise, the Jewish biblical commentator Rabbi David Kimchi stated,

> You [Israel] were not consumed as were the other peoples who have left no trace behind and have

ceased being nations. You have not disappeared, nor will you. You will always be distinguished from the others as a nation alone on earth. Just as I [the Lord] shall not change, so shall you not be consumed; and in the latter days, you will regain your ascendancy and will be supreme over all the nations of the earth.[1]

Although most of the nations of the world are blind to this future fact, this promise of God's reign and blessing from Zion has not escaped the understanding of *Christians* among the nations. It has been the theme of countless Christian hymns and songs, including titles such as "Jesus Shall Reign," "Come, Thou Almighty King," "Crown Him with Many Crowns," "Our God Reigns," and "The King Is Coming." These songs remind us that the longing of redeemed people is to be ruled by their Redeemer.

Today, unredeemed humanity longs for one man to make the world run right. The successful candidate is expected to bring world peace and prosperity, unite all peoples and nations as one community, and assure an ecologically better future. The terms used by the world to express this hope are varied: the New Age, the Age of Aquarius, the Golden Age, Utopia, Shangri-la, and so on. But when the world finally gets its universal man, he will be a dictator and a tyrant, a devil. He will be the forewarned Antichrist who will lead the world into the worst kind of deception, darkness, and devastation ever known to mankind. This will take place during that ominous time known as the Tribulation.

By contrast, the world on the other side of the Tribulation will be a vastly different place. The prayer prayed for thousands of years—"Thy kingdom come. Thy will be done, on earth as it is in heaven"—will finally come to fruition. The Antichrist will have been dethroned and replaced by Christ, and Gentile dominion will have been replaced by a redeemed and restored Israel. The apostle John, when he surveyed the scene of Messiah's rule, said, "And I looked, and behold, the Lamb was standing on Mount Zion" (Revelation 14:1).

The Messianic kingdom has always been linked with Jerusalem as evidenced by the Davidic Covenant, which prophesied of an enduring rule by one of King David's descendants (2 Samuel 7:8-17). For this reason one of the psalms of the sons of Korah attributed this title to Jerusalem: "City of the great King" (Psalm 48:2). By "great king" did the psalmist mean King David, since the prophecy had said David's name would be "great" (2 Samuel 7:9)? However, the opening words of Psalm 48 speak of "the city of our God" (verse 1), and the very next words after "great King" are "God, in her palaces, has made Himself known . . ." (verse 3). Who, then, is the king in verse 2? What we do know is that David (Acts 2:29) and David's own line ended without the promise being fulfilled in Jerusalem. And even though Jesus at His first advent fulfilled the role of David's descendant (Matthew 1:1), He did not *sit on David's throne* in Jerusalem. To understand how the prophecy in 2 Samuel 7:8-17 will find fulfillment, let's consider it in more detail.

David's Covenant, Messiah's Completion

God's unconditional promise to continue David's descendants on the throne of Judea did not guarantee uninterrupted rule (2 Samuel 7:14). Such an interruption occurred with the Babylonian destruction and the exile of the last of David's royal family, King Zedekiah (2 Kings 25:7). When that happened, Ezekiel the prophet proclaimed, " . . . the prince of Israel [Zedekiah], whose day has come, in the time of the punishment.... This also will be no more [the Davidic throne], until He comes whose right it is; and I [the Lord] shall give it to Him" (Ezekiel 21:25,27). This prophecy is about the Messiah, who as the son of David has the right to the dynastic promise. However, this prophecy could not be fulfilled during the first advent because Messiah's purpose was spiritual, not political: "My kingdom is not of this world" (John 18:36). But earlier, Jesus made it clear that His kingdom would one day be in this world: "the Son of Man will sit on His glorious throne . . ." (Matthew 19:28). Daniel prophesied about this future rule when he saw one "like a Son of Man" who "was given dominion, glory and a kingdom, that all the peoples, nations, and men of every language might serve Him" (Daniel 7:13-14). We know this universal king and kingdom have never before existed, for the text also says, "His dominion is an everlasting dominion which *will not pass away;* and His kingdom is one which will *not be destroyed*" (verse 14, emphasis added).

Every kingdom that has existed until now and sought to rule the nations has eventually vanished into the dust. The list includes Assyria, Babylon, Persia, Egypt, Greece, and Rome. However, Daniel predicted that one of these kingdoms would be revived, consist of ten kingdoms, and be the last kingdom of man on earth (Daniel 2:41-44). Daniel also revealed that this revived kingdom would be destroyed and followed by a final kingdom which, like its King, would not come from earth but from heaven (Daniel 2:44-45). The revived kingdom Daniel saw will be the kingdom of the Antichrist during the Tribulation period. And, as Daniel was shown, it will be destroyed by the return of Christ, who will come to set up His own kingdom.

In order to understand when this will take place, we need to examine what Jesus said about His future reign in Matthew 19:28 and Luke 22:28-30:

Matthew 19:28	**Luke 22:28-30**
Truly I say to you, that you who have followed Me, in the regeneration when the Son of Man will sit on His glorious throne, you also shall sit upon twelve thrones, judging the twelve tribes of Israel.	You are those who have stood by Me in My trials; and just as My Father has granted Me a kingdom, I grant you that you may eat and drink at My table in My kingdom, and you will sit on thrones judging the twelve tribes of Israel.

The question arises as to the time and place to which Jesus was referring—during the eternal state in heaven, or the Millennial kingdom on earth? Notice first that the rulership being spoken of here is over "the twelve tribes of Israel," and that it is a rule Jesus delegates to His earthly disciples ("you who have followed Me," "you . . . who have stood by Me in My trials"). Given that the disciples would have heard Jesus' words with an Old Testament frame of reference, their expectation of "the twelve tribes" would have been the predicted restoration of Israel with the tribes reunited (Jeremiah 3:18; 50:4; Ezekiel 37:22). These people will "ask for the way to Zion" (Jeremiah 50:5), now designated "The Throne of the Lord" (Jeremiah 3:17), where "David My servant shall be their prince forever" (Ezekiel 37:25).

Note, too, that Jesus refers to "the glorious throne" (literally "throne of glory") of "the Son of Man" in Matthew 19:28. In Matthew 25:31 we read that "He will sit on His glorious throne" when He "comes in His glory." This obviously refers to the second advent, for immediately following is the judgment of the Gentile nations ("and all the nations will be gathered before Him"—verse 32), which, as we have seen in chapter 9, occurs in the Valley of Jehoshaphat in Jerusalem. Furthermore, if we look into the Old Testament for a reference to this "Son of Man" and the acquisition of a throne, or kingdom, we find the elements combined in Daniel's prophecy in the vision of the Ancient of Days (Daniel 7:13-14). In this prophecy we read:

> Behold, with the clouds of heaven one like a Son of Man was coming, and He came up to the Ancient of Days and was presented before Him. And to Him was given dominion, glory and a kingdom, that all the peoples, nations, and men of every language might serve Him. His dominion is an everlasting dominion which will not pass away; and His kingdom is one which will not be destroyed.

From this passage we can see that the kingdom is universal, unending, and indestructible. As in Matthew 25:31-32, the rule here is seen as over the Gentiles ("the peoples, nations, and men of every language"). In addition, the statement in Luke 22:29, "just as My Father has granted Me a kingdom," is comparable to "He came up to the Ancient of Days . . . to Him was given a dominion" (Daniel 7:13-14). Concerning this kingdom the Luke 22 text also notes that the disciples will "eat and drink" at Messiah's table. Earlier in that same chapter, in verse 18, Jesus said this was the time when He would again share the cup with His disciples. Here, and in the parallel passage in Matthew 26:29, it is said that this will be "fulfilled in the kingdom of God." The term in the Matthew 19:28 text that determines precisely what this "kingdom of God" is (heaven or earth) is the term "regeneration." This same expression (Greek: *palingenesia*) is used in

Characteristics of the Millennium

Geographical	Social	Spiritual	Environmental
Increase in territory (Genesis 15:18; Isaiah 26:15; Obadiah 1:17-21)	Universal knowledge of Lord (Isaiah 11:9; 54:13; Habakkuk 2:14)	Universal worship (Isaiah 19:21; 52:1,7-10; Malachi 1:11; Zechariah 8:23)	Conditions of holiness (Isaiah 1:26-27; 35:8-10; Zephaniah 3:11)
Topographical changes (Ezekiel 47:8-12; Isaiah 2:2; Zechariah 14:4,8,10)	Reproduction by saints (Isaiah 65:23; Ezekiel 47:21-22; Zechariah 10:8)	Rebuilt Temple (Ezekiel 37:26-28; Ezekiel 40-48; Haggai 2:7-9; Joel 3:18)	Restoration of Edenic conditions (Isaiah 11:6-9; 65:25)
Jerusalem as center of world's worship (Isaiah 2:2-3; Micah 4:1-2; Zechariah 8:3; 14:16-21)	Unimpaired labor (Ezekiel 48:18-19; Isaiah 62:8-9; 65:21-23)	Return of the Shekinah Glory (Ezekiel 43:1-7; 48:35; Zechariah 2:10-13; Jeremiah 3:17)	Removal of harmful effects (Isaiah 33:24; 35:5-7; Zephaniah 3:19)
Enlargement of Jerusalem (Ezekiel 48:35; Jeremiah 3:17)	Universal language (Zephaniah 3:9)	Revival of sacrificial system (Ezekiel 43:13-27; 45:13-25; Isaiah 56:7)	Restoration of longevity (Isaiah 65:20)
Name of Jerusalem changed (Isaiah 62:2-4)	Freedom from war/enemies (Isaiah 2:4; 14:3-7; Zechariah 9:8; 14:10-11; Amos 9:15)	Restoration of Sabbath and ritual feasts (Ezekiel 44:24; Zechariah 14:16)	Increase in daylight (Isaiah 4:5-6; 30:26; 60:19-20; Zechariah 2:5)
Jews return and live in Land (Ezekiel 36:24; 37:25)	Peaceful society (Isaiah 11:6-9; 65:21; Hosea 2:18; Zechariah 9:10)	Spiritual obedience under New Covenant (Ezekiel 36:25-28; 37; Jeremiah 31:31-34)	Economic prosperity (Isaiah 30:23-25; 35:1-7; Amos 9:13-15; Joel 2:21-27)
Reversal of Land's desolate condition (Ezekiel 36:33-36; 62:4)	Justice (Isaiah 9:6-7; 32:16; Jeremiah 30:9; Ezekiel 34:23; Hosea 3:5)	Satan/demons bound; No spiritual deception (Revelation 20:1-3)	Universal access to Israel (Isaiah 2:2:3; 11:16; 56:6; Jeremiah 3:14-15)

Titus 3:5, where it is refers to the spiritual rebirth by the Holy Spirit. Here we must again consider the prophetic context, since Jesus is speaking with reference to a future time. While this term for regeneration does not appear in the Old Testament, it was used by the Jewish historian Josephus to speak of the restoration (rebirth) of the Jewish nation after the return from the Babylonian exile. The term also appears in Jewish apocalyptic literature (including the Dead Sea Scrolls) to speak of the "consummation of the kingdom" at the end of the age (see also Isaiah 65:17; 66:22).[2] Thus, taking the context established by Jesus and the disciples, the best understanding of these texts is to see Jesus as the Messianic King reigning over the restored Jewish kingdom with His disciples in positions of delegated jurisdiction, enjoying fellowship with their Messiah.

One additional scripture connected with the purpose and timing of the Millennial reign in relation to the Davidic Covenant needs to be considered. In Amos 9:11 we read, "In that day I will restore David's fallen tent. I will repair its broken places, restore its ruins, and build it as it used to be" (NIV). According to the apostle Peter, this restoration of rule to the Davidic dynasty was to occur *after* the church age. This is indicated in Acts 15:16-18 in the context of a debate over Gentile conversion (Acts 15:7-14). Peter opens his quotation of this text by interpreting Amos' words "in that day" as "after these things" because he understood the time of Israel's restoration ("restore David's fallen tent") to come *after* the time of Gentile inclusion in the present church age.

The Redeemer: Born to Reign

From the first time that the Old Testament prophesied the coming of the Messiah it was evident that He would be

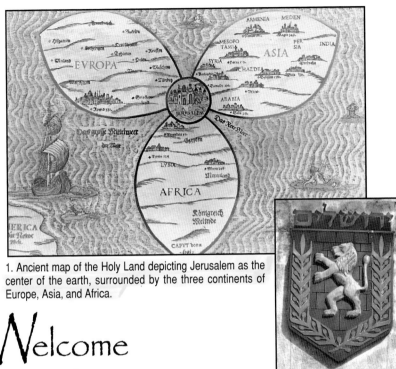

1. Ancient map of the Holy Land depicting Jerusalem as the center of the earth, surrounded by the three continents of Europe, Asia, and Africa.

Welcome to Jerusalem ...

2. *The Lion of the Tribe of Judah,* a Messianic symbol of protection and strength, the insignia of the municipality of the city of Jerusalem.

3. The large tapestry welcoming new immigrants and visitors to Israel in Ben-Gurion airport. The scene is of the prophetic in-gathering of the exiles to a restored Jerusalem based on the prophecy of Jeremiah 31:17.

4. Fireworks over the Old City in celebrations ending Jerusalem's 3000th anniversary as Israel's capital seem to foreshadow the future attack on Jerusalem by the nations of the world.

6. A poster reflecting the prophecy in Isaiah 6:13 that life would remain in fallen Israel and would sprout anew in the time of the future redemption. The view the poster portrays is that the Jewish State is fulfilling this prophecy.

5. Jewish poster reminding that God's future program for Israel and Jerusalem will take place in the same Land God brought His people to in the past.

7. Flags in Jerusalem celebrate Israel's 50th anniversary (Jubilee) as a modern state, considered by Jews as the first stage of prophetic fulfillment according to Ezekiel 36 and 37.

Where Past and Future Are Intertwined ...

8. Jewish soldiers reflect on Jerusalem's future as they overlook the city from the Mount of Olives on Independence Day, May 1998.

Famous Faces

COUNTERCLOCKWISE, FROM UPPER LEFT— 9. Present mayor of Jerusalem Ehud Olmert (left), a defender of Jerusalem's united status as Israel's capital, with the author. 10. Eliyahu Tal, author of *Whose Jerusalem?* and a commander in the Israel Defense Forces in 1948 who witnessed the siege of Jerusalem's Old City. He is also the founder of the International Forum for a United Jerusalem, which champions Jewish sovereignty over the city. 11. The body of slain Prime Minister Yitzhak Rabin lies in state at the Knesset, the seat of the Israeli Parliament, in Jerusalem. Rabin was assassinated because of fear he would redivide the Holy City. 12. Posters in Jerusalem as late as 1998 still show loyalty to Menachem Mendel Schneerson (who died in 1994) as the Jewish Messiah. The signs in Hebrew read "King Messiah" and "Blessed is he who comes, King Messiah." The movement reflects the Jewish revival and yearning for the coming of Messiah.

and
Famous
Places

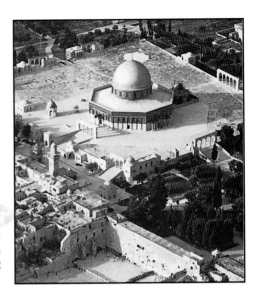

13. The Arab Dome of the Rock (top) on the Temple Mount near the Jewish Western Wall (bottom) reflects the tension over the site which will one day see the Antichrist make a covenant with the city.

14. One of Jesus' last views on earth from the Garden of Gethsemane was of the Eastern Gate and the Temple (its position is indicated by the dome to the left), sites connected with His return to Jerusalem in glory.

Past Victories ...

15. ABOVE—The bullet-scarred walls of the Zion Gate remember the battle fought here in 1967 to liberate the Old City of Jerusalem from Jordanian occupation.   16. INSET—The faint trace of the fisted hand drawn on the wall is the symbol of Kach, a right-wing Jewish organization defending a united Jerusalem. The fist can be seen in the larger photo at bottom, left.

17. Israeli soldiers stand guard at the Western Wall (the 2,000-year-old remnant from Temple times regarded by Orthodox Jews as part of the Holy Temple where the Presence of God continues to dwell) during Jerusalem Independence Day ceremonies (May 1, 1998). The return of Jews to the wall was won in the Six-Day War (June 6, 1967).

18. ABOVE—Hasidic Jews discuss plans to resettle "East Jerusalem" in order to retain sovereignty over the city. In this area ultra-orthodox Jews have purchased properties and opened a Jewish Yeshiva (seminary).

19. LEFT—A demonstration at the controversial site of Har Homa (May 1, 1998). Although the site is within Jerusalem's legitimate boundaries, the Palestinians have made it the object of renewed conflict by claiming it and all of eastern Jerusalem for the capital of their proposed Palestinian state.

... and Present Struggles

And I will bring them back, and they will live in the midst of Jerusalem

Zechariah 8:8

20. RIGHT—Anti-pope graffiti in Jerusalem's Jewish Quarter after the Israeli-Vatican diplomatic pact.

21. BELOW—A demonstration by the Temple Mount Faithful during the Feast of Tabernacles outside the walls of the Old City of Jerusalem. They are praying for the coming of the Messiah and calling for the rebuilding of the Third Temple.

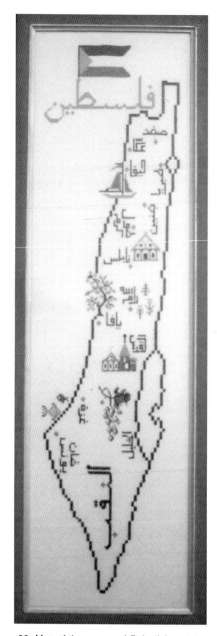

23. Painting of PLO leader Yasser Arafat on Arab merchant's shop in Jericho. Such images of Arafat as a promoter of peace (note doves and olive branches in gun barrel) became prominent after the September 13, 1993 signing of the Declaration of Principles with Israel.

24. The Orient House, a former hotel turned into the PLO's governmental offices in Jerusalem in violation of the Oslo accord. Foreign diplomats regularly visit these offices in recognition (against Israel) of the PLO's right to Jerusalem.

22. Map of the proposed Palestinian state in an office at the Orient House in Jerusalem, the PLO's unofficial government headquarters. The map has no names of Israeli cities and all of Jerusalem is called by the Arabic name, Al-Quds, "The Holy."

The Shadow of Terrorism:
Living "in a Bad Neighborhood"

25. The ghostly remains of burned-out bus along a road. Hamas terrorism has launched suicide bombers at city buses in Jerusalem causing terrible fatalities.

26. BELOW—Author with Feisal Husseini, Minister for Jerusalem Affairs in the Palestinian Authority, who is the chief negotiator for the PLO and has declared that Arabs will go to war if their demands in Jerusalem are not met.

27. ABOVE—Former Jerusalem Mayor Teddy Kollek inspects the damage at a Jerusalem café after a bomb planted by terrorists exploded in the Ben-Yehuda mall.

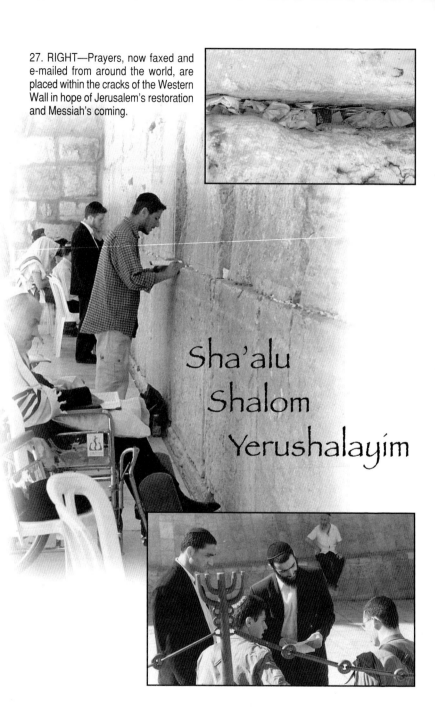

27. RIGHT—Prayers, now faxed and e-mailed from around the world, are placed within the cracks of the Western Wall in hope of Jerusalem's restoration and Messiah's coming.

Sha'alu
Shalom
Yerushalayim

Praying for the
Peace of Jerusalem:
Israelis pray at
the Western Wall

A Hope for the Future

28. Author with model of the Third Temple to be built in Jerusalem according to prophecies in the Old and New Testaments (see chapter 12). This model is in the Temple model museum of Atara Leyoshna.

Restoring the Temple

The redemption of all the world is connected, and the condition, the first step, is the redemption of the Temple Mount ... and the rebuilding of the Third Temple.
—Gershon Salomon

29. Author with Gershon Salomon, founder and director of the Temple Mount and Land of Israel Faithful, who demonstrate for Jewish sovereignty over Jerusalem and the right of Jews to rebuild the Third Temple.

30. The Islamic Dome of the Rock on the site of the Jerusalem Temple has been off limits to Jews for worship activities since Israel returned jurisdiction to the Muslim holy places shortly after the Six-Day War in 1967.

31. Author inspects new gold dome on Muslim Dome of the Rock during renovation by Jordan's King Hussein in 1995.

A Challenging Obstacle

Even so, come Messiah!

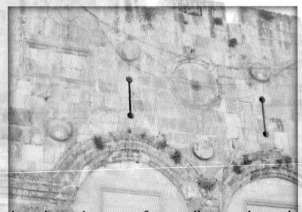

And in that day His feet will stand on the Mount
of Olives, which is in front of Jerusalem on the east.

—Zechariah 14:4

31. ABOVE—The Golden Gate (the Eastern Gate to the
Temple Mount), sealed by order of the Ottoman Sultan in
1541 to prevent the entry of the Jewish Messiah. The
cemetery in the foreground is for the same purpose. Nevertheless, Hebrew graffiti on the wall reads "Come Messiah" and "Israel waits."

32. The Valley of Jehoshaphat (Kidron Valley) and Mount
of Olives, where the final battle of the Armageddon campaign will be fought and the Messiah will ascend (Zechariah 13–14).

born to reign. The language of the first Messianic prophecy, known as the *proevangelium* ("first [preaching of the] good news") in Genesis 3:15 contains the imagery of rule, as the seed of the woman (Christ) crushes the head of the seed of the serpent (Satan). This metaphor of conquest has appeared on war reliefs from earliest times, depicting a king crushing the head of his enemy ruler with a battle-ax or club (see Numbers 24:17; Psalm 74:14). The interpretation of the prophecy in Genesis 3:15 is that the Messiah, who will be born of a woman (Isaiah 7:14; Galatians 4:4), will defeat Satan—both at His first coming through the cross (Colossians 2:15), and at His second coming when Satan is bound (Revelation 20:1-3), and finally when Satan is thrown into the Lake of Fire at the end of Christ's Millennial reign (Revelation 20:10; see also Romans 16:20).

Additional confirmation that Christ was born to rule is found in Isaiah 9 and Micah 5. Both passages proclaim that the purpose of the Messiah is to rule: "the government will rest on His shoulders. . . . There will be no end to the increase of His government or of peace, on the throne of David and over his kingdom . . . forevermore" (Isaiah 9:6-7); "one will go forth for Me [God] to be ruler" (Micah 5:2). Both prophecies appear in passages that combine elements of the first and second advents in order to present a complete picture of Israel's spiritual and national deliverance. Isaiah 9:1-2 found fulfillment with Jesus' Galilean ministry and outreach to the region's Gentile decapolis (Matthew 4:12-16). The next three verses, however—which depict Israel's national revival and restoration (Isaiah 9:3) through Messiah's vengeance on their oppressors (Isaiah 9:4-5; see also Psalm 2:9) will take place at the second advent (Zechariah 14:3; Revelation 12:5; 19:15). Micah's prophecy is similar, but specifies when this rule is to be expected: "He will give them up until the time when she who is in labor has borne a child. Then the remainder of His brethren will return to the sons of Israel" (Micah 5:3). The timing of prophetic events presented here correlates well with Romans 11:25-27, which describes the end of the period of Gentile rule and the establishment of Messiah's rule through a redeemed Israel. Micah says that the Jewish nation would be "given up" (not fulfill their theocratic purpose) until the time Messiah had been born (first advent) and regathered His scattered people (second advent). The period of the "giving up" corresponds to the "times of the Gentiles" (begun in 586 B.C.), which ends with the second advent and the restoration of Israel (Matthew 24:30-31; Romans 11:25). In this context Micah, like Isaiah, includes a promise that the time of Gentile rule would eventually end (Micah 5:15). However, Messiah had to first come and provide the spiritual basis for a future return (since it begins with "all Israel" being "saved"—Romans 11:26).

Jerusalem figures prominently in both Isaiah and Micah with respect to the Millennial reign. In Isaiah the city is the place of the restored Davidic rule (Isaiah 9:7), while in Micah the birth text is preceded by this declaration about Millennial Jerusalem: "The LORD will reign over them in Mount Zion from now on and forever. And as for you, tower of the flock, hill of the daughter of Zion, to you it will come—even the former dominion will come, the kingdom of the daughter of Jerusalem" (Micah 4:7-8). The same metaphor of shepherding appears in the birth text: "He will arise and shepherd His flock in the strength of the LORD, in the majesty of the name of the LORD His God. And they will remain, because at that time He will be great to the ends of the earth. And this One will be our peace" (Micah 5:4-5). Jerusalem's destiny is to watch over (shepherd) all of Israel (and the world) through its restored role as the center of divine revelation and righteous judgment (Isaiah 2:2-4). This will be fulfilled during the Millennium when Messiah, the Shepherd of Israel (see Ezekiel 34:11-16; John 10:14), maintains a universal rule from Jerusalem ("great to the ends of the earth," Micah 5:4) and establishes peace between Israel and the nations (Micah 5:5; Isaiah 2:4).

Events in Jerusalem During the Millennium

Beginning of the Millennium	Course of the Millennium	End of the Millennium
Resurrection of Old Testament and Tribulation saints (Revelation 20:4)	Descent and Presence of the New Jerusalem (Revelation 21:10–22:5)	Satan Loosed from Bondage (Revelation 20:7)
Son of Man on Throne of David (Jeremiah 23:5; Zechariah 14:9; Matthew 25:31)	Restoration of Israel's Promised Land and of the Natural Order (Ezekiel 37:25; Isaiah 11:6-16; 66:18-23)	Final "Gog and Magog" War (Revelation 20:8-10)
Judgment of Jewish Rebels and Gentile Nations (Ezekiel 20:33-38; Matthew 25:32-46)	Sacrificial Services at Millennial Temple by Jews and Gentiles (Isaiah 56:7; Zechariah 14:16-20; Ezekiel 40–48)	Resurrection of Unbelieving Dead (Revelation 20:5,13)
Messiah Builds Millennial Temple (Zechariah 6:12-15; Ezekiel 37:26-27)	Exaltation of Jerusalem and Instruction of Gentile Nations by Restored Jewish Nations (Isaiah 2:2-4; Zechariah 8:1-23; Habakkuk 2:14)	Great White Throne Judgment (Revelation 20:11-15)

Jerusalem, Center of the Millennial Kingdom

For ages Jerusalem has been the center of Jewish prayer, and in the final age it will become the center of worship and government for the whole world. The prophets Isaiah and Micah are foremost in teaching this truth:

> Now it will come about that in the last days, the mountain of the house of the LORD will be established as the chief of the mountains, and will be raised above the hills; and all the nations will stream to it. And many peoples will come and say, "Come, let us go up to the mountain of the LORD, to the house of the God of Jacob; that He may teach us concerning His ways, and that we may walk in His paths." For the law will go forth from Zion, and the word of the LORD from Jerusalem. And He will judge between the nations, and will render decisions for many peoples (Isaiah 2:2-4; see also Micah 4:2-3).

Earlier, in chapter 11, we saw that Jerusalem will be topographically elevated to assume a new position as the chief hill in the region with the Millennial Temple of Messiah atop the Temple Mount. Jerusalem will become the place to which every earthly government must submit for both its worship and judicial legislation.

The Center of Spiritual Worship

At the end of the Tribulation, Jerusalem will be established as the center for spiritual renewal for the people in the city and then for all the Land (Zechariah 13:1-2). As the spiritual center of the earth, Jerusalem will have an uncontested and incomparable holiness among the cities of that age (Ezekiel 43:12; Zechariah 14:20-21). Because of the Lord's presence in Jerusalem, Ezekiel says that from the commencement of the Millennium onward, the city will bear the ceremonial name *YHWH Shammah*, "the LORD is there" (Ezekiel 48:35). The Millennial worship in Jerusalem will be centered on the Messiah (Zechariah 14:9,16) and regulated by His priests (Ezekiel 44:1-31). Spiritual instruction will apparently involve the Jewish saints as teachers of the nations (Zechariah 8:21-23), although all saints under the New Covenant will have a personal knowledge of the Lord (Jeremiah 31:34). The instruction will most likely concern matters of law related to life in a ceremonial society (Isaiah 2:3)—laws that Jews, as those receiving this kingdom as their national restoration, would rightly administer. Therefore, all the inhabitants of this kingdom (Jew and Gentile) will worship the King Messiah through the ceremonial structure surrounding the Temple.

Though many consider the Temple ceremonies to be related to Jewish worship, the Temple, from the time of its dedication in the Old Testament, has invited a universal worship (see 1 Kings 8:41-43; 2 Chronicles 6:32-33). During the Millennium, the worship of God will take place in ritual or ceremonial form (at a Temple, with sacrifices) because this is the holy way God has prescribed that He be approached when resident on earth with His people (see Leviticus 1–10; Ezekiel 43–46). The Gentile nations that enter into the Millennium will be comprised of believing Gentiles who will abide by this biblical order of worship. These redeemed Gentiles will join Israel in commemorating the Millennial feasts (Ezekiel 44:24), but they will also have a special obligation because they represent national entities that formerly oppressed the Jewish people and their Messiah. This seems to be the meaning of Zechariah 14:16, which says: "Then the survivors from all the nations that have attacked Jerusalem will go up year after year to worship the King, the LORD Almighty, and to celebrate the Feast of Tabernacles" (NIV).

The worship offered during the Millennium will enjoy freedom from one specific source of spiritual warfare—Satan and his demons, who will be bound during this period (Revelation 20:1-3). There will still be spiritual conflicts, however, because the major source of sin, the flesh, will still be present in the Millennial saints who entered this era from the Tribulation period as well as in those who are born during the Millennium itself. It is for this reason that Christ will "rule…with a rod of iron" (Revelation 19:15). This rule of uncompromising standards, enforced by an all-powerful King, will create an outward safeguard against sin that will permit a world to worship without distraction or division. It is only at the end of the Millennium, when Satan is released (Revelation 20:3,7), that socially restrained unbelief will be manifest on a widespread scale (Revelation 20:8-9), demonstrating one last time the folly of the humanist belief that perfect social conditions can perfect man. This unbelief will culminate in a final assault on Jerusalem: "Satan will … gather them together for war. … And they came up on the broad plain of the earth and surrounded the camp of the saints [note the Millennial geography; see Zechariah 14:10-11] and the beloved city [Jerusalem]" (Revelation 20:7-9). Apparently God will allow this assault in order to make a last great separation among mankind. He allows it to prove, despite life in a perfect environment, the unchangeable nature of fallen man apart from the new birth (Jeremiah 13:23), to reveal His previously unseen power to the new generation of people born during the Millennium (Isaiah 65:18-23), and to justly conclude the devil's career in the Lake of Fire (Revelation 20:10).

The Center of Political Government

A Kingdom of Justice

In Jerusalem, which will become the world center for law and justice, God's law and His Word will become the universal basis for order. It will be the civil obligation of every national entity on earth to send representatives to

Jerusalem to receive biblical instruction. How different this age will be than our own, in which countries with the greatest biblical heritage (such as the United States) have legislated *against* biblical instruction in any government-sponsored agency or institution! What a difference also to one day see those nations that formerly banned the Bible from their citizens, persecuted the Jewish people, and aligned their foreign policy agendas against Israel come to Israel to learn the Bible from the Jews!

The Millennial Jerusalem will also have more than just the written Word of God, the city will also have the Living Word of God, the Messiah. For legal and spiritual matters that cannot be resolved by the respective nations even with a biblical foundation, the Messiah will be resident in Jerusalem to "judge between the nations and . . . render decisions for many peoples" (Isaiah 2:4). Messiah's legal decisions, unlike today, will not be subject to appeal or reversal by a higher court, for "the LORD will be king over all the earth; in that day the LORD will be the only one, and His name the only one" (Zechariah 14:9). Thus, this world government will be one in which "the LORD of hosts will reign on Mount Zion and in Jerusalem, and His glory will be before His elders" (Isaiah 24:23).

A Kingdom of Grace and Holiness

The Messiah's government will also be the most benevolent and charitable ever known: "In that day . . . I will gather the lame; I will assemble the exiles and those I have brought to grief. I will make the lame a remnant, those driven away a strong nation. The LORD will rule over them in Mount Zion from that day and forever" (Micah 4:6-7 NIV). During the Millennium, the Jewish people will experience the Lord's grace as they formerly experienced His wrath. Furthermore, in contrast to every government that has ever existed, the Millennial government will be gloriously holy—not only because the Holy One will be present, but because Satan and his demons will be absent and all the world's inhabitants will be required to maintain a state of ritual purity: "Awake, awake, O Zion, clothe yourself with strength. Put on your garments of splendor, O Jerusalem, the holy city. The uncircumcised and defiled will not enter you again" (Isaiah 52:1). Instead, in every corner of the earth there will be a knowledge of the Lord (Isaiah 11:9; Habakkuk 2:14). In every home, school, and community and on every occasion, God and His Word will control the conversations and activities. Whether or not the children born to believers in the Millennium are believers or not, they will have to act as believers, producing a spiritual and stable society. As a result, the world will be incredibly free of crime and the problems associated with it. Under the rule of the Messiah, Jerusalem will experience unparalleled peace, as will the world.

A Kingdom of Peace

On the entrance to the United Nations building in New York City is engraved a single verse of Scripture: "And they will hammer their swords into plowshares, and their spears into pruning hooks. Nation will not lift up sword against nation, and never again will they learn war" (Isaiah 2:4). We can clearly see that the United Nations has failed to achieve this goal by virtue of its unbalanced condemnations of Israel, the nation in which lived the very prophet who penned those words! But no human nation or nations can ever bring peace to the planet because peace requires a foundation in truth and justice: "These are the things which you should do: speak the truth to one another; judge with truth and judgment for peace in your gates. . . . so love truth and peace" (Zechariah 8:16,19; see also Jeremiah 33:6). Since truth and justice have not yet been attained by the nations of this world, neither can peace.

This peace will be made by the Messiah as the "Prince of Peace" (Isaiah 9:6) through a "covenant of peace" (Ezekiel 37:26). This covenant, unlike the pseudopeace of the Antichrist's covenant with Israel (Daniel 9:27), will be "everlasting" (Isaiah 9:7; Ezekiel 37:26). This peace, unparalleled in Israel's turbulent history, will be a testimony to it and the nations that God's promise of restoration has finally been fulfilled (Jeremiah 33:9). This peace will be so dependent upon the Messiah that He will destroy even Israel's own military armaments (Micah 5:10-14) so that the nation has nowhere to turn for security except the Lord Himself. Left without the means for war or a reason for war, Isaiah's prophecy will be fulfilled as intended: "Nation will not lift up sword against nation, and *never again* will they learn war" (Isaiah 2:4).

Those who are alive during the Millennium will know that the Messiah is all they need for their security, for many of them will have witnessed Jesus' victorious ascent to the Mount of Olives in the aftermath of Antichrist's defeat. And just as a "Song of the Sea" resulted from the display of the Lord's power at the Red Sea (Exodus 15:1-21), we could very well see a similar song sung by the saints throughout the Millennium (see Revelation 15:3-4). The prophet Joel put these elements together in his prophecy about the future peace that would flow from the Lord's throne in Jerusalem:

> The LORD will roar from Zion and thunder from Jerusalem; the earth and the sky will tremble. But the LORD will be a refuge for his people, a stronghold for the people of Israel. Then you will know that I, the LORD your God, dwell in Zion, my holy

hill. Jerusalem will be holy; never again will for-
eigners invade her. In that day the mountains will
drip new wine, and the hills will flow with milk
(Joel 3:16-18 NIV).

As a result, Jerusalem will be a "strong city" (Isaiah 26:1;
see also 60:18), whose "peace ... like a river" (Isaiah 66:12;
see also Zechariah 9:10) will flow throughout the earth.

The experience of true peace on a social, spiritual, and
even natural level (Isaiah 11:6-9; 66:25) will so fill the post-
Tribulation saints—who experienced a world of idolatry,
persecutions, and hostile animal attacks (Revelation 6:8)—
that they "will go out in joy and be led forth in peace; the
mountains and hills will burst into song...and all the trees
of the field will clap their hands" (Isaiah 55:12 NIV). This
will also be the experience of the Millennial saints, because
"at that time He [the Messiah] will be great to the ends of
the earth. And this One will be our peace" (Micah 5:4-5).

The Center of the World Economy

Throughout most of its history, Jerusalem has been,
and still is (by Western standards), a city whose economy
has never been envied by the world. Situated in a desert
region and having no natural resources of its own, ancient
Jerusalem was largely dependent on the economy gener-
ated by the Temple. After the Temple's destruction, the city
depended on charitable donations from Jewish people who
lived elsewhere, and today many Jews who make *aliyah*
there must be financed by religious institutions or supported by parents outside the country. But with Messiah on
the throne and Jerusalem's status as the central city of the
Millennium, it will become the international trade center
as well. Its wealth will come from two sources:

Tribute from the Nations

Because the Gentile nations had sought to destroy Jerusalem during the Tribulation (Zechariah 12:3; 14:2) and profited from the Jewish people's persecution (Micah 4:13), they will be required to contribute to its restoration:

> Foreigners will build up your walls, and their kings will minister to you.... your gates will be open continually; they will not be closed day or night, so that men may bring to you the wealth of the nations, with their kings led in procession. For the nation and the kingdom which will not serve you will perish (Isaiah 60:10-12; see also 66:12).

These nations will also be involved in rebuilding the Millennial Temple (Zechariah 6:15) and take part in its ceremonial maintenance (Isaiah 56:6).

Blessings from the Lord

The second source of Jerusalem's prosperity will be its unique blessing by the Lord. Perhaps its geographic transformation (Ezekiel 47:1-12; Zechariah 14:8-11) combined with the restoration of nature (Isaiah 35:1; Ezekiel 36:36) will have a part in making Jerusalem and the Land more productive. In addition, the city's citizens will see to it that it is appropriately adorned: "All the nations will call you blessed, for you shall be a delightful land" (Malachi 3:12; see also Psalm 132:15; Joel 2:23-27).

A Glorious Future Indeed!

The Jerusalem of the Millennium will find the glory it was denied throughout the ages, and a worshiping world will say, "The LORD has built up Zion; He has appeared in His glory" (Psalm 102:16). Yet as great and glorious as the

Millennial Jerusalem will be, the city has a heavenly coun-
terpart that will be exceedingly spectacular. That's the focus
of our next chapter: the New Jerusalem, our heavenly
home.

By faith Abraham. . . . was looking for
the city which has foundations,
whose architect and builder is God.

—Hebrews 11:8,10

You have come to Mount Zion and to the city
of the living God, the heavenly Jerusalem. . . .

—Hebrews 12:22

I saw the holy city, New Jerusalem, coming
down out of heaven from God, made ready
as a bride adorned for her husband.

—Revelation 21:2

He carried me away in the Spirit to a great
and high mountain, and showed me the holy
city, Jerusalem, coming down out of heaven
from God, having the glory of God.

—Revelation 21:10-11

14

THE JERUSALEM ABOVE:

The New Jerusalem as Our Heavenly Home

Not only on the face of this earth is there a Jerusalem, called in Hebrew Yerushalayim Shel Matta *("Jerusalem the Lower"), but also in heaven is there such a city:* Yerushalayim Shel Maalah *("Jerusalem the Upper").*[1]

—Zev Vilnay
Legends of Jerusalem

By the end times, Jerusalem will have had a long history of sin, scandal, deception, and destruction. Worn by the ravages of wars and stained by struggles over sovereignty, it awaits a new day when its faded past will greet a glorious future. It alone of all cities on earth has a promise of eternally abiding. For when time ends and eternity begins, Jerusalem will still be standing, the city and home of God's people forever!

But how can this be? Doesn't everything on earth have an end? Yes and no. There will be an end to the earth, as well as the heavens, and a new earth and heavens will take their place. Yet, as we will see, there will also be a New Jerusalem—not from earth, but heaven, yet on earth. If this seems confusing, you are in good company. Even the best of prophecy scholars and experts disagree on how to interpret the biblical doctrine of the New Jerusalem. Has it always existed or never existed, being a symbol rather than substance? If it exists, does it exist only in the eternal state or will it also be present during the Millennium? Is the believer's home to be in heaven or in the New Jerusalem on earth? Though the answers that have been offered to these questions have been varied, it seems fitting that as we come to the end of our look at Jerusalem in prophecy that we seek to understand the Jerusalem that waits at earth's end. Since both Jews and Christians anticipate the New Jerusalem, let's consider how each views this heavenly hope.

The New Jerusalem in the Old Testament

The New Testament book of Hebrews states that the goal of the godly—who by faith follow God and trust Him to take them to His promised final destination—is a heavenly city (Hebrews 13:14). This hope goes all the way back to Israel's beginning in Abraham: "By faith Abraham.... was looking for the city which has foundations, whose architect and builder is God" (Hebrews 11:8,10). It is passages like that which help us to see a clear contrast between an earthly Temple and the heavenly Temple. Both Moses (Exodus 25:9,40) and David (1 Chronicles 28:11-19) were shown the heavenly Temple and used it as a blueprint or pattern for the later construction of the earthly Sanctuary

(Tabernacle and First Temple). Davidic psalms frequently refer to God being in His house or Temple (Psalm 11:4; 23:6; 26:8; 27:4; 138:2), even though the Temple was not built until after David's death. It's possible David was referring to the heavenly Temple, an identification that one psalm seems to make: "The LORD is in His holy Temple; the LORD's throne is in heaven" (Psalm 11:4). Based on the parallel structure of the Hebrew text, "holy Temple" and the "throne...in heaven" seem to be one and the same. If there is a heavenly Temple, would there not also be a heavenly Jerusalem, since the earthly structures were copied after the heavenly (Hebrews 9:23)?

One objection to this last point is that the Temple and Tabernacle appear in heaven (Revelation 11:19; 15:5-8)—the same Tabernacle/Temple where Christ returned at His ascension (Hebrews 9:11)—and the New Jerusalem is to come from heaven (Revelation 21:2,10). Furthermore, the New Jerusalem is specifically stated *not* to have a Temple (Revelation 21:22). But, even if David's psalms do not describe the New Jerusalem, but rather the heavenly court of God (the Third Heaven), they still prepare us for the fact that the promise of our future existence in heaven will become a reality.

While the concept of the New Jerusalem is not *explicitly* taught in the Old Testament, it is *implicit* in those texts that deal with the eternality and inviolability of Jerusalem. For example, in a text that combines both of those elements we read, "Those who trust in the LORD are as Mount Zion, which cannot be moved, but abides forever" (Psalm 125:1). However, the Old Testament prophets also predicted that neither the present earth nor heaven would continue (Isaiah 34:4). Old Testament theologians, seeking to harmonize this seeming contradiction, have reasoned that if

Jerusalem is to remain eternally, God will have to create a New Jerusalem in order to fulfill the prophecies about a city that abides forever. This is, in fact, what is implied in those passages in Isaiah where the prophecies of a restored Jerusalem is joined to those of a new heaven and new earth:

> Behold, I create new heavens and a new earth; and the former things shall not be remembered or come to mind. But be glad and rejoice forever in what I create; for behold, I create Jerusalem . . . (Isaiah 65:17).

> "My holy mountain Jerusalem. . . . I will also take some of them for priests and Levites," says the LORD. "For just as the new heavens and the new earth which I make will endure before Me," declares the LORD, "so your offspring and your name will endure" (Isaiah 66:20-22).

Despite Isaiah's association of Jerusalem with a new creation, there is still some ambiguity in these contexts. The context of Isaiah 65:17-25 reveals that it is the Millennial kingdom that is in view, since there is death (verse 20), decay (verse 22), and birth (verse 23). However, the opening statement of that passage (verse 17) mentions the new heavens and earth. This could be a general introduction with the Millennial description following as "preliminary specifics," but we can't be certain. In Isaiah 66 we seem to be looking at one time period in verses 10-21 (the Millennial Age), but verse 22 moves to the new heavens and earth and the eternal state (note the statement about eternal punishment in verse 24). Regardless of the lack of distinctions between these times in the text, later Jewish teachers apparently understood the implications and built upon them, as we'll see next.

The New Jerusalem in Later Judaism

The Jewish perception of the promised restoration of Jerusalem was that the city would become the ideal place described by both the pre-exilic and post-exilic prophets. But the earthly restoration that took place after the exile fell far short of this expectation. The idea of a future heavenly Jerusalem, then, first began to appear in the Jewish apocalyptic literature and the Jewish midrashim of the post-exilic Second Temple period. In general these extrabiblical documents describe a heavenly Jerusalem, perfect in every respect, that either replaces or transforms the imperfect earthly Jerusalem as the pinnacle of restoration. Also included among these apocalyptic writings[2] are the famous Dead Sea Scrolls, written before the birth of Jesus. In one document, known as *The New Jerusalem*, which is preserved in several fragmentary copies (1Q32, 2Q24, 4Q554-555, 5Q15, 11Q18), a vision of the New Jerusalem is given that is similar to Ezekiel's vision of Millennial Jerusalem and the Temple (Ezekiel 40–48), but differing in a number of details. In this extrabiblical vision the dimensions of the city are much greater than those of the ancient city of Jerusalem. And, similar to what we see in Ezekiel and Revelation, this vision mentions a city with 12 gates, each named for one of the 12 tribes. It's interesting to note that the extrabiblical material places the appearance of this New Jerusalem to be after the final end-time battle in which Israel emerges victorious over the Gentile nations and has been restored to glory.[3]

In the Talmudic age, the sages sought to instruct a Jewish community that had no access to earthly Jerusalem. The people had lost both their Temple and city, but not their promises. Therefore, as in Christianity, an emphasis was placed on what could not be lost or destroyed: the heavenly Jerusalem (even while retaining the hope of restoration of the earthly Jerusalem). For example, the rabbis tell us, "Not only on the face of this earth is there a Jerusalem, called in Hebrew *Yerushalayim Shel Matta* ("Jerusalem the Lower"), but also in heaven is there such a city: *Yerushalayim Shel Maalah* ("Jerusalem the Upper"). Summarizing Judaism's concept, the Jewish authority on the heavenly Jerusalem, Yitzhak I. Hayutman, writes:

> In these legends the heavenly Jerusalem is the archetype of the good to come, which will be revealed to all at the redemption of the world. At present she hovers above the earthly Jerusalem, even when the latter lies in ruin or sin, but only the most righteous can see her, in moments of grace. In Christian tradition, she is described at the end of the New Testament as descending out of heaven perfect and complete at the consummation of history, while Jewish legends emphasize the building from below to actualize the heavenly Jerusalem.[4]

As can be seen in this summary, according to the Judaism of the Second Temple and the Talmudic periods, the New Jerusalem appears as both present and future. Yet, while it exists at the present time and exerts an influence, it will not be realized completely until the age in which the Jerusalem on earth has fully attained its redemption. Earlier, in chapter 11, we briefly considered this Jewish Age of Redemption; however, in Jewish theology, this is still not the final age. The final age is what is called *'Olam ha-Ba'* ("the World to Come") and sometimes compared to *gan ha-'eden* ("the Garden of Eden"). This age is equivalent to the Christian concept of the eternal state, which follows the Millennium. Although in Judaism we do not find a detailed description for this age (as we do for the Millennium in the New Testament), it is clearly distinguished from the Millennium in that there is "no eating and drinking, no begetting of children, no bargaining, no jealousy and hatred, and no strife; but the righteous sit with their crowns on their heads enjoying the effulgence of the *Shekinah* ("Presence of God")" (*Bab. Berakot* 17a).

The Jewish Talmud records that the heavenly city, which would not be realized until the Age of Redemption, could already be seen by the righteous in moments of grace (and they could receive inspiration from it as well). It was depicted as positioned directly above earthly Jerusalem, with the earthly and heavenly Holy of Holies in direct alignment. Even so, the Talmud makes the heavenly Jerusalem subservient to the earthly Jerusalem—probably in reaction to Christianity, which emphasizes the heavenly Jerusalem and identifies with it as a replacement of the earthly Jerusalem.

There are also several references to the heavenly Jerusalem in the Zohar, the extrabiblical text revered by Kabbalistic (mystical) Judaism. It says that the heavenly Jerusalem was created by God to house the souls of the righteous. The Zohar also makes a distinction between earthly Jerusalem, which it identified with the kingdom or the Shekinah (the presence of God), and the heavenly Jerusalem, which it identified with the higher Shekinah, the *sefira* of *binah* ("understanding"), and also the World to Come. Thus it appears that Judaism understood a presently existing New Jerusalem that would be realized in the Millennial era yet continue into the final age, the World to Come.

The New Jerusalem in the New Testament

The only biblical use of the phrase "New Jerusalem" is found in the book of Revelation, which was written by the apostle John at the end of the reign of the Roman emperor Domitian (about A.D. 90, which would place it after the destruction of the Temple in Jerusalem in A.D. 70). Some commentators believe that the concept of a New Jerusalem was developed in response to this disaster. However, as we have just seen, the Jewish concept of a New Jerusalem had existed long before the Temple's destruction. John, as a Jew, would have been quite familiar with this perspective, and Israeli scholar David Flusser has noted a close parallel between Revelation 21:22-23 (which describes the New Jerusalem in relation to the Temple), and an earlier Jewish midrash on Isaiah 60:19, which is fused with a midrash on Psalm 132:17.[5] The similarities in these accounts do not mean that John borrowed his material from the Jewish midrashim; rather, they simply confirm that Jews and Christians had similar concepts of the New Jerusalem at this time.

The *concept* of the New Jerusalem does appear in several earlier New Testament texts. In Galatians 4:26 the apostle Paul speaks of "the Jerusalem above" in contrast to "the present Jerusalem" (verse 25). Even though this is an analogical (not allegorical) use for the sake of comparison, the concept of a heavenly Jerusalem clearly exists in his thinking. The author of the epistle to the Hebrews also understood this to be an established concept in the Jewish circles he addressed, for he writes of the heavenly Jerusalem (place of grace) in contrast to the earthly Mount Sinai (place of the law):

> But you have come to Mount Zion and to the city of the living God, the heavenly Jerusalem, and to myriads of angels, to the general assembly and church of the first-born who are enrolled in heaven, and to God, the Judge of all, and to the spirits of righteous

> men made perfect, and to Jesus, the mediator of a
> new covenant . . . (Hebrews 12:22-24).

In that passage, we read that the inhabitants of this "heavenly Jerusalem" are God the Father (Judge), Jesus the Son (Mediator), the angels, Old Testament believers ("righteous men made perfect"), and the church. This accords with the scriptural descriptions of both the heavenly court of God and the New Jerusalem in the book of Revelation. The writer provides more clarity for us in verses 26-29, where he wrote:

> Yet once more "I [God] will shake not only the earth, but also the heaven." And this expression, "Yet once more," denotes the removal of those things which can be shaken, as of created things, in order that those things which cannot be shaken may remain. Therefore, since we receive a kingdom which cannot be shaken, let us show gratitude . . . for our God is a consuming fire.

This explanation reveals that it is the new heavens and earth that is in view. The old created order (both the earth and the heavens) will be removed in fire and be replaced by an indestructible kingdom. This appears to be the same cosmic dissolution that Peter speaks of in 2 Peter 3:10-13— the climax of the Day of the Lord, which results in "new heavens and a new earth." Peter was not talking about the third heaven (which cannot be shaken), but the eternal state in the new cosmos.

Some individuals would also include the reference "our citizenship is in heaven" (Philippians 3:20a) in this discussion, but it's clear Paul is referring to the third heaven, because it is from this place that "we eagerly wait for a Savior, the Lord Jesus Christ" (Philippians 3:20b). Christ is presently at the "right hand of the throne of God" (Hebrews 12:2) rather than in the New Jerusalem.

The New Jerusalem in Revelation

What does the New Jerusalem look like?

The most complete description of the New Jerusalem is in the book of Revelation, chapters 21–22. John calls it "the bride, the wife of the Lamb" (Revelation 21:9). This description, along with its appearance as a city from outer space, its immense size and foursquare shape, its jeweled adornment, and its supernatural source of illumination have caused many Bible interpreters to decide that the whole picture is symbolic of the church (the redeemed on earth or in heaven). However, Revelation 22:3 makes it clear that the bond-servants of the Lamb (the church) are *separate* from the city itself, so the city cannot be a symbol of them. In addition, despite its unusual features, this city qualifies in every sense as a physical reality, with measurable architectural structures, planned design, building materials, rivers, trees, and human inhabitants. We also have to keep in mind that this incredible description of the New Jerusalem had to be written to accommodate our inability to grasp such future realities. After all, this eternal city for an eternal people is not of earth, but heaven, and as the handiwork of an infinite God, should not be expected to conform in every respect to the world we live in today (see Revelation 21:5). The New Jerusalem's dimensions are 1,500 miles equally in every direction,[6] or as one engineer has figured, an area of 2,250,000 square miles.[7] In our day of Hollywood special-effects with spaceships the size of cities (like those in the science-fiction film *Independence Day*), such proportions are no longer impossible to imagine. The

NEW JERUSALEM
Revelation 21

SIZE OF
NEW JERUSALEM
2,250,000
SQ. MILES

U.S.A.

1500 MI

1500 MI

NEW HEAVENS

NEW JERUSALEM

NEW EARTH

New Jerusalem is laid out as a square with connecting planes of equal size that apparently form a cube. This has long been recognized as the exact shape of the Holy of Holies, although 240,000 times as big! Thus, the place where God and the Lamb are the light (Revelation 21:11,23; 22:5)—as was the Shekinah Glory in the ancient Holy of Holies—is revealed as the dwelling place of God, but this time with no partitions, curtains, walls, or restrictions barring people from His presence!

The New Jerusalem's gates are inscribed with the names of the 12 tribes of Israel, and the foundation stones of its wall with the names of the 12 apostles (Revelation 21:12-14). Even though these are all Jewish, they represent the two dispensations of Israel and the church (or the Old and New Testament saints, as in Hebrews 12:23). That the church's "foundation of the apostles and prophets" (Ephesians 2:20) was Jewish reminds grafted Gentile Christians not to be arrogant toward the natural branches (Romans 11:18-23). As such, it is fitting that it was during the dispensation of Israel that Jesus the Jewish Messiah announced to His Jewish disciples that He was going away [to heaven] to prepare a place [this city] for them as His bride (John 14:2). Part of that preparation may be His entrance into the heavenly Holy of Holies as a High Priest in order to bring us there to serve the living God (see Hebrews 9:11-14; Revelation 22:3).

This is confirmed by John's description of a city with iridescent stones of every color and streets of pure gold that is transparent like glass. This language seeks to convey to us the vision of God's presence. In Exodus 24, when Moses and the elders of Israel were permitted to see the God of Israel, their vision was of His heavenly court, where the street was described as "a pavement of sapphire, as clear as the sky itself" (verse 10).

John also described the New Jerusalem as "having the glory of God" (Revelation 21:11); it is this that John emphasizes the most in his description of the city. The supernatural illumination provided to the city is the result of God's presence and is the reason there can be no night there (Revelation 21:5; 22:5). The archetype of the Garden of Eden is also present in the city, complete with "a river of the water of life" and "the tree of life" (Revelation 22:1-2).

Is the New Jerusalem in the Millennium?

One of the debates among those who hold to the premillennial view of prophecy is whether the New Jerusalem appears only in the eternal state or also during the Millennial kingdom. The New Jerusalem is described as "coming out of heaven from ...God" (Revelation 3:12 NIV; see also 21:2,10). The present participle indicates that John saw the city as being in the process of descent, thereby characterizing it as a "descending from heaven" kind of city. This is further emphasized by the prepositions "out of," indicating its origin (heaven), and "from," indicating its originator (God). These prepositions indicate that the New Jerusalem comes out of heaven, that is, it's heavenmade. The directional term "coming out of" also indicates that it comes from somewhere—from heaven to earth. This could imply that the New Jerusalem is created by God at the beginning of the eternal state, since John's words about it *follow* the creation of the new heavens and new earth (Revelation 21:1).

There's another possibility, however. If the New Jerusalem is intended to form a conduit between heaven and earth—that is, be a touchpoint where that which is heavenly connects with that which is earthly—then, as I suggest following, it is possible that the New Jerusalem is not created at the beginning of the eternal state, but is part of the eternally existing heavenly Temple that is brought down to enable those on earth to be in the presence of the Triune God. This would allow the New Jerusalem to exist in both the Millennium and the eternal state, although there are other factors we must consider.

One of these factors is the chronological progression of Revelation 19:11–22:5. There are some places in the book of Revelation where recapitulation takes place, but that doesn't seem to be the case in the section that presents the New Jerusalem. John is shown the city from afar in Revelation 21:2 and then taken to a closer vantage point in Revelation 21:9. Since Revelation 21:1 starts the section by mentioning the new heavens and new earth, it seems that the vision of the New Jerusalem is limited to the eternal state.

However, this chronological progression does not necessarily mean that the New Jerusalem could not be present during the Millennium. The Jewish concept is of a heavenly city suspended in space and positioned directly above and in alignment with the earthly city. Although there is no direct biblical support for this concept, many have pointed to Revelation 21:24-26 as suggesting this possibility. These verses have been a problem for the eternal-state-only view because they depict nations and kings of the earth walking by the light of the city and bringing the "glory and the honor of the nations into it." Who are these "nations" and "kings"? One of the best answers for those who hold to the eternal-state-only position is that they are saved but unresurrected human beings who survived the Millennium without dying but were transformed (during the creation of the new heavens and earth) and given immortal bodies to inhabit the new earth throughout eternity.[8] However, this explanation lacks any biblical support, and its proponents must concede that "this is an issue on which the text of Revelation is silent."[9]

If we consider the Old Testament prophecies that parallel these verses (Psalm 72:10-11; Isaiah 60:3,10a,11-12; 66:12), it seems to make sense to see these "nations" and "kings" as remnants of the Gentile nations that were once opposed to God and His people, became believers during the Tribulation, and in the Millennium will bring their wealth into the earthly Jerusalem. One immediate objection that could be raised is that the kings and nations in Revelation 21:24-26 are in the eternal state, not the Millennium. But John may be considering the position of the people (within and without the city) without regard to the position of the city itself (that is, in the Millennium or eternal state). If so, such considerations are not necessarily bound by the chronology of the immediate context, but rather are determined by whatever contexts establish their identity. In this case, it is those texts in the Old Testament which fit the Millennial kingdom. In fact, if we do *not* see the New Jerusalem as having been preexistent, we must look to another context to explain "the bride, the wife of the Lamb" as being in the New Jerusalem before the eternal state. Dallas Seminary professor J. Dwight Pentecost explains his reasoning in favor of the New Jerusalem in the Millennium:

> When the occupants of the city are described it must be seen that they are in the eternal state, possessing their eternal inheritance, in eternal relationship with God who has tabernacled among them. There will be no change in their position or relation whatsoever. When the occupants of the earth are described they are seen in the millennial age. They have an established relationship to the heavenly city which is above them, in whose light

they walk. Yet their position is not eternal nor
unchangeable, but rather millennial.[10]

This seems to me to be a more reasonable solution than
attempting to fit these "nations" and "kings" into the
eternal state by transforming them into a new race of
immortals, which is out of character with the rest of
redeemed humanity. Why should they remain eternal visitors if they are without sin and have their names written in
the Lamb's Book of Life, the qualification for entrance
(Revelation 21:27)? But if they are redeemed sinners, still
under the curse, as in the Millennium, it is obvious why
they can enter, but not remain. There is also the question of
why they bring their "glory and honor" into the New Jerusalem and not the Millennial city of Jerusalem. This can
best be answered by considering the contrast between the
earthly and heavenly Jerusalem—especially with relationship to the Temple.

The New Jerusalem and the Temple

The city of New Jerusalem is described with the *Shekinah* glory of God present (Revelation 21:11), *but with no
Temple* (Revelation 21:22)! Such a statement would be star-
tling to those accustomed to viewing the Temple as the
place of the divine presence. For this reason, Ezekiel uses
historic detail to depict the return of the Shekinah glory to
the Millennial Temple (Ezekiel 43:1-7). But, in my opinion,
John's description of the New Jerusalem has been built with
allusions to Ezekiel, in order to continue a ceremonial connection with the new earth through the New Jerusalem as a
"Temple-city."[11] But how can the New Jerusalem be considered a Temple-city if there is no Temple in it?

Let's remember that when John first introduced the New Jerusalem in Revelation 3:12 he spoke of believers in the New Jerusalem as "a pillar in the temple of My God." In the ancient Greek world, it was customary to place a pillar in a temple in order to honor a dignitary. Thus John is not in contradiction to the later statement omitting a Temple; rather, he may be implying that the New Jerusalem is something of a Temple itself. By comparison with all earthly Temples, including the Millennial Temple, the New Jerusalem is unique. Earthly Temples had restrictions, even for the righteous, and hid the *Shekinah* in an innermost chamber away from all human sight. The New Jerusalem is exceptional in that it has no such limitations, but goes beyond them just as an archetype exceeds the model. For example, in the New Jerusalem, God's bond-servants "shall see His face" (Revelation 22:4). This clearly indicates a new access without the previous restrictions given in Exodus 33:20: "You cannot see My face, for no man can see Me and live!" The text explains that the reason this is possible is because the New Jerusalem cannot be defiled *from within* by sin because there is no curse there (Revelation 22:3), nor *from without*, since no unclean person can enter (Revelation 21:27). Thus, as George Ladd has pointed out, "in the eternal state God will dwell among His people in a direct unmediated communion."[12]

Another contrast is that the New Jerusalem is not an earthly structure, as is the case with Israel's past and future Temples, but a structure transferred from heaven. Based on the parallels between the description of this city and the Garden of Eden and Ezekiel's Temple, we may conjecture a common source, namely the archetypal heavenly Temple that John depicted in his heavenly throne visions. Thus, the New Jerusalem is a heavenly Temple transferred to the new earth, and it will be an inviolable and eternal structure where God can be served by His redeemed creation.

The apostle John also tells us that the New Jerusalem is a "holy city" (Revelation 21:2) "having the glory of God" (Revelation 21:11). This is reinforced by the announcement in Revelation 21:3: "Behold, the tabernacle of God is among men, and He shall dwell among them, and they shall be His people, and God Himself shall be among them." What "tabernacle of God" is this? My suggestion is that it's the *heavenly* Tabernacle/Temple which has previously appeared (see Revelation 7:15; 13:6; 15:5) and has in view the Holy of Holies. This may imply that the Holy of Holies in the heavenly Tabernacle/Temple will separate from its heavenly courts[13] during the Millennium and form the New Jerusalem. This idea may also be supported by the dimensions of the Temple's Holy of Holies (see 1 Kings 6:19-20), which form the enlarged shape of the New Jerusalem (Revelation 21:16).

What we may have here, then, is the *entire city* as a Temple, or rather, an immense heavenly Holy of Holies.[14] If so, this is the Sanctuary *par excellence*, epitomizing the realization of the Temple's intended function, the communion of God and man. And within this Temple is what has always constituted a Temple and a holy place: the true Temple, God Himself. This fits with Revelation 21:22, which says "...the Lord God, the Almighty, and the Lamb, are its Temple." If we can then see this New Jerusalem as a Holy of Holies positioned above the earthly Jerusalem and its Temple during the Millennium, we can understand how it illumines the earthly city and turns it into the Throne of God (Jeremiah 3:17), how the Shekinah fills the earthly Temple while being in the New Jerusalem, and how the Lamb can be with His resurrected saints above and His millennial saints below. In the eternal state it becomes the conduit between a new heaven and the new earth, allowing God's creation, for whom the world was made, to enjoy its recreated wonders while dwelling in the place prepared by their Savior (John 14:2).

Forever in New Jerusalem!

The New Jerusalem will one day be the heavenly reality for the people of God, but only for the people of God. As the Puritan scholar William Gurnall reminds, "Nothing is more contrary to a heavenly hope than an earthly heart." Perhaps as we conclude this chapter, with all its detailed promise of our heavenly home, you will pause, consider your relationship with God, and regain a heavenly hope. Then, it will not be simply "Next year in Jerusalem," but "Forever in the New Jerusalem!"

> I am going to that city,
> the New Jerusalem.
> There I'll spend eternity in
> the New Jerusalem.
> Land of promise, home of glory,
> the New Jerusalem.
> I will know eternal joy in
> the New Jerusalem.[15]

PART FOUR

The Day
of
Decision

Thou wilt arise and have compassion on Zion;
for it is time to be gracious to her,
for the appointed time has come.

—Psalm 102:13

On your walls, O Jerusalem, I have appointed
watchmen; all day and all night they will never
keep silent. You who remind the LORD,
take no rest for yourselves;
and give Him no rest until He establishes
and makes Jerusalem a praise in the earth.

—Isaiah 62:7

Be glad and rejoice forever in what I create;
for behold, I create Jerusalem for rejoicing
and her people for gladness. I will also rejoice
in Jerusalem, and be glad in My people.

—Isaiah 65:18–19

15

JERUSALEM IS OURS!

Getting Ready
for God's Reign

---

*We are part of a much, much larger scheme. The
return of the Jewish people is not just a passing epi-
sode that will be wiped out by the force of ignorance and stupidity. The life-force of the friends of
the Jewish people around the world, especially the
Christian world, is enormous. And this partner-
ship will safeguard the Jewish land, will safeguard
Zion, will safeguard the eternal city.*[1]

—Benjamin Netanyahu,
Prime Minister of Israel

There is a slogan that appears frequently on bumper
stickers and banners in Jerusalem nowadays. In Hebrew it
reads *Yerushalayim shelanu!* ("Jerusalem is ours!"). Its message has become the rallying point for those who defend
Jewish sovereignty over all of Jerusalem. This is a cause we

should support, for the future of Jerusalem belongs to the Jews. But beyond the politics of our day, we have seen that Jerusalem stands at the center of God's plan for this age and the age to come. It also stands as the eternal hope of all who hope in God the Eternal. If you have come to understand these truths, then you can rally with God's people around His future purpose for this world and also say, "Jerusalem is ours!"

Preparing for What Is Ahead

One reason I wrote this book is to help prepare those in the twenty-first century for the prophetic events that will surely overtake their generation. As we observed at the beginning of this book, every good father wants his children to have an understanding of what lies ahead. Having grown up and gone before, wise fathers have a wealth of insight to share for the unseen path. Children do not always want to listen, but in going where they have not gone before, they half-realize that they need a guide for the road. God is our Father, and He wants His children to know what awaits us in the future—especially in relation to the central city of all time, Jerusalem. To understand God's control over this city is to gain assurance of His control over our lives as believers: "Those who trust in the LORD are as Mount Zion, which cannot be moved, but abides forever. As the mountains surround Jerusalem, so the LORD surrounds His people from this time forth and forever" (Psalm 125:1-2). God's control over Jerusalem will one day be "on earth as it is in heaven," for He is coming to reign the world from this city.

Therefore, in this closing chapter, I want to share about how we can get ready for God's reign. While it is my conviction that the Scriptures teach that believers in the Jewish

Messiah in this age will not have to face the Tribulation of the next (1 Thessalonians 1:10; 5:9; Revelation 3:9-10), our subjection to God as sovereign over our lives should include a concern for what will happen in the future, including the end times. Because Jerusalem occupies a central place in the panorama of prophecy, we should include the city and its people in our prayers. The disciples of our Lord, standing 2,000 years behind us in the prophetic plan, were instructed to pray: "Thy kingdom come . . ." (Matthew 6:10; Luke 11:2), even though the kingdom for which they were to pray waited far beyond their lives and on the other side of the Tribulation period. In like manner, the early church was told to be "looking for and hastening the coming day of God [the prophetic "Day of the Lord"] (2 Peter 3:12), even though this far-off event would destroy the earth only at the end of the kingdom age. We benefit when we pray for the fulfillment of God's prophetic plan; to do so orients us to God's future purposes, which are being prepared for during our lifetime. Peter put it this way: "Since all these things are to be destroyed in this way [by divine intervention], what sort of people ought you to be in holy conduct and godliness" (2 Peter 3:11). In the same manner, by encouraging you to not forget Jerusalem, you will not forget the direction God is taking this world— whose destiny, like our own, depends on God's promises to Jerusalem being fulfilled.

Remembering Jerusalem and Its People

From 605-586 B.C. the Babylonians deported the best of the people of Judah to Babylon before they destroyed Jerusalem. Although the Jews had been taken far from Jerusalem, Jerusalem was never far from the Jews. When these exiles sat down by the rivers of Babylon they wept and remembered their native Jerusalem, vowing:

> If I forget you, O Jerusalem, may my right hand forget her skill. May my tongue cleave to the roof of my mouth, if I do not remember you, if I do not exalt Jerusalem above my chief joy" (Psalm 137:5-6).

This vow may sound strange to modern ears, but its meaning is timeless. In the ancient world the right hand was the hand extended in friendship, and it was also used to wield a sword in battle. To lose the use of the right hand was to not only lose one's friends, but also one's life. The Jewish exiles understood that Jerusalem meant more than life itself, for despite personal ambition and achievement, without the fulfillment of the prophetic plan for Jerusalem, no one has a future. They exalted Jerusalem in their words, because they knew God would one day exalt it in the world. They reasoned that if they had no words for Jerusalem, it would be better for them to have no words at all! Throughout the intervening centuries, even though Jerusalem was by its devastated condition impossibly far from its fulfillment, Jewish hope continued true to the ancient vow. One example of this hope is found in a letter written by the famous rabbi Moshe ben Nachman (Rambam):

> I write you this letter from Jerusalem, the holy city . . . the most ruined of all cities. . . . The houses of the city are abandoned, and anyone could claim them. . . . May He who has granted us to see Jerusalem in its ruin allow us to witness its restoration and restitution when the Divine presence will return to its midst.

Today, the ancient vow is seen everywhere throughout the modern city on amulets and necklaces, reminding the present-day generation that Jerusalem is still in jeopardy and must never be forgotten.

Yet, the two millennia that have separated the church from its Jewish founder have also separated Christians from remembering to exalt Jerusalem. The church has too long rejoiced in the fulfillment of the Savior's prophecy of Jerusalem's ruin while forgetting His prediction of its restoration. Too, the church seems to have lived too long with a Jewish people in exile to recognize the significance of their returning home. It is easy to forget a Jerusalem that perished in the past, but the church must repent and remember a Jerusalem that is fighting for its future.

Jesus, like the exiles in Babylon, was exiled from Jerusalem, but His exile was from the hearts of its people (John 1:11). When He remembered Jerusalem He too wept over it (Matthew 23:37; Luke 19:41). But He never forgot Jerusalem; He rose from its tomb, ascended from its Mount, and "vowed" to return again (John 14:3,28; Acts 1:11) to establish it as the center of His kingdom on earth (Matthew 25:31; Luke 21:28; Acts 1:6-7). If the church forgets Jerusalem, it forgets this kingdom which the King of the Jews has promised (Matthew 26:29; see also Luke 22:18). So that we might help one another remember Jerusalem, let's consider four things that we can do: 1) perceive Jerusalem's situation, 2) provoke Jerusalem's senses, 3) pray for Jerusalem's security, and 4) proclaim Jerusalem's Savior.

Perceiving Jerusalem's Situation

Despite the fact that the background of our Bible is the Land of Israel, we usually will hear more about what is happening in Israel on the news than in church. The reason for this, I suspect, is that pastors in general are more focused on the Israel of the past than that of the present or future. By contrast, the world outside the church has an intense interest in Israel today and its plans for tomorrow. This was brought home to me when on the evening of April 15, 1998 more than 90 nations watched simultaneously via satellite as America celebrated Israel's fiftieth birthday. Throughout the telecast, Los Angeles was linked live to Jerusalem, and while it was night in America, the sun was just rising over the Old City of Jerusalem. As the cameras panned this most famous landscape in history, my thoughts could not help but turn to prophecy, for soon a new day will dawn over the City and the events predicted for it will be fulfilled. Yet how many millions of the people who watched that telecast around the world were aware of Jerusalem's present and predicted situation?

Many Christians today hold to the perception that because the Jewish people rejected the Messiah, they have fallen out of God's plan. This same perception apparently was held by Gentile Christians in Paul's day because he addressed this issue in the book of Romans. In Romans 11:11-15 he explained that Israel had not fallen out of the good purpose of God, but only been set aside for a time. He also said that the greater their present failure, the greater will be their future fulfillment.

Later on in Romans 11, after reviewing the prophetic scenario of Israel's return to Jesus and Jesus' return to Jerusalem (verses 25-27), Paul made the incredible statement that though the Jews are at present the enemies of the gospel, God has never become their enemy (verses 28-29). Rather, "they are beloved for the sake of the fathers" (verse 28). That is, God still loves them because of His unfulfilled promise to Abraham, Isaac, and Jacob to bless the world through them. After all, if God went back on His word, where would *we* be? If He were to fell the olive tree in order to rid Himself of its natural branches, would not we as grafted branches likewise suffer? In other words, if God does not fulfill His promises to Israel and Jerusalem, then on what basis will He fulfill His promises to us? His character cannot discriminate when it is His own reputation that's at stake. Therefore, concerning Israel, Paul has assured that "the gifts and the calling of God are irrevocable" (Romans 11:29). To act against Israel and judge Jerusalem as having no significance to the future of the church is to find ourselves, as Gamaliel cautioned, "fighting against God" (Acts 5:38-39).

The political situation involving Jerusalem is not just an Israeli or Jewish concern; it is a concern for everyone who believes the events of today are preparations for the fulfillment of God's prophecies tomorrow. Christians need to realize that the Israeli forfeiture of the cities of Gaza, Jericho, and Hebron as well as a large portion of the West Bank territories has almost returned Israel to its pre-1967 borders, excepting the city of Jerusalem. Israeli Prime Minister Benjamin Netanyahu once observed that Israel's survival in the almost disastrous Yom Kippur War depended on its secure boundaries. He said:

> There was an important lesson here for both Israelis and Arabs. On both the Egyptian and Syrian fronts, the Arabs had managed to penetrate as much as twenty miles before Israeli forces finally checked them. If the war had begun not on post-1967 lines, but on the *pre*-1967 lines, and if the Arab armies had advanced the same distances, Israel would have ceased to exist.[2]

Our awareness of these matters must not be deceived by sentimental pro-Palestinian scenes selectively shown by the modern media, or by anti-Semitic statements found in the popular press. Rather, we should endeavor to become apprised of the facts and support what is in harmony with the prophetic purposes of God, as J.C. Ryle, Bishop of Liverpool, England, wrote in 1867: "Is there anyone that desires God's special blessing? Then let him labour in the cause of Israel and he shall not fail to find it." This, of course, does not require that we ignore what is wrong (bigotry, brutality, harassment) while we regard what is right (biblical promises to the Jewish people). It simply requires that we perceive our responsibility as Gentile members of the church in relation to the Jews: "For if the Gentiles have shared in the Jews' [in context: Jews in Jerusalem] spiritual blessings, they owe it to the Jews to share with them their material blessings" (Romans 15:27 NIV).

Provoking Jerusalem's Senses

Not only are Christians to perceive Jerusalem's situation, they are also to provoke Jerusalem's senses. In Romans 11:13-14 Paul wrote, "I am speaking to you who are Gentiles . . . I magnify my ministry, if somehow I might *move to jealousy* my fellow countrymen and save some of them" (emphasis added). Based on this passage, Gentile Christians have an obligation to show their faith in such a way as to cause Jewish unbelievers to want what they have. This could include spiritual gifts, but I think it primarily has reference to material gifts which, given in acts of charity, were highly regarded in a Torah-observant community.

Throughout the Old Testament, God shows great concern for the poor, the alien, and the stranger (Deuteronomy 15:4-11; Psalm 72:13; Proverbs 19:17). It was also a special concern of the prophets (Isaiah 3:15; 10:2; Jeremiah 5:28; Ezekiel 16:49; Daniel 4:27; Amos 5:11-12; Zechariah 7:10). It is no wonder, then, that the early Jewish-Christian epistle of James should say, "This is pure and undefiled religion in the sight of our God and Father, to visit orphans and widows in their distress, and to keep oneself unstained by the world" (James 1:27). The care of the poor, widows, and orphans was a special concern of the early Jewish-Christian community (Acts 6:1-3; Romans 15:26; Galatians 2:10). Indeed, so generous were these early Christians with one another that it was boasted that "there was not a needy person among them" (Acts 4:34).

The ancient Israelites were required to make annual pilgrimages to Jerusalem's Temple, which allowed people in the city a special opportunity to show hospitality to those away from home. Poor people would also congregate in the Temple precincts (Acts 3:2-5,10), expecting their fellow Jews to observe the commandment of giving alms to the needy. When persecution and famine hit the Jewish-Christian community in Jerusalem, the apostles collected monies for their support among the far-flung Gentile provinces in Asia Minor (1 Corinthians 16:1-3; 2 Corinthians 8:1–9:15; Philippians 4:15-16). What a witness this must have been to the unbelieving Jewish community in Jerusalem! What envy they must have felt for their believing neighbors as they received such loving gifts from far-off members of their family in the faith.

Such giving will become the distinguishing mark of true believers during the Tribulation period, when, "because lawlessness is increased, most people's love will grow cold" (Matthew 24:12). This virtue will become a Gentile witness to the Jewish world at the conclusion of the Tribulation, when the Messiah will judge the nations on the

basis of their treatment of Israel: "I tell you the truth, whatever you did for one of the least of these brothers of mine,
you did for me" (Matthew 25:40). Knowing then the prov-
ocation such acts of faith have produced in the past and will
demonstrate in the future, how does the church today measure up in its duty to move Jews toward the gospel by its
Christian character?

My own answer to this question comes by way of an
experience I had many years ago. The story I am about to
tell may be convicting to many Christians—and it needs to
be! When my family and I returned from living in Israel, we
moved back to the Texas town where we had sublet (the
year before) to a seminary couple a house we were renting.
We had expected our transition to the States to be difficult,
but we never would have imagined what we were about to
encounter!

Earlier in the year, we had written to the seminary
couple about our return so that they would have adequate
time to find another place. However, upon our arrival, we
discovered that because they were unable to find other suit-
able housing, they had *bought* the house we were renting!
Furthermore, they had piled our furniture and belongings
in one room and wanted them moved immediately! Next I
checked on our station wagon, which had been loaned to
friends. It was raised up on blocks, having broken down
and been left unrepaired. We had come "home" with a two-
year-old child and an infant, but with no place to live, no
transportation, and no current contacts. At this point we
thought that the Christian community would be available
to provide advice and fellowship when we made known our
need for housing, a good church home, and a job. After all, I
had graduated from a well-known seminary in the city, had
previously planted and pastored a church, and had just

completed graduate studies in, of all places, Israel. But few Christians I contacted showed genuine concern, even though we visited church after church. Perhaps we should not have expected more, but given the Bible's encouragements to care for both brethren and the needy (Galatians 6:6-10) we were surprised at the lack of concern that greeted us.

After some hard weeks of storing furniture, fixing the car, and searching unsuccessfully for local work, I took a job at a Christian high school in another large city some distance away. There I faced more weeks of hardship, sleeping on a mattress on a floor while waiting for a reluctant Christian single to move out of a four-bedroom house I had rented. Once the home became available, I moved my family to town.

Shortly after the move, we visited an art gallery in one of the area malls. Worn out from weeks of working to get our lives back together, and with one child in our arms and another in a stroller, we found a happy diversion in a series of paintings depicting scenes in Jerusalem. A gallery employee noticed our obvious interest in the paintings and began talking to us. We told her that we had just moved to the States from Israel. Although we were complete strangers to her, she immediately forgot about us as potential customers and shot a volley of questions at us: Have you got a place to live? Do you have a job? Have you gotten into a congregation yet? Thinking we were Jewish, she offered to help us get connected, settled, and secured. Her great concern stood in contrast to the response we had gotten from Christians. A few Christians had shown some concern, but nothing like this! Here was the help we had so wanted, but, of course, couldn't receive. Eventually we found a wonderful church, made good friends in the community, and became actively involved in ministry, but I have never forgotten this "Jewish encounter."

I realize that what my family encountered is not true of all churches. There are good churches in our world that are actively committed to helping those who are in need. Yet I share this story because the concern shown by the Jewish woman at the gallery is the kind of concern we as Christians are called to show to the Jewish community. If my experience in this instance is typical, then we as modern Christians still have a way to go if we are to provoke the Jews to jealousy over what we have as believers!

Consider the appeal of a Messianic Jewish believer who, ostracized from the Jewish community, looks to Gentile Christians to fulfill their responsibility to his people:

> Are Gentile believers in Yeshua expected to be involved in what God is doing with Israel and the Jewish people? If the Jewish people are truly the Lord's brethren, then they are our brethren as well. Most well-balanced people are involved with their natural family, particularly if a member of the family is about to give birth. In these days we will see Israel go into labor, preparing to bring forth the Messianic kingdom. We have seen a nation born in one day, we have seen the miraculous restoration of the Hebrew language, and now we are witnessing that great final exodus of the Jewish people, returning to Israel from the four corners of the world. What a privilege to be involved in what God is doing! Imagine if we lived in the days of the first exodus, when Moses brought the children of Israel out of Egypt and through the Red Sea. Would we want to be involved in such a spectacular event? Yet the Bible says that this second exodus is so much greater than the first that the first will not

even be remembered! And yet, how few Christians
want to be involved.[3]

We can get involved by educating ourselves about Israel
and the Jewish people—what they believe (and their perspective of Christians) and why; getting to know Jewish people on
friendly terms (without a conversion agenda); seeking to
show our gratitude for their having given us our Bible, our
heritage, and our Messiah; and simply living out our own
faith in a biblically appropriate and appealing manner.

Praying for Jerusalem's Security

Prayer is to be the first feat of faith performed by the
Christian. Christian pastor and writer Thomas Watson
underscored this truth when he said, "You can do more
than pray *after* you have prayed, but you cannot do more
than pray *until* you have prayed."

There is an Old Testament account that demonstrates
to us the great power of prayer. This prayer was lifted up to
God by King Hezekiah when the defeat of Jerusalem was
imminent and deliverance seemed impossible. The prayer
itself is recorded in 2 Kings 19:15-19 and is a model prayer
for intercession. What's important to note is what God said
when Hezekiah finished praying: "Thus says the LORD, the
God of Israel, 'Because you have prayed to Me about Sen-
nacherib king of Assyria, I have heard you'" (2 Kings
19:20). Do you see the cause and effect in those words?
Jerusalem didn't have a prayer against the Assyrians, but
King Hezekiah knew that prayer was their only hope. The
result was one of the greatest and most miraculous deliver-
ances in all of history.

Because of the place that prayer plays in God's prophetic
program, David, Jerusalem's most celebrated king, charged

his people, "Pray for the peace of Jerusalem: May they prosper who love you. May peace be within your walls, and prosperity within your palaces" (Psalm 122:6-7). Observe that in these words it is the *peace* of Jerusalem that is requested. For a city whose name means peace, but has rarely known it in its history, this is appropriate. Yet the word "peace" (Hebrew: *shalom*) means more than a prevention of war. It is the word used today in the streets of Jerusalem (as well as among all those who speak Hebrew) when they greet someone, ask about their present well-being, and say farewell. It is a word that includes the full-orbed blessings of salvation, health, security, prosperity, and welfare.

Notice too that David's request is for those within the walls and palaces of Jerusalem (verse 7). This means the *people*, who in that day lived mostly within its walls (David's city to the south and on the Ophel Ridge), and the *leaders*, who dwelt in palaces. Jerusalem's leadership of today and tomorrow faces and will face a crisis over their city. The people now and in the future will stand on the threshold of salvation and need to recognize "the time of their visitation" by their Messiah, who came and is coming. Recognizing this, Christians need to pray both for Jerusalem's present and future.

Praying for Jerusalem's Present Security

There is first a need to pray for Jerusalem's present security. Even as I was writing this book the Palestinians continued to openly declare their designs on Jerusalem. On August of 1997, Palestinian Authority Chairman Yasser Arafat stated the following on Palestinian television:

> . . . let us commit ourselves before Allah and the Palestinian people that we shall lead the coming

> battle as we have led previous battles.... The whole world stands by us, while they [Israel] are alone.... The Palestinian people is faithful to its oath, the one which we swore upon the first day when the initial shot was fired and the first martyr fell.... We are marching together with the blessing of Allah, my brothers, we are marching together to Jerusalem, Jerusalem, Jerusalem.[4]

Arafat's words only expanded the threat voiced several months earlier by Feisal Husseini, the Palestinian Authority's Minister for Jerusalem Affairs: "Israel is attempting to obstruct peace.... The only option remaining for us will be an alternative option ... war."[5] However, despite the candor, Arafat and Husseini's words do not fully reveal the Arab agenda. To hear this we must listen to their Muslim clerics and scholars, who base their beliefs on the Koran. For example, Sheikh Hamed Bitawi, Chairman of the Palestinian Religious Scholars Association, stated on July 27, 1997, "That which befell the infidel nations will also occur to the State of Israel. We are certain that Allah will destroy the State of Israel either through natural disasters, such as an earthquake, or at the hands of the Muslims, or both."[6] Hearing such statements against any people should provoke us to pray. But in Jerusalem's case, the call for prayer is not merely a matter of spiritual compassion, it is a matter of scriptural command!

Praying for Jerusalem's Future Security

There is also need for Christians to pray for Jerusalem's future security. I asked my good friend Noam Hendren, pastor of the Israeli congregation Keren Yeshua in Tel Aviv, to give his unique perspective on the Christian's obligation to pray for Jerusalem's future. He wrote:

In view of biblical prophecies concerning the sufferings of Jerusalem in the period leading up to the
second coming of Yeshua (Jesus), the injunction to
"pray for the peace of Jerusalem" (Psalm 122:6)
should take on new meaning for every believer.
That call is made "for the sake of my brothers and
friends" (verse 8). In other words, "for the sake of
the Jewish people in the Land," whose fate is bound
tightly to that of the Holy City.

When Jesus considered the coming judgment of
Jerusalem, He did not rejoice in the fulfillment of
God's purposes . . . He wept (Luke 19:41). When the
apostle Paul considered the fate of Israel without
faith in the Messiah, his heart broke (Romans 9:1-5),
he prayed earnestly (Romans 10:1), and he did
everything he could to see some of his brethren
saved (Romans 11:13-14).

When you consider the prophetic truths concerning
Israel and Jerusalem, please do not forget that this
country and this city are inhabited by families with
children, citizens, singles, and young couples who
will suffer terribly as prophecy is fulfilled. Pray that
many might come to know their Messiah before the
"time of Jacob's trouble" begins, and thus be spared
the horrors of that period. Pray for the individual
believers and Messianic congregations throughout
the Land, that we might boldly and fearlessly bring
the message of salvation through Yeshua to our
people while it is yet day. And pray for our leaders,
who sit in Jerusalem, that they would reject the
ongoing attempts to pass laws and use other "legal"
means to restrict or prevent altogether the proclamation of the Hope of Israel; the Prince of Peace,
who alone can bring true peace to Jerusalem.[7]

Praying for peace for those who daily experience conflict and who may soon suffer in war and worse is a necessary part of our prayer for Jerusalem, but there is more. While we pray for peace to preserve from difficulties, we also need to pray for peace as a product of deliverance. Immediately after his command to pray, the psalmist added, "For the sake of the house of the LORD our God I will seek your good" (Psalm 122:9). I believe this is a prayer for the peace that will prevail in the day of restoration. It has in view the rebuilding of the Temple ("the house of the LORD our God") and the Millennial blessings that will come with it. Ultimately, it is a prayer that stretches beyond time to God's final future for the city:

> Behold, I will create new heavens and a new earth. The former things will not be remembered, nor will they come to mind. But be glad and rejoice forever in what I will create, for I will create Jerusalem to be a delight and its people a joy. I will rejoice over Jerusalem and take joy in my people; the sound of weeping and of crying will be heard in it no more (Isaiah 65:17-19 NIV).

In light of this future salvation for Jerusalem and the Jewish people, Christians need to speak to the people of the Messiah about His salvation today.

Proclaiming Jerusalem's Savior

There is a Jewish maxim that says, "Whoever saves one Jewish soul saves the whole world." Our understanding of the role of the Jewish people in prophecy assures us that in at least one sense this will be so. Perhaps the apostle Paul had this in mind when he spoke to Gentiles about proclaiming the salvation they had received; he was careful to call them to speak first to the people from whom that salvation had come: "I am not ashamed of the gospel, for it is the power of God for salvation to everyone who believes, to the Jew *first* and also to the Greek [Gentile]" (Romans 1:16-17). This order recognizes the historic priority of God sending His Son as a Jew to the Jewish people: "You shall call His name Jesus [God's salvation], for it is He who will save *His people* from their sins" (Matthew 1:21), and "For you first [the Jewish nation], God raised up His Servant, and sent Him to bless you by turning every one of you from your wicked ways" (Acts 3:26). If God first brought the Word in this way, it is a way we should follow.

There are several specifics in Romans 1:16-17 that we need to observe in relation to some extreme perspectives of our day. First, it is "the power of God" resident in the message of the gospel that saves—not human persuasion. One extreme position some Gentiles take in their outreach to Jewish people is to try to "become Jewish" by observing the Sabbath, keeping kosher, dressing in teffilin and prayer shawls, studying the Talmud, and worshiping with Jews in the synagogue. All this is done in order to build a bridge to the Jewish community, and while the intentions may be good and sincere, according to Romans 1:16-17, this will not help bring Jewish people any closer to their Messiah's salvation. Only the clear, prayerful, loving, patient, culturally sensitive teaching of the truth to Jewish souls will, by the will of God, bring this to pass.

There's a second extreme that is far worse: the belief that the Jewish people are in a special category with regards to the Abrahamic Covenant and do not need salvation as do the Gentiles. Paul's words in Romans 1:16-17 stand in strong contrast to that view. He was "not ashamed" to preach the gospel *"to the Jews."* In addition, he not only thought it essential to preach to them, but to preach to them *"first."* Jewish people often think our preaching to the Jews is anti-Semitic. But should we do good to all people except the Jews? Or rescue only Gentiles and let the Jews perish? To do this would be the height of anti-Semitism. On the contrary, out of love and obligation we are to go to them before all others.

Finally, he made it clear that salvation is only to those who believe, and that it is the *same* for both Gentiles and Jews. This same point is made by the apostle Peter when, in Acts 15, Paul reported to the Jerusalem Council that Gentiles were receiving salvation in Christ. This apparently raised some questions: How are the Gentiles to be saved? Must they become Jews in order to enjoy the salvation brought by the Jewish Messiah? Peter concluded that was not the case when he responded, "We believe that we [Jews] are saved through the grace of the Lord Jesus, in the same way as they [Gentiles] also are" (Acts 15:11). In other words, Gentiles do not need to become Jewish, nor are Jews as Jews saved already, but both Jews and Gentiles must be "saved through the grace of the Lord Jesus," the Messiah.

One obstacle to the Jewish people coming to Jesus as their Messiah today has been competing religious claims and traditions. Nevertheless, Israeli pastor Noam Hendren believes even these are part of the prophetic plan to bring Israel to repentance and the Messiah:

> As we consider all that is going on in the Land today, and all that the Scriptures say concerning what will take place with the Jewish people in the Land, I believe that the stage is being set for just such an event. There is a desperate search among the Jewish people in the Land of Israel for true meaning. The people are polarized: There are those

who are looking in New Age philosophies and mysticism, in occult ideas, and other religions; there are others who are seeking through rabbinic Judaism and a return to the roots of the rabbis. Many times those roots are being found in Poland and Russia more than in the Land of Israel. Yet [these people] are seeking desperately for something to give Jewish meaning to their lives. As all of these things are coming to pass in our Land, as we anticipate the coming against Israel by nations around the world and the pressure that will come to conform to world opinion and the threat to the ultimate existence of Israel which will result, we can expect that that cry for meaning will become far more focused. If we look in Zechariah 12, the passage which speaks about the nations coming against Israel and the threat to the continued existence of the Jewish people in this Land, we know that . . . at the crisis point, at the point of no return, at that point in which the very existence of the Jewish people is threatened totally in this Land and in the world, God intends to pour out His Spirit upon the Jewish people—a "Spirit of grace and supplication" (Zechariah 12:10) which will cause the Jewish people finally to realize that Jesus was the one who was pierced 2,000 years ago and that He is the only hope of deliverance from the threat which is coming against our people. As Paul on the Damascus Road was confronted with the truth he could no longer deny, so will the people of Israel be confronted with the truth that Jesus is the Messiah. And as the Messiah, He is the only hope for deliverance from the threat coming against our people.[8]

This is what we have been called to proclaim to our Jewish friends today so that Jerusalem may one day enjoy its prophesied blessing: "No longer will violence be heard in your land, nor ruin or destruction within your borders, but you will call your walls *Salvation* and your gates *Praise*" (Isaiah 60:18 NIV, emphasis added).

Remaining Faithful to Jerusalem

That day is coming soon. And until that day, our responsibility is clear: "You will arise and have compassion on Zion, for it is time to show favor to her; the appointed time has come. . . . For the LORD will rebuild Zion and appear in his glory" (Psalm 102:13,16 NIV). No matter what our theological orientation, if we can agree on this, then we can join in the declaration *"Jerusalem is ours!"* It is ours in prophecy, it is ours in prayer. As those who want to be ready for God's reign, let us be faithful to favor it—our hope on earth and our home in heaven.

> O Jerusalem, Jerusalem,
> My prayer for you shall be
> That Messiah long awaited,
> Will come to set you free.
>
> Through the years your gates have seen
> The nations come in power,
> Soon, O soon, Jerusalem,
> Will come your chosen hour.
>
> In that bright day the world shall know,
> What favor God has had,
> For trodden-down Jerusalem,
> The city now made glad.
>
> O Jerusalem, Jerusalem
> May all the earth soon see,
> The blessings that are longed for
> All await for thee.
>
> —Author

JERUSALEM IN HISTORY AND PROPHECY
A Chronology of Jerusalem Past, Present, and Future

Historical periods are indicated by italics in the subheads. Descriptions of events on dates with prophetic significance are indicated in the main text by *italics*.

Jerusalem in History

Jerusalem Past

DATES B.C. (B.C.E.)
Pre-biblical Period (2000–1450)

2000   Jerusalem first mentioned in Egyptian Execration Texts as Urusalim.

1900   Abraham met Mechizedek, king of Salem (Jerusalem) and high priest of God Most High (Genesis 14:18-24).

Biblical Period (1450–400)

1450   Joshua conquered Canaan and defeated Amorite king (Adoni-zedek) of Jerusalem at Gibeon (Joshua 10; 12:10), but Jerusalem remained a hostile enclave.

1425   Jerusalem taken by tribe of Judah who shared it with Jebusites (Judges 1:8,21).

347

996   *King David captured Jerusalem from Jebusites and makes it the capital of Israel (2 Samuel 5:6-10) according to Moses' prediction (Exodus 15:17).*

First Temple Period (960–586)

967   *King Solomon began building the First Temple in Jerusalem (1 Kings 5–6; 2 Chronicles 2–4) according to the prophets Moses' and Samuel's predictions (Deuteronomy 2:11; 2 Samuel 7:13).*

930   The 10 northern tribes rebelled against Rehoboam king of Jerusalem and kingdom divided, but Jerusalem remained capital of Judah and only legitimate central Sanctuary (1 Kings 12:16-27).

605   Daniel and noble families of Jerusalem deported to Babylon by Nebuchadnezzar, king of Babylon (Daniel 1:1-3).

597   Jehoiachin, king of Jerusalem, and Ezekiel the prophet exiled to Babylon (2 Kings 24:10-16; Ezekiel 1:1; 3:15,24).

586   *The city of Jerusalem destroyed by Nebuchadnezzar and its Temple burned by Nebuzaradan, captain of the Babylonian army (2 Kings 25:1-10; 2 Chronicles 36:17-21), fulfilling the prophets' predictions of divine punishment through the Babylonians (see, for example, Isaiah 39:5-7).*

Persian Period (539–332)

538   *Daniel prayed concerning Jerusalem's restoration and received prophecy of the seventy weeks concerning the Messiah's death in Jerusalem, the destruction of the Second Temple, and its future rebuilding and desecration by Antichrist (Daniel 9:1-27).*

538   Cyrus, king of Persia, issued edict releasing Judean exiles to return to Jerusalem and rebuild city and Temple (2 Chronicles 36:22-23; Ezra 1:1-11).

Second Temple Period (515 B.C.–A.D. 70)

515   Zerubbabel dedicated Second Temple in Jerusalem on March 12 (Ezra 6:16-18).

445   Nehemiah returned to Jerusalem from Persia to re-build the walls of the city (Nehemiah 1–7:4).

332   *Alexander the Great rules, as predicted by Daniel (Daniel 11:3-4),* and may have (according to legend) visited Jerusalem and been welcomed by high priest.

Hellenistic/Hasmonean Period (320–152)

301   *Ptolemy I (a general and the historian of Alexander the Great) captured Jerusalem and began rule under the Ptolemaic dynasty as predicted by Daniel (Daniel 11:4,20).*

167   *The Seleucid ruler Antiochus IV Epiphanes desecrated the Temple with statue of Zeus Olympias and pagan sacrifices as Daniel prophesied (Daniel 11:21-35).*

164   Hasmonean revolt, led by Judas Maccabeus, liber-ated Jerusalem and reconsecrated the Temple. Event is commemorated by Feast of Dedication or *Hanuk-kah* (John 10:22).

Roman Period (68 B.C.–A.D. 324)

63   The Roman general Pompey besieged Jerusalem, en-tered the Temple, and placed the city under Roman rule.

37   Herod I (the Great), with Roman Legions, captured Jerusalem from Hasmonean-Partian alliance that took city in 40 B.C. and was appointed new Judean king (although of Idumean [Edomite] descent).

20   King Herod began reconstruction of Jerusalem Temple to win favor of Jewish citizenry and impress Rome. The building continued throughout the earthly life of Jesus (John 2:20) and was completed only a few years before the Temple's destruction in

A.D. 70, making the total time of reconstruction about 86 years.

6   *Birth of Jesus the Messiah in Bethlehem (Matthew 1:18–2:1; Luke 2:1-20) in fulfillment of prophecy (Isaiah 7:14; Micah 5:2).* He is dedicated in the Jerusalem Temple (Luke 2:21-38).

4   The wise men (Greek: *magoi*) arrived in Jerusalem looking for newborn Messiah (Matthew 2:1-12). Herod I died, was buried at the Herodium, and succeeded by his son Archeleaus (who ruled until A.D. 6).

DATES A.D. (C.E.)

7   Jesus came to Jerusalem for His bar-mitzvah, remained in Temple for three days, and discussed Torah with the Jewish scribes (Luke 2:39-51).

27   Satan took Jesus to pinnacle of Temple in Jerusalem during testing at the commencement of His ministry (Matthew 4:5; Luke 4:9). *Jesus drove money changers from outer courts of Temple (John 2:13-17), fulfilling prophecy of Messiah's zeal for the Temple (Psalm 69:9).*

30   *Jesus entered Eastern Gate on donkey in fulfillment of prophecy (Zechariah 9:9; Matthew 21:1-11; Luke 19:37-44), prophesies destruction of Jerusalem and Temple (Matthew 24:1-2; Mark 13:1-2; Luke 21:6, 20-24), was crucified under Roman and Jewish law (Deuteronomy 21:22; Galatians 3:10-14) in fulfillment of prophecy (Isaiah 53; Psalm 22) was buried, but rose from the dead in fulfillment of prophecy (Psalm 16:8-11; Acts 2:24-32), and returned to heaven to await day of Israel's repentance and Jerusalem's restoration (Matthew 23:28-39; Acts 1:6-11; Romans 11:25-27).*

56   Paul (Saul) went to Jerusalem Temple to complete Nazirite vow and was wrongly accused and arrested (Acts 21:26-28).

70   *The Roman Tenth Legion under the command of Titus (son of the Roman emperor Vespasian) destroys the city and completely burns and tears down the stones of the Temple, fulfilling the prediction of Jesus.*

132   The Jewish revolt led by Jewish commander (and proclaimed messiah) Bar-Kokhba drove Roman troops of emperor Hadrian from Jerusalem and restored Jewish rule for a period of three years.

Byzantine Period (324–638)

326   Queen Helena, mother of the Roman emperor Constantine the Great (who made Christianity the new state religion), traveled to Jerusalem to identify the holy places connected with Jesus.

335   Dedication of the Church of the Holy Sepulcher, built by order of the emperor Constantine, over the sites of Jesus' crucifixion, burial, and resurrection.

363   Byzantine Roman emperor Julian (the Apostate) permitted Jews to return to Jerusalem and rebuild the Temple, but effort ended when explosion during preparation for construction was taken as a sign of God's condemnation of the project.

565   Mosaic map of the Holy Land, with Jerusalem as most detailed scene at its center, was built in the city of Madaba (in present-day Jordan). Discovered in 1884, it is the oldest known map of Byzantine Jerusalem.

614   The Persians, under Khursau II, captured Jerusalem with the help of Jewish fighters from Galilee. Jews again allowed to settle in the city. Persian rule lasted only until A.D. 629 when emperor Heraclius restored Byzantine rule.

Early Muslim Period (638–1099)

638   Muslim Caliph Omar Ibn al-Khatab captured Jerusalem (with Jewish help) six years after the death of the Islamic prophet Muhammad and two years after the defeat of the Byzantines at the battle of Yarmuk.

691   The Muslim Caliph Abd-al-Malik completed wooden structure of present-day Dome of the Rock on the site of the Jewish Temple (on the Temple Mount).

701   The Muslim Caliph al-Walid completed the Al-Aksa
              Mosque on the site of a Byzantine church (on southern
              portion of Temple Mount).

Crusader Period (1099–1187)

1099   Jerusalem is captured by Crusader army under com-
              mand of Godfrey de Bouillon, its Jewish and Muslim
              inhabitants were slaughtered, and his brother Bald-
              win was crowned King of Jerusalem (in Bethlehem in
              1011).

Ayyubid Period (1187–1260)

1187   The Muslim Turkish emperor Saladin defeated the
              Crusaders at the battle at the Horns of Hittin (in Gali-
              lee); permitted Jews and Muslims to return to Jerusa-
              lem.

1229   The Crusaders briefly regain control of Jerusalem
              through a ten-year treaty between the Emperor
              Frederick II of Germany and Sicily and the Egyptian
              Sultan al-Kamil.

Mamluk Period (1260–1516)

1260   The Mamluks (descendants of Turkish and Cauca-
              sians) captured Jerusalem.

1275   The famed explorer Marco Polo, en route to China,
              made a stop in Jerusalem.

Ottoman Period (1516–1917)

1516   The Sultan Selim I of Turkey captured Jerusalem
              and placed it under the rule of the Ottoman empire.

1535   The Ottoman Sultan Suleiman I (the Magnificent)
              began to rebuild the walls of Jerusalem and desig-
              nated the Western Wall as the official place for Jewish
              worship.

1541   *The Golden Gate is sealed to prevent Jesus (or the
              expected Jewish Messiah), who, according to tradition*

(based on prophecy in Ezekiel 44:2-3), is to enter the gate and rule Jerusalem.

1667 The false messiah Shabbetai Zvi arrived in Jerusalem and was enthusiastically embraced, but later excommunicated, by its Jewish community.

1799 The French emperor Napoleon Bonaparte invaded Palestine, announced that he would restore Jerusalem to the Jews, but was defeated at Acre (on the northern Mediterranean coast).

1865 The British Palestine Exploration Fund launched first archaeological surveys of underground Jerusalem, especially the vaulted passageways and ancient cisterns beneath the Temple Mount. Jewish majority in the city for the first time in 1,800 years.

1883 British General Gordon, hero of Khartoum, identified hill resembling skull at Jeremiah's Grotto in eastern Jerusalem as site of the crucifixion of Jesus.

1900 The archaeological research facility known formerly as the American School of Oriental Research (now the Albright Institute, named after William Foxwell Albright, who directed it from 1920–29) was founded in eastern Jerusalem.

British Mandate Period (1917–1948)

1917 The British General Sir Edmund Allenby defeated Turks and received Jerusalem's surrender; walked into city through Jaffa Gate, rather than rode in as conqueror, because he wanted to show respect to it as the City of the Great King. Jewish Legion participated in liberating Galilee, Samaria, and Transjordan. Balfour Declaration issued in Britain called for establishment of homeland in Palestine for the Jews.

1921 British mandate administration appoints Haj Amin al-Husseini as Grand Mufti in Jerusalem.

1925 The Hebrew University opened on Mount Scopus in Jerusalem with inauguration by Lord Balfour.

1936   Arab Higher Committee established under Jerusalem Mufti, general strike called, and Arab riot caused high death toll among Jews and moderate Arabs (killed by Arab extremists).

1939   Britain issued infamous White Paper, announced end to plan for a Jewish national home in Palestine by restricting Jewish immigration to Palestine. World War II began and Jerusalem became military headquarters of British.

1941   The Grand Mufti Haj Amin al-Husseini relocated to Berlin, met with German Chancellor Adolf Hitler and offered to assist in his campaign to exterminate world Jewry by creating a "fascist" Arab state.

1947   The United Nations General Assembly issued a partition plan for Palestine with Jerusalem as an international city. The Arab States rejected this plan and the Jews in Jerusalem came under combined Jordanian Arab, Egyptian, and British siege with shelling for three months, ended with opening of "Burma Road" bypass.

Jerusalem Present

Israeli Period (1948–Present)

1948   *The period of British mandate ended and the first Jewish Prime Minister, David Ben-Gurion, declared the independent Jewish State of Israel with Jerusalem as its capital. This event is proclaimed by Ben-Gurion as the beginning of the fulfillment of the prophetic redemption of the nation.*

1948   Arab forces invaded Israel in an attempt to prevent the establishment of a Jewish State, announcing a policy of mass-annihilation toward the Jewish population ("drive Israel into the sea").

1949   After the war (War of Independence), which was won by Israel, Jerusalem was divided. West Jerusalem was retained by the Israelis, but East Jerusalem with the Old City and Temple Mount remained under Jordanian control. Despite U.N. supervision, Jordanians deny Jews access to the Western Wall, the Hebrew University, and Hadassah Hospital on Mount Scopus, all now within their territory.

1951   King Abdullah of Jordan (grandfather of King Hussein) was assassinated on the Temple Mount by Arab extremists.

1953   The national Holocaust memorial museum, Yad Vashem, was established on Jerusalem's Memorial Hill as a research and document center for the six million victims and families of the Nazi Holocaust.

1964   First visit by a Roman Catholic Pope (Pope Paul IV) to East Jerusalem since the establishment of the State of Israel.

1965   Israel Museum (national museum) founded in Jerusalem with the Shrine of the Book to house the Dead Sea Scrolls in Israel's possession. Teddy Kollek was elected Mayor of Jerusalem.

1967   *During the Six-Day War, Jordanian troops attacked West Jerusalem and in battle, East Jerusalem fell into Israeli control on June 7. The divided city was reunited, the flag of Israel hoisted (temporarily) atop the Dome of the Rock, and Mayor Teddy Kollek ordered Arab houses removed to expand Western Wall plaza for thousands of Jews returning to worship at the Western Wall for the first time in two decades. This marked the first return of Jewish sovereignty to united Jerusalem since the destruction of the Temple 2,000 years previous. This event prepares Jerusalem for the fulfillment of future prophecies.*

1969   Australian Christian cult member Dennis Ronan set fire to the Al-Aksa Mosque on the Temple Mount; Muslim officials claimed the Israeli government was trying to destroy the site in order to rebuild the Jerusalem Temple.

1977   Egyptian president Anwar Sadat came to Jerusalem and met with Israeli Prime Minister Menachem Begin and addressed the Israeli Knesset. His message called for the establishment of a Palestinian State with Jerusalem under Muslim control.

1980   The Israeli Knesset by special law re-affirmed that united Jerusalem is the capital of Israel by officially annexing East Jerusalem; foreign embassies moved to Tel Aviv in protest.

1987   Palestinian Intifada ("uprising") began under orders of Yasser Arafat, Chairman of the PLO (in Tunisia) with general strikes in the Old City and East Jerusalem and riots and bombings in Jewish sectors of the city. PLO was banned in the U.S. and placed on top-ten terrorist organizations.

1989   The Temple Institute was founded in the Jewish Quarter of Jerusalem by Rabbi Yisrael Ariel to research and prepare items for the Third Temple. The Temple Mount and Land of Israel Faithful Movement, directed by Gershon Salomon, attempted to lay cornerstone for the Third Temple, but the group was turned away by police.

1990   Arabs contended that followers of the Temple Mount Faithful were attempting to "take over" the Temple Mount and rioted at the Western Wall and on the Temple Mount with 18 casualties. Saddam Hussein of Iraq sent Scud missiles against Israel in attempt to launch a *jihad* and "liberate" Jerusalem and Israel for the Palestinians. The Gulf War with Saddam Hussein ended with an American-led international coalition victory and sanctions against Iraq.

1991   Middle East Peace Conference convened in Madrid, Spain, and ended with Syrian Foreign Minister Farouk Al-Shara declaring that all of East Jerusalem must be returned to the Arabs and become the capital of a Palestinian State.

1993   On September 13 the Israeli-PLO accord was signed in Washington, D.C., by PLO Chairman Yasser Arafat and Israeli Prime Minister Yitzhak Rabin. The Declaration of Principles agreed to postpone the resolution of the status of Jerusalem until the final phase of the negotiation talks. On the same day, however, Arafat declared that the Palestinian flag would fly over the walls of Jerusalem as the capital of a Palestinian State.

1994   The United States brokered a peace treaty between Jordan and Israel, signed by Jordan's King Hussein and Israel's Prime Minister Yitzhak Rabin. The treaty made Jordan the protector of the Muslim holy sites in Jerusalem and Jordan installed their own Mufti over the sites.

1995   King Hussein began restoration of the Dome of the Rock, primarily replacing the aluminumized gold dome with a copper-nickel alloy covered with pure gold.

1996   Jerusalem celebrated its 3,000[th] anniversary as the capital of Israel with celebrations throughout the city. Many countries worldwide joined the Arab boycott against the celebrations, claiming that Israel was trying to "create a history" in the Palestinian city.

1996   Israeli Prime Minister Yitzhak Rabin was assassinated in Tel Aviv by an Israeli extremist because of his giving away much of the biblical territories of Judea and Samaria and the fear he would re-divide Jerusalem. He had a state funeral on Jerusalem's Mount Herzl attended by PLO Chairman Yasser Arafat, Jordan's King Hussein, Egyptian president Hosni Mubarak, and American President Bill Clinton.

1997   Likud candidate Benjamin Netanyahu is elected Israeli Prime Minister by a large Jewish majority largely because he vowed to defend united Jerusalem as Israel's capital in any final status negotiations.

1997   Israeli Orthodox Jew Yehuda Etzion is arrested for attempting to pray on the Temple Mount; appealed to Supreme Court, which upheld his right (and Jewish right) of access to the Temple Mount for worship. However, attempts by his organization Chal ve-Kaiyam continued to be rebuffed by police fearing Arab riots.

1998   A slowdown in the peace process caused Yasser Arafat to openly embrace Hamas terrorists and Saddam Hussein and pledge a renewal of the Intifada and war if Jerusalem did not become the capital of a new Palestinian state to be declared on May 4, 1999. (That's the date chosen as of the time of this writing.) Jerusalem celebrated Independence Day on April 29-30 as part of Israel's fiftieth anniversary celebrations. The celebrations were protested worldwide by Arab ads in newspapers condemning the event.

Jerusalem in Prophecy

The order of events here are subject to varying placement based on legitimate interpretations of the biblical texts and should not be taken as my final judgment.

Jerusalem Future

TRIBULATION PERIOD (7 YEARS)
First Half of the Tribulation (3½ years)

First Quarter of First Half   The Antichrist makes a covenant with Israel, bringing peace to Jerusalem and Israel (Daniel 9:27; Isaiah 28:14-15).

The Jewish Temple is rebuilt in Jerusalem, perhaps as a part of the provisions of the covenant made with the Antichrist (Daniel 9:27; Revelation 11:1).

The seal judgments are opened, bringing judgment on the world, although no specific effects are mentioned for Jerusalem (Revelation 6:1-17; 8:1-2).

Between the seventh and eighth seals God brings forth 144,000 "bond-servants of God" for worldwide revival (Revelation 7).

Second Quarter of First Half

The trumpet judgments occur, bringing more destruction on the earth (Revelation 9:1-21; 11:15-19). During these judgments it may be that Israel and Jerusalem become fearful and alarmed (Revelation 9:13-21; see also Joel 1:15–2:11).

Midpoint of the Tribulation

The Antichrist breaks his covenant with Israel by desecrating the Jerusalem Temple with the Abomination of Desolation and stopping the sacrificial system (Matthew 24:15; Mark 13:14; 2 Thessalonians 2:4).

The Antichrist will break his covenant with the Jews and invade Israel (Daniel 11:40-45; Isaiah 28:14-22). During that time the Abomination of Desolation takes place in Jerusalem (Daniel 9:27; 12:11; Matthew 24:15-16; 2 Thessalonians 2:3-4,8-12; Revelation 13:11-15) and the Antichrist forces his godless worship on Jerusalem and the world (Daniel 11:36-39; Revelation 13:1-18).

Jews flee Jerusalem after the Antichrist ends his pseudopeace, knowing that the Abomination of Desolation in the Temple signals the escalation of the Tribulation judgments (Matthew 25:16-22; Mark 13:14-20).

The two witnesses serve the "Lord of the earth" (Revelation 11:4-14) for the last half of the Tribulation. Their appearance may be in response to the Antichrist's desecration of the Temple and placing it under his control (Revelation 11:1-2). It may also come as a means of thwarting the Antichrist's persecution of the Jews.

Second Half of the Tribulation (3½ years)

First Quarter of Second Half

The bowl judgments begin the second half of the Tribulation (Revelation 16).

War breaks out and apparently the Antichrist is killed during this worldwide conflict (Daniel 11:40-45; Revelation 13:3).

Satan is cast down from heaven and makes war against the woman, who is Israel (Revelation 12:7-17). Jerusalem's inhabitants will experience his wrath. The Antichrist, empowered by Satan, is resuscitated and rises to worldwide dominance and worship (Revelation 13:2-3).

The Antichrist blasphemes God (Revelation 13:4-10) and a false prophet arises, performing false miracles to encourage the false worship of the Antichrist (Revelation 13:11-15).

Second Quarter of Second Half During the last quarter of the Tribulation, Jerusalem and all Israel will greatly suffer (Isaiah 3:1–4:1; 40:1-2; Jeremiah 30:4-7).

The Antichrist will subdue three kings and seven others will submit to him (Daniel 7:24; Revelation 17:12-13,17).

Campaign of Armageddon begins with sixth bowl judgment and Antichrist assembling his allies together at Armageddon (Revelation 16:12-16).

The enemies of Antichrist destroy his commercial center of Babylon. Many will flee to Jerusalem to announce Babylon's fall (Revelation 17:1-13,18; 18:1-24; see also Jeremiah 50:28).

The Antichrist will move against Jerusalem in a satanic desire to destroy the Jews (Zechariah 12:1-3; 14:1). Briefly, Jewish forces will control the city (Zechariah 12:4-9; Micah 4:11–5:1), possibly with the help of the two witnesses. Ultimately, half the city will be destroyed (Zechariah 14:2).

During this battle the Antichrist kills the two witnesses and leaves their bodies on display in the streets of Jerusalem (Revelation 11:7-10).

The two witnesses are resurrected in the streets of Jerusalem and visibly taken up to heaven (Revelation 11:11-12). Their resurrection makes that of the Antichrist less unique and is superior because it involves two, rather than one, and involves ascension. It is also accompanied by an earthquake, which rocks Jerusalem, killing 7,000 people and terrifying all (Revelation 11:13). Against all of this the Antichrist is powerless, and their ascension, along with the terrible conditions brought about by the war, may stimulate Jewish national repentance.

The remnant of Jews in the city will receive the spirit of grace and supplication, which will cause them to cry out for Messiah to deliver them (Zechariah 12:10–13:1; Joel 2:28-32).

Christ's second coming is first to Bozrah, where the Jews have fled and also called out in repentance (Isaiah 34:1-7; 63:1-6; Habakkuk 3:3), where He will confront Antichrist forces.

In desperation, the Antichrist will move his forces to Jerusalem for a final assault on the city to destroy it, but Christ will destroy the Antichrist's forces in the Kidron Valley (Isaiah 14:3-21; Zechariah 12:7; 14:12-15; Joel 3:12-13; Revelation 14:14-20).

After the battle, Christ ascends the Mount of Olives on the east of Jerusalem in a victory procession (Zechariah 14:3-4).

A great earthquake will split Jerusalem into three parts (Zechariah 14:4-5; Revelation 16:18-19; see also Joel 3:14-17), and a blackout will also occur at this time (Joel 3:14-17; Matthew 24:29).

TRANSITION BETWEEN TRIBULATION AND MILLENNIUM (75 DAYS)

The interval between the end of the Tribulation and beginning of the kingdom age (Daniel 12:11-12) will include the following events: the Antichrist will be removed (Revelation 19:20), the Abomination of Desolation will be removed (Daniel 12:11-12), the

Gentiles will be judged (Joel 3:1; Matthew 25:31-46), the Old Testament and Tribulation saints will be resurrected (Isaiah 26:19; Daniel 2:2; Revelation 20:4).

Millennial Kingdom Period (1,000 years)

According to some scholars, the new heavens and new earth will be renovations of the existing heavens and earth and will take place at the beginning of the Millennium.

The topography of Jerusalem will be transformed and rise above its present height (Zechariah 14:9-10; see also Isaiah 2:2-4). It will be a place of great beauty (Ezekiel 17:22-24).

Jerusalem and Israel will be the home of regathered Jews (Deuteronomy 29:1–30:20) and a place of unparalleled quietness and security (Isaiah 30:20-24).

In the Messianic kingdom Jerusalem will be the throne of God (Psalm 48:1-3; Jeremiah 3:17) and the capital city of King Messiah.

The Millennial Temple will be built by Christ (Ezekiel 40:5–43:27; Zechariah 6:12-15) and a river will flow east and west from beneath the altar of the Temple (Ezekiel 47:1-12).

The Shekinah glory will return to the Millennial Temple (Ezekiel 43:1-7) and the entire city will be a place of holiness, righteousness, and justice (Isaiah 1:26-27; 2:2-4; 65:17-25; Zechariah 14:20-21; Micah 4:1-5).

Jerusalem will be the center for world peace (Isaiah 2:2-4) and law (Psalm 147:15,19-20; Isaiah 2:3) and especially the center for universal worship (Isaiah 27:13; 56:6-8; 66:20; Ezekiel 20:40-41; Micah 4:1-2), and, as evidence of a new order, for Gentile worship (Zechariah 8:20-23; 14:14-16).

According to many scholars, the New Jerusalem may descend and be suspended above the earthly Jerusalem, providing a heavenly illumination in which the nations will walk when they bring their tribute to the city (Revelation 21:23-24).

The Eternal State

The Great White Throne judgment ushers in the eternal state (Revelation 21:1-2). According to some scholars, the new heavens and new earth will be a complete recreation at the beginning of the eternal state.

The New Jerusalem, as part of the creation of the new heavens and new earth, appears at the beginning of eternity, coming down from the new heavens (Revelation 21:2-3).

GLOSSARY

Abomination of Desolation (Hebrew: *hashiqutz meshomem*, "the abomination that makes desolate"): The expression used to describe the act of setting up an idolatrous image in the Holy Place, thus defiling or "making desolate" the Temple, and ending the offering of all sacrifices. This was done in the past by Antiochus Epiphanes (Daniel 11:31), whose act reflects the future defilement by the Antichrist (Daniel 9:27). Both Daniel and Jesus indicated that the future act done by the Antichrist would signal the start of the Great Tribulation (Daniel 12:11; Matthew 24:15; Mark 13:14).

Abrahamic Covenant: The covenant made by God with Abraham that unconditionally promised his descendants a land (the Land of Israel), a seed (the Jewish people), and a blessing (to the nations), Genesis 12:1-3; see restatements in Genesis 13:14-17; 15:1-7. Its boundaries were given as from the "river of Egypt" (wadi el-Arish) to the river Euphrates (Genesis 15:18).

'Acharit ha-yamim (Hebrew, "end of the days"): The Hebrew term used eschatologically to designate that period of the end-time described by the biblical prophets. It is inclusive of *Yom YHWH* ("the Day of the Lord"), in which God's judgment falls upon Israel's adversaries, as well as *Yemot ha-Mashiach* ("the days of Messiah"), the period preceding the judgment. It is followed by *'olam ha-ba* ("the world to come"), the eschatological future world.

Age of Redemption (Hebrew: *ge'ullah*): In later Judaism it refers to the time of the arrival of the Davidic Messiah, in which the Land and people of Israel are restored, salvation enjoyed, and oppression and suffering ended with the establishment on earth of the kingdom of God in the end of days. In Zionism it refers to the physical buying back of the land of Israel for Jewish ownership.

Aggadah, adj. aggadic: The portion of rabbinic literature and tradition that consists of stories about biblical and rabbinic figures, ethical teachings, or interpretations of Scripture that teach the principles of Jewish thought and theology.

Aliyah (Hebrew, "to go up, ascend"): The Jewish expression used for the act of returning or making immigration to the Land of Israel, the first wave of which began in the early 1880s.

Amillennialism (Latin, "no millennium"): The theological view that Christ and His saints will *not* reign for 1,000 years in connection with His final return.

Amoraim, adj. Amoraic: The teachers of the Talmud from A.D. 200–500 whose main activity was interpreting the Mishnah and tannaitic (earlier rabbinic) traditions.

Anti-Semitism: The term applied to the hostile attitude of non-Jews toward Jews, individually and collectively. The consequences of this viewpoint have ranged from restrictive laws against Jews and the social isolation of Jewish groups to *pogroms* and attempted genocide in the Nazi Holocaust. *Christian* anti-Semitism has historically resulted from an adoption of *Replacement Theology.*

Apocalyptic: Pertaining to a genre of literature that divulges otherwise unknown secrets about the nature of God and the heavens and the end of days. Especially prominent is the concept of divine intervention and the dualistic idea of a cosmic/earthly conflict between evil angels, their agents and God, His Messiah and holy angels. The term is also used to describe the imminent Messianism that is often part of these texts.

Apocrypha: Pseudobiblical books composed by Jewish authors in the Second Temple period which were not included in the Hebrew Bible. Most of these works survive only in translation; some are included in the Septuagint and others were preserved by various Christian sects.

Apocalyptic Literature: Prophetic writings concerning the end of the world and/or God's final judgment, both in and outside the canon of Scripture. In particular it has reference to that body of Jewish prophetic writing that developed between the sixth century B.C. and the first century A.D.

'Aksa (Arabic, "the farther"): Term used for the farther mosque in the *Koran* (Surah 17). It probably originally indicated a mosque located in the northern corner of Mecca, but the tradition was later moved to Jerusalem, hence the *Al-Aksa Mosque.*

Armageddon (Hebrew: *har-Megiddo,* "mount of Megiddo"): The place to which the armies of the world are gathered together for one of the central battles at the end of the Tribulation period (Revelation 16:16). In popular usage it is a term used to speak of the end of the world.

Ashkenazi (Yiddish pl. *Ashkenazim*): Those Jews and their descendants who came from Germany or parts of Western, Central, or Eastern Europe as contrasted with *Sephardi[m]* (Jews from Spain or Portugal).

Atara Leyoshna (Hebrew, "crown to its original [form]"): The name of an activist organization in the Temple Movement, which seeks to restore Jewish life to its former state; i.e., biblical Judaism with complete Jewish sovereignty and a rebuilt Temple. It is involved primarily with Jewish settlement in the Muslim Quarter.

Ateret Cohanim (Hebrew, "crown of the priests"): The name of an activist organization in the Temple Movement that maintains a *yeshiva* for the training of priests for future Temple service. It is affiliated with *Atara Leyoshna* in settlement activities.

Babylonian Exile: The deportation of the Jewish people from Judea during three periods of invasion (605–586 B.C.). Daniel the prophet was taken in the first deportation and Ezekiel the prophet in the last. Jeremiah the prophet had prophesied that the exile would continue for 70 years (Jeremiah 25:11-13; Daniel 9:2; see also Jeremiah 27:19-22; Isaiah 52:11-12), after which the Jews would be allowed to return. The exile was ended as predicted by the Medo-Persian conquest of Babylon in 539 B.C., and 50,000 Judeans returned to Jerusalem under the edict of the Persian emperor Cyrus (2 Chronicles 36:22-23; Ezra 1:1-11).

Bar Kokhba: Literally "Son of the Star," it is the designation of Simeon bar Kosiba, who led the second Jewish revolt against Rome in A.D. 132–135.

The discovery of the Bar-Kokhba letters among the Scrolls at Wadi Muraba'at revealed his real name for the first time as Bar Kosiba.

Bar mitzvah (Hebrew, "son of the covenant"): The ceremony that marks the initiation of a Jewish boy (at the age of 13) into the Jewish religious community.

Brit milah (Hebrew, "covenant of circumcision"): The act of removing the foreskin, usually on the eighth day after birth, in fulfillment of the provision of the Abrahamic Covenant (Genesis 17:10-14).

Byzantine: The period of Roman Christian rule in Jerusalem (A.D. 313–638) during which Christianity was made the official religion of the Roman Empire, and the center of imperial power was moved to Byzantium. The Byzantine Period is divided into the early period (313–491), the great Christian architectural period, and the late period (491–638), which saw a temporary conquest by the Persians and ended with the Islamic invasion under *Caliph* Omar Ibn el-Khattab.

Caliph (Arabic, "succeed"): The title of an official successor to Muhammad. Wherever a *Caliph* prayed, a mosque had to be built by his followers on the now-hallowed spot.

Canaanites (from Hurrian, "belonging to the land of red-purple"): The original inhabitants of the land of Canaan (the ancient name of the Land of Israel west of the Jordan—Numbers 34:3-12), which include a lengthy list of various nationalities (Genesis 10:6; 15:8).

Chabad: The initials of the three Hebrew words *chokmah* ("wisdom"), *binah* ("understanding"), *da'at* ("knowledge"), which are used as the name of the Hasidic Movement founded in White Russia by Shneur Zalman of Lyady. *Chabad Lubavitch* is a specific organization of Chabad, headquartered in Brooklyn, New York, whose spiritual leader is Rabbi Menachem M. Schneerson.

Chasidism/Chasidic (Hebrew, "righteous, pious"): A religious movement founded by Israel ben Eliezer Ba'al Shem Tov in the first half of the eighteenth century. Originally it was a religious revivalist movement of popular mysticism that began in West Germany in the Middle Ages.

Chronology (Greek, "study of time"): A study of the time sequence of important events. A biblical chronology is an attempt to order the various dates preserved in Scripture to arrive at a complete list of events without gaps in time.

Cohen (Hebrew, "priest," pl. *Cohanim*): An Israelite descendant of the family of Aaron, which was the priestly line (Exodus 28:1,41). Because this family belonged to the tribe of Levi, they are referred to as the Levitical priesthood. Their functions were ritualistic in nature and revolved around service in the Temple during Temple times.

Constantinople: The capital of the Byzantine (Christian) Empire, named after its Roman conqueror, the emperor Constantine I (c. A.D. 324), and located on the European shore at the southern end of the narrow straits of the Bosporus that connect the Black Sea with the Sea of Mamara (present-day Istanbul, Turkey). Because legend attributes its founding to a Megarian captain by the name of Byzas (c. 667 B.C.), it was later called Byzantium.

Crusaders: Medieval armies comprised of western European "Christians" who waged holy wars at the order of the papacy to recapture the Church of the Holy Sepulcher from the Muslims. During the First Crusades the Crusaders sought to avenge the blood of Jesus on the Jews and began an extermination of Jewish communities, and killed all the Jews of Jerusalem when they took the city in A.D. 1099.

Davidic Covenant: A further guarantee of the "seed" provision of the Abrahamic Covenant, which promised to David as king a succession of heirs on the Judean throne (2 Samuel 7:12-14; 22:51). This covenant will be fulfilled by Jesus as Messiah, a "son of David" (Matthew 1:1) during His Millennial reign in Jerusalem (Psalm 2; 22; 110; Isaiah 9:6-7; see also Acts 2:24-36).

Dead Sea Scrolls: A collection of some 1,100 manuscript documents written on either parchment or papyrus and discovered in caves in the Dead Sea region. The documents contain copies of all of the books of the Old Testament except the book of Esther, largely eschatologically oriented commentaries on biblical books, extrabiblical apocryphal and pseudepigraphical works, sectarian writings, and additional works of Jewish concern. They are believed to have been written by an apocalyptic

Jewish sect known as the Essenes that inhabited the community at Qumran, a plateau area on the shores of the Dead Sea surrounded by high limestone cliffs with caves. The scrolls are dated from around 250 B.C. to A.D. 68, the date of the Roman invasion of the Qumran community and its abandonment by the Essenes.

Diaspora: Greek for "dispersion," referring to the Jewish population outside the Land of Israel. During the time the Dead Sea scrolls were being written, the Diaspora communities were in Babylon and Egypt.

Dispensationalism: The view of biblical history that maintains one plan of salvation in which God reveals Himself to man and deals with man in different ways in each successive period of their relationship or economy (*dispensation*) of time.

Divine Presence: (See *Shekinah.*)

East Jerusalem: The term used by most non-Jewish media and sources for the eastern section of the city which, since 1967, has continued to be inhabited by an Arab population. It also includes within the Old City the Temple Mount and the Church of the Holy Sepulcher. Jews lived alongside Arabs in this section before 1948 and built the Hebrew University and Hadassah Hospital on Mount Scopus. The division of Jerusalem after the War of Independence in 1948 left East Jerusalem and the Old City in Jordanian control. The Jordanians barred Jews from access to the Western Wall and destroyed the Jewish synagogues. Israel captured the area in the Six-Day War of 1967 and officially annexed it and united it with the rest of the city in 1980 as Israel's capital.

Eastern Gate: The gate of Second Temple times that served as the eastern entrance into the Temple. The original name of this gate during that period was the *Shushan Gate*, which probably exists today beneath the present sealed double gate called the *Golden Gate.* The term *golden* was mistakenly applied to this gate because the reference in Acts 3:2, to another inner Temple gate, used the Greek word *horaia* ("beautiful"), which was misunderstood as *aurea* ("golden"). It is thought that this Eastern Gate might also be the *Double Gate* mentioned in the Copper Scroll, in which are hidden the red heifer urn and a scroll describing its ceremony.

End of Days/End Time (Hebrew: *qetz ha-yammim*): A biblical term that Jewish and Christian tradition have understood to refer to the eschatological Messianic era. It is inclusive of both *Yom YHWH* ("the Day of the Lord"), in which God's judgment falls upon Israel's adversaries, as well as *Yemot ha-Mashiach* ("the days of Messiah"), the period preceding the judgment. It is followed by *'olam ha-ba* ("the world to come"), the eschatological future world.

Era of Redemption: (See *Age of Redemption*.)

'Eretz Israel (Hebrew, "Land of Israel"): The Hebrew term used by Jews to designate the biblical Promised Land, the historical homeland of the Jewish people.

es-Sakhra: (see *Sakhra*.)

Eschatology (Greek, "study of last things"): The study of things relating to the end of the world, the final judgment, and the life and world to come.

Eternal State: The condition that will prevail after the Millennium in which a new heavens and a new earth will exist and the glorified saints of God (Old Testament, church, Tribulational, and Millennial) will enjoy fellowship with and service for the Lord in the New Jerusalem.

Eusebius: A fourth-century A.D. bishop of Caesarea who was the leading church historian and apologist of his day. His works are notably anti-Semitic and advanced the Replacement Theology position of the Roman Church.

'Even Shtiyah (Hebrew, "Foundation Stone"): The stone, which according to ancient Jewish sources existed within the Holy of Holies in the Temple, and upon which the Ark of the Covenant rested in First Temple times. According to tradition this stone is identified with the rock inside the Muslim Dome of the Rock.

Exegesis, adj. exegetical: Used in this book primarily to refer to interpretation of the Bible.

Falasha: Ethiopian Jews who claim descent from Israel through Menelik I, an offspring of a supposed liaison between King Solomon and the Queen of Sheba. While their Jewish identity is still disputed by some, the State of Israel has recognized them as "black Jews" and has aided in their immigration to Israel in two operations, Operation Moses and Operation Solomon.

First Temple: The Jerusalem Temple, erected by Solomon ca. 960 B.C., which was destroyed by the Babylonians in 586 B.C.

Gemara (Hebrew, "study"): The commentary material included in the Talmud from Jewish tradition, as opposed to material from the Bible or logical reasoning.

Gihon (Hebrew, "gush" or "burst forth"): The spring on the eastern slope of the *Ophel,* which served as the chief water source for Jerusalem in the days during the biblical period.

Great White Throne: The final judgment at which all unbelievers will appear before the throne of God for condemnation and punishment in the Lake of Fire (Revelation 20:11-15).

Gush Emunim (Hebrew, "Bloc of the faithful"): The movement to foster Jewish settlements in the West Bank in order to continue the national stream of Zionism. Activist by definition, members of this movement have been involved with attempting to blow up the Dome of the Rock and anti-Arab attacks and demonstrations.

Haganah: The underground Jewish organization for armed self-defense under the British Mandate period in Israel, which became the basis for the Israeli army.

Haggadah (noun from Hebrew *maggid,* "telling, recounting"): The written story of the Exodus from Egypt that has been put into an orderly account (seder), which is used by Jewish families in the home liturgy on the first two nights of the Passover celebration.

Halakah (Hebrew, "walk", pl. *halakot*): The official or lawful way according to which a Jew ought to conduct his life. The Jewish Halakah contains various moral laws and ritual prescriptions, based on the Bible, that embrace all of the teachings of Judaism. It also refers to those parts of the Talmud which deal with legal matters.

Haram (Arabic, "enclosure"): The present platform upon which the Dome of the Rock is built and which is thought to approximate the original Herodian Temple platform. The full title used by the Muslims is *Haram es-Sharif* ("The Noble Enclosure").

Hamas: A terrorist organization with ties to the PLO who follow the Palestinian Covenant calling for the removal of the State of Israel. They employ terrorist tactics against Israel, especially suicide bombings, for which they promise immediate entrance into the Islamic Paradise.

Har Homa: A wooded hillside located near the site of Ramat Rachel within the boundaries of the city of Jerusalem, but contested by the Palestinians since they claim the area as part of where they expect to have the capital of their proposed Palestinian State. It has become a point of international contention and the rallying point for Palestinians and their supporters, who seek to use it to force Israel to greater territorial concessions or renewed conflict.

Hegira (Arabic: *hijrah,* "immigration"): Muhammad's immigration from Mecca to Medina in A.D. 622, which became the date marking the beginning of the Muslim era.

Holocaust (Hebrew *shoah,* "a burnt offering or sacrifice"): Term applied to the mass persecution and attempted genocide of European Jewry by the Nazis during the Second World War (1933–1945). More than six million men, women, and children were systematically exterminated in this *sacrifice* of Jewish lives.

Imam (Arabic, "prayer leader"): The spiritual leader of the Muslim community.

Imminency: The biblical concept that Christ could return at any moment. This means that there is nothing that must occur in the prophetic program *before* the rapture of the church can take place.

Intifada (Arabic, "shake-off, uprising, strike"): The Palestinian revolt against Israeli rule in the so-called "occupied territories," that began in December 1987 and was abated temporarily after the signing of the Declaration of Principles on September 13, 1994, between Israel and the PLO.

Islam: A monotheistic religion whose only deity is *'Allah* ("God"), and whose prophet is Muhammad. It venerates certain Old Testament figures and traditions and accepts some traditions about Jesus, who is considered a lesser prophet. Its primary religious text is the *Koran*, a set of divine revelations made to Muhammad.

Jebusites: The original Canaanite inhabitants of Jerusalem at the first conquest of Jerusalem by Joshua (Joshua 10:23; 12:10), and the second, and complete, conquest of the city by David (2 Samuel 5:6-8; 1 Chronicles 11:4-9). The water shaft entered by David and his men to breach the walls, which was later connected by Solomon and others to reach the upper city by tunnels, was of Jebusite origin.

Jihad (Arabic, "striving"): The term used in Muslim religious law for the holy war waged against all infidels until the end of time.

Josephus, Flavius: The Roman name of a Jewish historian and military leader known in Hebrew as *Yosef ben Mattiyahu* (Mattathias). His many historical writings, apparently intended for a Roman audience, constitute the best extrabiblical source for the study of Jewish life during the period of the Second Temple.

Jubilee Year: The last year in a cycle of 50. The Jubilee is preceded by seven units of seven years, each culminating in a Sabbatical year.

Judgment Seat of Christ: The heavenly judgment of church age believers that will occur after the rapture (2 Corinthians 5:10).

Kabbalah (Hebrew: *mikkubalim*): The Jewish mystical tradition; *Kabbalist:* A Jewish mystic or student of the Kabbalah.

Kach (Hebrew, "thus"): The name of the Israeli party created by the late Rabbi Meir Kahane, advocating the deportation of all Arabs from the Land of Israel after due compensation was paid. Members of Kach have attempted to take over the Temple Mount in the past.

Kingdom of God: The manifestation of God's dominion and divine justice on earth in a spiritual sense, and especially the literal period of God's restoration of His divine plan in history at the end of days.

Knesset (Hebrew, "assembly"): The parliament of the State of Israel, located on Mount Herzl in Jerusalem.

Koran (also *Qur'an*, Arabic, "recitation"): The most holy book in Islam, believed by Muslims to be 114 chapters dictated or recited by the archangel Gabriel to the prophet Muhammad at Mecca and Medina.

Kotel (Hebrew, "wall," from *kathal*, "to join together, make into blocks"): The Western or "Wailing" Wall, popularly called *Ha-Kotel*, "The Wall." This section of wall after the destruction of the Second Temple was the only remnant of the Temple (a retaining wall) accessible to the Jewish people. It first became accessible to Jews for worship in modern times on June 7, 1967.

Latter Days/Last Days (Hebrew: '*Acharit ha-yamim*): A biblical term that can indicate a final period in history climaxed by severe judgments ("latter days") or the final days of history prior to the end time or end of days.

Lubavitch (lit., "town of love"): The town in White Russia that served as the center of *Habad* Hasidism from 1813 to 1915 and whose name has become synonymous with the movement.

Likud (Hebrew, "union, alignment"): The right-wing bloc or political party in the Israeli system of representation. The representative of Likud, at the time of this writing, is Prime Minister Benjamin Netanyahu.

Maccabees: The family of Judah the Maccabee, who led a revolt of the Jews against the Seleucid rulers of Syria in 168–164 B.C. Their victory and re-purification of the Temple is celebrated by the Jewish holiday of Hanukkah.

Maimonides: Rabbi Moshe ben Maimon (A.D. 1135–1204), also referred to as the Rambam (see *Rambam*). One of the foremost Jewish scholars of the Middle Ages. His *Misheh Torah* is one of the classic texts of Jewish law, and his *Guide to the Perplexed* is one of the classics of Jewish philosophy. In the former work, of special interest are his treatises "The Laws of the King Messiah" and "The Laws of the Temple."

Menorah (Hebrew, "lamp"; pl. *menorot*): A term used for the seven-branched oil lamps, or candelabras, used both in the Tabernacle and the Temple.

Menorot: (See *Menorah.*)

Messiah (Hebrew: *Mashiah*, lit. "anointed [one]"): Equivalent to the Greek term *Christos,* from which is derived the English "Christ." In traditional Orthodox Jewish definition this is a human political-military deliverer who is sent by God to usher in the age of redemption for Israel as promised by the biblical prophets. In historic Orthodox Christian definition the Jewish concept is further developed by God the Son being sent to fulfill this role. Thus, Christians accept a divine Messiah whom they identify as the Jewish man Jesus of Nazareth.

Messianic Age (or Messianic Era = The Era of Redemption): That period that spans the beginning of redemption for the Jewish people in the Land of Israel (interpreted by some as 1948) through the coming and rule of King Messiah at the end of the 6,000 years of history to bring a reign of universal peace, moral justice, and spiritual life.

Messianic Jews: Orthodox Jews who believe the Messianic times are imminent. Most Messianic Jews in Israel are actively preparing for the Messiah's coming through the adoption of more biblical life-styles and in research and activism toward rebuilding the Temple.

Middot (Hebrew, "measurements"): A tractate of the Jewish *Mishnah* that deals specifically with the measurements of the Temple.

Midrash (Hebrew, "interpretation"): A written collection of rabbinical interpretation of the Bible compiled by the *Soferim* ("scribes") in the fourth century A.D. The *midrashic* method of interpreting Scripture was employed to clarify legal points or to bring out lessons by the use of stories.

Midrash, adj. midrashic: A Hebrew term for the method of biblical interpretation that was current in rabbinic times and earlier. The term can also designate a collection of such interpretations produced by the rabbis.

Millennium (Latin, "thousand"): The final period of Jewish history, lasting 1,000 years (Revelation 20:1), which follows the Tribulation and the second advent of Christ. It is characterized by a restoration of the Jewish nation and the reign of Christ on earth. See also *Kingdom of God.*

Miqveh, pl. *miqva'ot:* A ritual bath that may be used to fulfill the Jewish requirement of immersion after contraction of ritual impurity.

Mishnah (Hebrew, "learning, repetition"): The earliest written collection of Jewish Oral Law (i.e., Jewish religious and legal teachings handed down orally). It was compiled about A.D. 200 by Rabbi Judah ha-Nasi ("the Prince"). It comprises the first part of the Talmud and appears in the form of homiletical discourses by the Jewish sages.

Mitzvah (Hebrew, "commandment," pl. *mitzvot*): The term for a religious and moral obligation, whether one of the 613 biblical commandments or any other traditional ordinance, observance, teaching, or statute.

Mitzvot: (See *Mitzvah.*)

Moshiach: The Ashkenazi-accented Hebrew spelling of *Messiah,* literally, "anointed one." The Messiah in contemporary Orthodox Judaism is envisioned as a human political and military leader who will usher in the Day of Redemption for the Jewish people. Christians are more familiar with the term through the Greek *Christos,* translated "Christ."

Moslem: (See *Muslim.*)

Mufti: Muslim cleric who is competent to render an opinion on a case of Islamic law. In Jerusalem there are currently two competing Mufti—the Jordanian Mufti and the Palestinian Mufti.

Muhammad (from Arabic *hmd,* "to praise," also *Mohammad*): The founder and prophet of Islam, who was born in A.D. 570 and died at Medina in A.D. 632.

Mujaheddin (Arabic, "warriors of Jihad"): The term used by Islamic terrorists for those who join in the fight to annihilate the State of Israel and the Jewish people in the holy war commanded in the Koran.

Muslim (from Arabic *'aslama,* "to submit, convert to Islam"): A believer or follower of Islam.

New Covenant: The covenant God made with Israel which enlarges the blessing promise of the Abrahamic Covenant. Believers in the church age through Christ enjoy the spiritual aspects of this blessing (Matthew 26:28; 2 Corinthians 3:6), which regenerated Israel will enjoy along with Land blessings in the Millennial kingdom (Jeremiah 31:31-34). Unlike the Mosaic Covenant it will be unconditional (Hebrews 8:6-13) and guarantee Israel's new relationship with the Lord (Isaiah 59:20-21; Jeremiah 32:37-40; Ezekiel 16:60-63; 37:21-28).

Olivet Discourse: The eschatological teaching of Jesus in response to questions raised by His disciples while they were sitting on the Mount of Olives on the east of the city of Jerusalem (Matthew 24–25; Mark 13; Luke 21).

'Ophel (Hebrew, "hill, mound"): The southeastern spur north of the City of David, which is the oldest known part of Jerusalem. It is the section of Jebusite territory captured by King David and was the site of the Tabernacle during his days.

Oral Law: A second Torah (law), consisting of interpretations of the written Torah, which was studied and passed down by oral tradition. In rabbinic Judaism, this oral Torah, believed to have been given by God at Sinai along with the written Torah, constitutes the authoritative interpretation of the written law.

Orthodox (Greek, "straight"): Those holding to religious views that have been traditionally accepted and taught. *Orthodox Jews* are those accepting the *Tanakh* (Old Testament) as divine revelation, and the *Talmud* as divine direction for the interpretation of the *Tanakh*, and are observant (practitioners) of Jewish law. *Orthodox Christians* are those who accept the cardinal doctrines of the historic faith, whether as formulated by various creeds or by personal affirmation to the basic scriptural tenets of the triune nature of the One God (Father, Son, and Holy Spirit), the deity, virgin birth, and mediatorial work of Christ as an atoning Savior, and salvation by grace through personal faith in Christ apart from works. There are many different divisions within both Orthodox Judaism and Christianity today.

Palestine/Palestinian: A pejorative term for the country west of the Jordan River, first coined by the Greeks and Romans after the word *Philistine*, the name of the enemies of Israel who inhabited the Mediterranean coastal plain. The Bible refers to the same territory as *Canaan*, after its pre-Israelite inhabitants, though Jews have always called it *'Eretz Israel*, the Land of Israel. Often used by writers to refer to Second Temple period Judaism resident in the Land of Israel, hence "Palestinian Judaism."

Passover: A Jewish springtime festival commemorating the exodus of the Jews from Egyptian bondage in biblical times. It is celebrated with the eating of *matzah* (unleavened bread).

Pax Romana (Latin "peace of Rome"): The peaceful conditions maintained by Roman law and culture that was imposed on all captured lands, including the Land of Israel. It made possible the means to universal communication and travel in the late Second Temple period, during which the Greek language was used throughout Jewish cities and to translate the Old Testament (Septuagint) and write the New Testament.

Pentateuch: The first five books of the Bible, also termed the Torah, or the Five Books of Moses.

Pesach (Hebrew, "Passover"): The Hebrew term for the festival of Passover, which commemorates the exodus from Egypt (Exodus 12:1-36) and was celebrated at the last great reform of the Second Temple, at which the Ark was reinstalled (2 Chronicles 35:1-3). Prophetically, it looks toward the final exodus of God's people under Messiah (see 1 Corinthians 5:7; Revelation 15:3-4 based on Exodus 15).

Pharisees: A group of Jews in Second Temple times who constituted the spiritual forebears of the talmudic rabbis. Led by lay teachers of the Torah, they became the dominant sect. The word derives from Hebrew *perushim*, "separate."

Phylacteries: Cubical compartments of leather that contain biblical passages emphasizing God's sovereignty and the obligation of the Jew to observe His commandments, which are affixed to the head and arm with leather thongs. They are known in Hebrew as *tefillin*.

Pogrom (Russian, "devastation"): An organized persecution, massacre, or attack on the Jewish people in the Diaspora.

Polemics, Polemical (Greek, "to make war"): An argument or refutation, usually of an idea or practice and/or the group that holds the idea or practice. In the case of the Dead Sea scrolls, the manner in which other sectarian groups may be described (i.e., by example in order to refute the group).

Postmillennialism (Latin, "after millennium"): The theological view that Christ and/or His saints will reign on the earth *before* His final return.

Predestination: The belief that the process of history and the destiny of man are determined in advance by God.

Premillennialism (Latin, "before millennium"): The theological view that Christ and His saints will reign on the earth for 1,000 years *after* His final return.

Preterism: The eschatological view that holds that the destruction of Jerusalem in A.D. 70 by the Roman army fulfilled the prophecies of the Olivet Discourse and the book of Revelation, except for the second advent. More extreme preterism holds that the second advent also occurred at this point.

Proselyte: A non-Jew who formally converts to Judaism.

Pseudepigrapha (Greek, "false writings"): A collection of non-canonical works of mystical Jewish-Hellenistic origin, generally composed after the sixth century B.C. These writings were influenced by Persian cosmology (view of the universe) and are highly *apocalyptic* in nature. More generally, the term is used to designate much of the religious literature of the various groups within Second Temple Judaism.

Ptolemies: The rulers of Egypt and its empire in the Hellenistic era. This dynasty took its name from Ptolemy, the general of Alexander the Great who retained control of Egypt after Alexander's death.

Quds̄ (Arabic, "holy"): Arabic term used for both Jerusalem and the Temple Mount area (the Sanctuary), as in *Al Quds,* "the Holy City."

Qumran: A site on the western shore of the Dead Sea. The Dead Sea Scrolls were uncovered in nearby caves. Qumran itself preserves the ruins of a building complex that served as the headquarters of the sect during the Second Temple period.

Rabbi (Hebrew, "master"): Derived from the Hebrew verb *rabab,* "to be great," the term was an honorable title for an ordained Jewish teacher of the law or a leader of a Jewish community. Roughly equivalent to the Christian term "pastor" or "bishop."

Rambam: Acronym for **R**abbi **M**oshe **b**en **M**aimon (A.D. 1135–1204) or Maimonides. One of Judaism's leading Torah authorities and philosophers who wrote a commentary on the Mishnah in Arabic known as the *Book of Illumination,* which the term may also denote.

Rapture (from Latin *rapturo* after Greek *harpadzo,* "seize, catching away"): The first phase of the second advent of Christ according to premillennial interpretation, in which the church (both dead and living saints) is translated to meet the Lord in the air (1 Corinthians 15:51-52; 1 Thessalonians 4:16-17; Titus 2:13) and taken to heaven for the Judgment Seat of Christ (2 Corinthians 5:10). In dispensational premillennialism the Rapture precedes the Tribulation period.

Rashi: Acronym of **R**abbi **Sh**lomo (ben **Yi**tzkak) **Y**archi (A.D. 1040–1105), the medieval author of the most important commentary on the Bible and Talmud. His commentary on the Torah was the first known Hebrew book to be printed.

Redemption: (see *Age of Redemption.*)

Replacement Theology: A theological view among both Catholics and Protestants that the Jews have been rejected and replaced by "the true Israel," the church. Those who espouse this view disavow any distinct ethnic future for the Jewish people in connection with the biblical covenants, believing that their only spiritual destiny is either to perish or become a part of the Christian church.

Revelation: The process by which God is believed to have revealed His will to the people of Israel and the world.

Rosh Hashanah (Hebrew, "head of the year"): The Jewish festival of the civil New Year, celebrated on the first and second days of the month *Tishri* (equivalent to September/October on the Julian calendar). In postbiblical Judaism, it is a time for celebration of God's kingship and for introspection and repentance.

Sabbath: The seventh day of the Jewish week, upon which it is forbidden to work. This day is considered holy, and there are many special prayers, customs, and ceremonies connected with it.

Sadducees: A sect of Second Temple-period Jews, connected primarily with the priestly aristocracy, which accepted only the authority of teachings based strictly on the Bible and its interpretation. The word derives from the name Zadok, the high priest in the time of King Solomon.

Sakhra (Arabic, "rock"): The Muslim term for the sacred rock within the Islamic shrine of the Temple Mount, hence the full expression *Qubbet es-Sakhra,* "Dome of the Rock."

Samaritans: A Jewish sect comprised of a mixed people descended from those original northern Israelites who were not exiled in 722 B.C. and the tribes introduced into the area by the Assyrians. They separated from the rest of the Jewish people early in the Second Commonwealth and set up their own religious center on Mount Gerizim, situated above the city of Shechem (modern Nablus).

Sanhedrin: The assembly of ordained Jewish scholars which functioned both as a supreme court and as a legislature in Israel before A.D. 70. With the destruction of the Temple and the end of Jewish independence, the Sanhedrin ceased to function.

Second Advent: The eschatological designation for the final Messianic return of Jesus. In premillennialism it consist of two phases: the *rapture,* being the return of Christ "in the air" (1 Thessalonians 4:13-17) and the *revelation,* being the return of Christ "to the earth," which, according to Zechariah 14:4, will be to Jerusalem.

Second Commonwealth: The political organization of the Jewish people in the Land of Israel beginning with the return from exile in the sixth century B.C. and ending with the final dismantling of the Herodian dynasty in the first century A.D.

Second Temple: The Temple in Jerusalem that was constructed in 515 B.C. by Zerubbabel, reconstructed by Herod the Great (beginning c. 20 B.C.), and lasted until its destruction by the Romans in A.D. 70. The term can also designate the period during which this Temple stood.

Sect, adj. sectarian: The term designates the various groups of Jews and their particular approaches to Judaism in Second Temple times. Such usage does not imply that any one of the groups is considered mainstream.

Seleucid: The name given to the dynasty of Macedonian rulers who ruled a large part of the Greek Empire after Alexander the Great. This empire stretched from Syria eastward and at various times (Hellenistic times) included Palestine.

Septuagint: The Greek translation of the Hebrew Old Testament, produced in Egypt during the Hellenistic period.

Shabbetai Zvi (or Tsevi): The charismatic kabbalistic Jew (1626–1676) who said he was born on the Ninth of Av, the traditional date believed to be that of the Messiah. He proclaimed himself as King Messiah at the synagogue in Smyrna in December 1665, gained a prophet (Natan of Gaza), and a following by a large portion of the Jewish world, who believed he would raise an army and march to Jerusalem. However, he converted to Islam in a ploy to save his life after being arrested upon his arrival in Constantinople. Nevertheless, a Messianic movement, known as Shabbateanism, continued claiming that his "sham" conversion was only part of a divine plan.

Shavuot: The Jewish holiday of Pentecost, which in biblical times was connected with the offering of the first fruits of the wheat harvest. Later, Shavuot came to commemorate the giving of the Torah at Sinai as well.

Sheikh (Arabic, "elder, chief"): A Muslim high priest, ruler, or head of an Arab tribe or family.

Shekinah (Hebrew, "dwelling, resting"): A term developed by the rabbis and used for the "Divine Presence" of God that was manifested by "dwelling" between the wings of the cherubim on the Ark (see 1 Chronicles 13:6). It represented the immanence of God with the Israelites, first in the Tabernacle and later in the First Temple. The word is derived from the verbal form *shakan* ("to dwell") as is the word for the Tabernacle, *mishkan* ("dwelling").

Sho'ah (Hebrew, "burnt offering, sacrifice"): (See Holocaust).

Siloam (Hebrew: *Shiloah*, "the one sent"): Greek (New Testament) term for the pool located at the end of the water tunnel of King Hezekiah, which collected water from the Gihon Spring on the eastern slope of the *'Ophel*. During the ancient *Hoshana Rabba* water was drawn from this source for the libation poured on the altar in the Temple.

Six-Day War: The war that occurred from June 5-10, 1967, when Israel reacted to Arab threats and a blockade by defeating the Egyptian, Jordanian, and Syrian forces. The Sinai Peninsula, the West Bank, and the Golan Heights fell to Israel in this conflict. The Sinai was returned to Egypt in 1979 as a condition of the Camp David Peace Treaty. For Jerusalem the war was a three-day conflict from June 5-7 that resulted in the liberation of East Jerusalem and the Temple Mount from Jordan.

Sukkah, pl. *Succot* (Hebrew for "booth"): This term designates the temporary shelter Jews erect in observance of the fall festival of Succot, the Jewish holiday of Tabernacles, which is connected with the fall harvest and which also commemorates both the exodus from Egypt and God's protection of the people of Israel during their time of wandering in the desert.

Sukkot (Hebrew, "booths"): The Hebrew term for the one-week Feast of Tabernacles or Booths; the last of the three pilgrim festivals that begins on the fifteenth of Tishri (approximately September–October on the Julian calendar). The word *sukkot* is the plural of *sukkah*, a booth or tabernacle that the Israelites dwelled in during their time of wandering in the wilderness (Leviticus 23:42).

Synagogue (Greek, "gathering together"): An institution that was developed by Jews in the *Diaspora*, after the destruction of the First Temple, for worship and study of the Bible. In Hellenistic usage, the term also referred to a Jewish community.

Tabnit: The Hebrew term first used in Exodus 25:8 and then in repeated commands and discussions (Exodus 25:40; 1 Chronicles 28:11-12,19) to describe the "plan" or "design" for the earthly Temple based on the heavenly Temple as a prototype.

Talmud (Hebrew, "teaching"): The entire corpus of Jewish Oral Law including the *Mishnah* together with a written compendium of discussions and commentary on the Mishnah called *Gemara*. Its teachings and rulings span a period between Ezra in the Old Testament (c. 450 B.C.) and the middle of the Roman period (c. A.D. 550). Because it includes rulings made by generations of scholars and jurists in many academies in both Palestine and Babylon it exists in two versions: the *Jerusalem,* referred to as Talmud Yerushalmi, consisting of discussions held in the Jerusalem academies, and compiled in Israel at the end of the fourth century A.D., and the *Babylonian,* referred to as *Talmud Babli,* consisting of discussions in the Babylonian academies and edited at the end of the fifth-century A.D. Talmudic Judaism is that defined by the rabbis in the first two centuries A.D. and further expounded until the end of the fifth century.

Tanakh: Term used for the Jewish Bible, comprised of the Hebrew initials for the words *Torah* ("law"), *Neveim* ("prophets"), *Ketubim* ("writings"), the three divisions of the Old Testament.

Tannaim, adj. Tannaitic: The earliest teachers of the Mishnah, Tosefta, and halakhic Midrashim who flourished c. 50 B.C.–A.D. 200.

Targum (Hebrew, "translation"): The authorized Aramaic translation of the Torah by the proselyte Onkelos (c. A.D. 90). In Talmudic times, it was read along with the Torah so that the congregation could understand what was being read (see Nehemiah 8:7-8). In many cases, the Targum renders the text homelitically rather than literally.

Tefillin: Cubical compartments of leather that contain biblical passages emphasizing God's sovereignty and the obligation of the Jew to observe His commandments, which are affixed to the head and arm with leather thongs. (See also *phylacteries.*)

Times of the Gentiles: The period of Gentile domination over Jerusalem, beginning in 586 B.C. and ending with the final battle of the Armageddon campaign by the second advent of Christ and His

destruction of the Antichrist's armies as recorded in Zechariah 14 and
Revelation 19.

Tisha B'Av (Hebrew, "Ninth of Av"): A fast day commemorating the
destruction of the First and Second Temples that occurs on the ninth
day of *Av*, the first month of the Jewish religious year, approximating
July-August on the Julian (Christian) calendar.

Topography (Greek, "study of place"): The description of a particular
place, including its physical structures and elevation.

Torah (Hebrew, "law"): Used either of the first five books of the Old
Testament, the Pentateuch, or of the entire body of traditional Jewish
teaching and literature. The Hebrew word *torah* literally means
"instruction, teaching."

Tosefta: A collection of early rabbinic traditions that were not included
in the Mishnah. The Tosefta is the earliest commentary to the Mishnah
and is organized in approximately the same manner.

Tribulation: That period of time, according to the biblical prophets,
during which Israel as a nation will experience unparalleled distress as a
part of the "Day of the Lord." In Jewish theology it is the time of "Messianic woes" or "Messianic birthpangs" prior to the coming of the Messiah. In the dispensational premillennial interpretation of prophecy it
is the period that follows the rapture of the church and lasts for seven
years. The first three-and-one-half years are a time of peace that witness
the rise of Antichrist and the rebuilding of the Jewish Temple. The last
three-and-one-half years are a time of divine judgment known in the
Old Testament as "the time of Jacob's trouble." At the end of this
period, climaxed by the Battle of Armageddon, Christ returns to rescue
Israel and set up His Millennial kingdom.

Typology (Greek: *tupos*, "type"): The study of the various types in the
Bible which foreshadowed later, more developed revelations of charac-
ters or figures (the antitypes), whether positive or negative. A positive
example is David as a type of Christ (Psalm 22:1; Matthew 27:46). A
negative example is Antiochus as a type of Antichrist (see Daniel 11:21-
35,36-45).

Tzitzit (Hebrew, "fringes"): The tassels attached to the four corners of
the *Tallit*, the traditional prayer shawl or garment, with a blue thread

included in each tassel to remind Jews to keep God's commandments (Numbers 15:37-39).

Wadi (or *Wady*): An Arabic word (Hebrew: *nahal*) for a riverbed that is dry during most of the year and carries water only during the rainy season. Most early settlements were built near wadis for access to water, hence settlements and wadis often share the same place name (e.g., Wadi Qumran, Khirbet Qumran).

Wakf (also *Waqf*): The land or property whose income is deeded to the construction of mosques or madrashes and the support of its faculty and students. The term is also used for the Supreme Muslim Council, which maintains religious jurisdiction over Islamic holy places, especially those on the Temple Mount.

West Bank: The term employed in most non-Jewish media and sources for the territory of biblical Judea and Samaria (including East Jerusalem) captured by Israel in the Six-Day War of 1967 and the Yom Kippur War of 1973 and presently in dispute by the international community. It is the area demanded by the Palestinians for a new Palestinian State with Jerusalem as its capital.

Western Wall (Hebrew *kotel*, "wall"): The name given to the ancient remnant of the Herodian retaining wall on the western side of the Temple Mount platform. It was not the western wall of the Temple itself, but since the destruction of the Temple in A.D. 70 it has become the focus of Jewish prayer as the only (at that time) known portion of the Temple complex. Today it is still the only portion of the area accessible to Jews, the Temple Mount being under the jurisdiction of Arab Muslims. Orthodox Judaism believes that the presence of God "hides behind" the wall and that prayers made or directed to this spot have a special efficacy.

World to Come (Hebrew, *'olam ha-ba'*): The final period in Jewish eschatology, in which the heavenly blessings are realized. Equivalent to the Christian concept of the eternal state, in which a new heavens and new earth are created.

Valley of Jehoshaphat: Name given to the valley situated between Jerusalem and the Mount of Olives, also known as the Kidron Valley, which has been used as a cemetery by the Jewish people. It was in this valley that the Judean king Jehoshaphat overthrew the united enemies of Israel (2 Chronicles 20:26). According to biblical prophecy, this is where God will destroy the armies of the Antichrist at the end of the Tribulation (Joel 3:2,12).

Valley of Jezreel: The valley in the city of Jezreel, in the tribal allotment of Issachar, lying on the northern side of the city between the ridges of Gilboa and Moreh. The name was extended to the entire plain of Esdraelon (Joshua 17:16; Judges 6:33; Hosea 1:5). In prophecy it is the place where the armies of the world will gather in the battle of Armageddon (Hosea 1:5-11; see also Zechariah 12:11; Revelation 16:16).

Year of Jubilee: (See *Jubilee Year.*)

Yeshiva (Hebrew, "sitting"): A Jewish traditional Torah academy, or school, devoted primarily to the advanced study of the Talmud and rabbinic literature; roughly equivalent to a Christian seminary.

Yom Kippur (Hebrew, "Day of Atonement"): The most solemn day of the Jewish year, celebrated on the ninth day of Tishri (September–October on the Julian calendar), ten days after the Jewish New Year. Considered the day of judgment and reckoning, it is a time when Jews, individually and as a nation, are cleansed of sin and granted atonement. It was on this day alone that the high priest was permitted to enter the Holy of Holies in the Temple. In postbiblical tradition, the theme of the day is human repentance, which leads to divine forgiveness.

Zion (Hebrew disputed): Originally the hill area north of the City of David, the *'Ophel*, where the Tabernacle resided. Through poetic usage it became a synonym for the city of Jerusalem and Israel itself, and spiritually it came to represent the eschatological idea of God's chosen place on earth.

Zionism: The movement to establish an autonomous Jewish national home in the Land of Israel, so called because of the historical desire of Jews to return to *Zion*. Zionism as a political movement of world Jewry

(*The World Zionist Organization*) began with the first Zionist Congress (1897) convened by Theodor Herzl. With the establishment of the State of Israel, the political aspirations were attained, and the organization now assists in development of the State and as a bridge between Israel and Jewish communities in the *Diaspora*.

Zohar (lit., "radiance"): The classical Jewish religious work embodying the mystical teachings of the *Kabbalah* (lit., "received tradition"), the body of classical Jewish mysticism.

NOTES

An Invitation to Visit Jerusalem

1. Testimony of Luana Fabry, New Jerusalem Ministries web site.

Chapter 1: Why Study Prophecy?

1. Charles H. Dyer, *World News and Bible Prophecy* (Wheaton, IL: Tyndale House Publishers, 1995), p. 270.
2. Thomas Ice and Randall Price, *Ready to Rebuild: The Imminent Plan to Rebuild the Last Days Temple* (Eugene, OR: Harvest House Publishers, 1992).
3. Peter W. Stoner, *Science Speaks* (Chicago: Moody Press, 1963), pp. 100-01.

Chapter 2: Focusing on the Future

1. Letter to John A. Washington in *George Washington, Programs and Papers* (Washington: U.S. George Washington Bicentennial Commission, 1932), p. 33.
2. As quoted in David Barton, *The Bulletproof George Washington* (Aledo, TX: WallBuilder, Inc., Winter 1993), pp. 50-51.
3. As cited by Charles Colson on his radio program "Breakpoint," February 26, 1998.
4. As noted by Willem A. VanGemeren, "Psalms," *The Expositor's Bible Commentary,* eds. Frank Gabelein and Richard Polcyn (Grand Rapids: Zondervan Publishing House, 1991), 5:67.

Chapter 3: Jerusalem at the Center

1. Arnold Olson, *Inside Jerusalem, City of Destiny* (Glendale, CA: Regal Books/Gospel Light Publications, 1969), p. 25.
2. The forms (and states) are: Jerusalem (Arizona, Arkansas, Georgia), Salem (Alabama, Florida, Illinois, Indiana, Iowa, Kentucky, Maine, Massachusetts, Missouri, Nebraska, New Mexico, New York, North Dakota,

Ohio, Oregon, Pennsylvania, South Dakota, Tennessee, Utah, West Virginia), Zion (Arizona, Arkansas, Illinois, Indiana, Kentucky, Missouri, Utah).

3. Mark Twain, *Innocents Abroad* (1869).

4. Chaim Hazaz, *The Right of Righteousness* (1977), as cited by Eliyahu Tal, *Whose Jerusalem?* (Tel Aviv: International Forum for a United Jerusalem, 1994), pp. 297-98.

5. Aryeh Dean Cohen, "4% of new immigrants live in Jerusalem," *The Jerusalem Post International Edition* (February 28, 1998): 5.

6. *Washington Post* Service story "Separating religion, politics called answer to status of Jerusalem," *San Antonio Express-News* (Monday, September 27, 1993): 3A.

7. As cited in Fouad Ajami, World Report: "An old city's dreams," *U.S. News & World Report* (December 13, 1993): 68.

8. As cited in Lisa Beyer and Dean Fischer, "Men of the Year: Yitzhak Rabin & Yasser Arafat," *Time* (January 3, 1994): 49.

9. Interview with Mayor Ehud Olmert, Mayor's office, Jerusalem, November 10, 1995.

10. Interview with Prime Minister Benjamin Netanyahu by Steve Rodan, *The Jerusalem Post International Edition* (May 3, 1997): 7.

Chapter 4: Jerusalem's Place in Prophecy

1. Amos Elon as cited in the review by Gene R. Garthwaite of Martin Gilbert's *Jerusalem in the Twentieth Century*, *History Book Club Review* (December 1996), p. 12.

2. Harold D. Foos, "Jerusalem in Biblical Prophecy," *Dictionary of Premillennial Theology*, ed. Mal Couch (Grand Rapids: Kregel Publications, 1996), p. 207.

3. From a letter sent to Manchester Alderman Moser when the Zionist movement was still undecided over the alternative of Uganda to Palestine for a Jewish national homeland—as cited in the forthcoming book by Martin Gilbert, *Churchill and the Jews*.

Chapter 5: Zealous for Zion

1. Eliyahu Tal, *Whose Jerusalem?* (Tel Aviv: International Forum for a United Jerusalem, 1994), p. 11.

2. Meron Medzni, "Complicated City: A Review of the Politics of Jerusalem Since 1967 by Michael Dumper," *The Jerusalem Post International Edition* (February 14, 1998): 22.

3. Interview with David Cassuto, Jerusalem Municipality, June 29, 1995.

4. The identification of these boundaries have been difficult to determine. Some interpret the "river of Egypt," marking the southern boundary, as

the Nile; however, others believe (and I think more accurately) that it is better understood as the Wadi el-'Arish, about 50 miles southwest of Gaza and 90 miles northeast of the Suez Canal. With this latter identification note the southern border of Israel stated in Amos 6:14 as the "brook of the Arabah," which is almost certainly the same as the present Wadi el-'Arish. While the identification of the "river Euphrates" as the northern boundary seems straightforward, the reference to "Great River" has been made with a river running through the valley between the modern northern boundary of Lebanon and the southern boundary of Syria.

5. According to this text the southern boundary stretched from the Salt Sea (Dead Sea) southwest along the border of Edom (Jordan) and across the northern half of the Negev, then northwest to the brook of Egypt (the Wadi el-'Arish). The western boundary was the Great Sea (Mediterranean Sea), and the eastern was from the Sea of Chinnereth (Sea of Galilee) running southward along the Jordan River to the Dead Sea. The northern boundary included Mount Mermon and the towns of Lebo-hamath (in southern Syria), Zedad, Ziphron, and Hazar-Enan (all near Damascus in modern Syria).

6. Edward Gibbon, *The History of the Decline and Fall of the Roman Empire,* ed. J.B. Bury (London: Meuthen & Co., 1909), vol. 5, ch. 58.

7. For a discussion of these factors and the theological views of the church see Peter Walker, "Jerusalem in the Early Christian Centuries," *Jerusalem Past and Present in the Purposes of God,* ed. P.W.L. Walker (Grand Rapids: Baker Book House, 1994), pp. 79-97.

8. The edict placed "circumcised persons" under penalty of death for staying within the area of Aelia Capitolina (Hadrianic Jerusalem); however, it is unclear how enforceable or enforced such an edict was by the Roman authorities. For the edict itself see Michael Avi-Yonah, *The Jews of Palestine* (Oxford: University Press, 1976), and for its discussion, Peter Walker, *Holy City, Holy Places? Christian Attitudes to Jerusalem and the Holy Land in the Fourth Century* (Oxford: University Press), p. 8, n. 12.

9. An exception to this was the proposal of Cyril, bishop of Jerusalem (A.D. 320–386), that since Jerusalem was now a Christian Jerusalem, it was not the same city as that Jewish one judged by God. Furthermore, since the Christian Jerusalem worshiped Christ, it was now a "holy city" and deserved to be at the center of the new Christian world that was being formed. Even though Cyril's positive view of Jerusalem is distinct from the negative view of Eusebius, it nevertheless is based on the same theological premises, which are against a future reestablishment of a Jewish Jerusalem.

10. An example of this thinking in Luther is his famous statement, "A Jew or a Jewish heart is so wood, stone, iron, devil-hardened, that it can in no way be moved."

11. For a good discussion on why and how this took place, see Pinchas Lapaide, *Hebrew in the Church* (Grand Rapids: Wm. B. Eerdmans Publishing Co., 1987).

12. As cited in Peter Toon, ed., *Puritans, the Millennium, and the Future of Israel: Puritan Eschatology 1600 to 1660* (Cambridge: James Clarke, 1970).

13. Salo W. Baron, *A Social and Religious History of the Jews* (New York, 1952), 2:329.

14. David L. Larsen, *Jews, Gentiles, & the Church: A New Perspective on History and Prophecy* (Nashville, TN: Discovery House Publishers, 1995), p. 130. The original citation is in M.M. Noah, *Discourse on the Restoration of the Jews*, pp. 1-55.

15. For the details of Truman's leadership in support of Jewish nationalism see Abba Eban, *My People* (New York: Random House, 1968), pp. 453-58.

16. Interview with Noam Hendren, Independence Park, Jerusalem, June 1997.

Chapter 6: The Zion Factor

1. Statement by Keith L. Brooks, president of the American Prophetic League, Inc., in a foreword to Robert L. Evans, *The Jew in the Plan of God* (New York: Loizeaux Brothers, Inc., 1950), p. 6. Even though these comments originally addressed the circumstances of the 1948–49 War of Independence when Israel became a new state, world events have continued to follow the *same course* in conformity with the scriptural predictions.

2. John F. Walvoord, *Armageddon, Oil and the Middle East Crisis: What the Bible Says About the Future of the Middle East and the End of Western Civilization*, rev. ed. (Grand Rapids: Zondervan Publishing House, 1990), p. 120.

3. For a more complete treatment of this point see Clarence Wagner, "The Year of Jubilee," *Bridges for Peace Israel Teaching Letter* No. 98-3 (Jerusalem, March 1998).

4. For more discussion on the future aspects of the Jubilee Year, see Kevin L. Howard, "The Jubilee Year," *Zion's Fire* 7:4 (July/August 1996): 15-16.

5. Hendrikus Berkhof, *Christ, the Meaning of History* (Richmond, VA: John Knox Press, 1966), p. 148.

6. For a detailed examination of this objection from Zechariah, as well as additional objections to the past fulfillment view, see Walter C. Kaiser, Jr., "The Land of Israel and the Future Return (Zechariah 10:6-12)," *Israel, the Land and the People: An Evangelical Affirmation of God's Promises*, ed. H. Wayne House (Grand Rapids: Kregel Publications, 1998), pp. 209-27, esp. 213-24.

7. For further support for this view and discussion see *Dictionary of Premillennial Theology*, ed. Mal Couch, s.v. "Eschatological Terms," by Ed Hindson

(Grand Rapids: Kregel Publications, 1996), pp. 108-09; and Thomas Ice & Timothy Demy, *The Truth About the Signs of the Times* (Eugene, OR: Harvest House Publishers, 1997).

8. For more discussion about this see Thomas Ice & Timothy Demy, *The Truth About A.D. 2000 & Predicting Christ's Return* (Eugene, OR: Harvest House Publishers, 1996).

9. Interview with Noam Hendren, Independence Park, Jerusalem, June 1997.

Chapter 7: Dark Before the Dawn

1. George Will, "Palestinian promises rest on violence, lies," *San Antonio Express-News,* March 31, 1997, p. 13A.

2. For a presentation of these terms see the author's chapter "Old Testament Tribulation Terms" in *When the Trumpet Sounds,* eds. Thomas Ice & Timothy Demy (Eugene, OR: Harvest House Publishers, 1995), pp. 57-83, and "NT Tribulation Terms" charts in Wayne House & Randall Price, *Charts on Biblical Prophecy & Eschatology* (Grand Rapids: Zondervan Publishing House, 1998).

3. For the arguments for this conclusion see Robert L. Thomas, *Revelation 8–22: An Exegetical Commentary* (Chicago: Moody Press, 1995), pp. 86-100. For the argument that the two witnesses occupy the first half of the Tribulation and die at the midpoint, see Arnold G. Fruchtenbaum, *The Footsteps of the Messiah: A Study of the Sequence of Prophetic Events* (Tustin, CA: Ariel Press, 1982), pp. 158-60, 168-70.

4. A similar statement was made by Yasser Arafat on *Voice of Palestine* radio, Algiers, October 24, 1993.

5. As cited by John Wheeler, Jr. in the *Christian American* 5:2 (February 1994): 4. An earlier, more detailed version of this statement was given by Arafat in Arabic to the Palestinian people on Jordanian television on the day of the signing of the Declaration of Principles with the Israelis at the White House in Washington, D.C., September 13, 1993.

6. This excerpt was taken from the contents of the recorded speech first reported by the offshore radio station Arutz Sheva, February 7, 1996, and published in the *Jerusalem Post,* February 23, 1996.

7. As cited by Cal Thomas, "Preaching hate OK for one side," syndicated column for Monday, July 28, 1997.

8. As quoted in an interview with Feisal Husseini in the Jordanian newspaper *Al-Aswak.*

9. As broadcast on the *Voice of Palestine* radio and cited in *Dispatch from Jerusalem* (January, February, 1998), p. 19.

10. Quoted in an interview with Feisal Husseini published in *Al-Quds,* the official newspaper of the Palestinian press.

11. Interview with Clarence Wagner, Bridges for Peace office, Jerusalem, November 8, 1995.
12. Statement made by Hussein in Amman, Jordan and reported by the Washington Post Service on September 27, 1993.
13. See Jeff Jacoby, "In Arabic Not a Word of Peace from Arafat," *Prophecy Update* magazine 2:1 (1998): 15, 23.

Chapter 8: Destined for Disaster

1. This was the suggestion made by J. Dwight Pentecost, *Things to Come* (Finley, OH: Duhnam Publishing Co., 1958), p. 357.
2. "The Status of Jerusalem," s.v. "The International Position on Jerusalem," prepared for and under the guidance of the Committee on the Exercise of the Inalienable Rights of the Palestinian People" (United Nations, New York, 1997).
3. *Eternal Jerusalem: A Reader and Teaching Manual*, ed. Ariel Eisenberg (New York: Jewish Education Press, 1971), p. 125 (emphasis added).
4. Recorded on May 10, 1994 and reported by Arutz Sheva offshore radio.
5. There are at least six different interpretations of the placement of this war. For these see my chart in H. Wayne House and Randall Price, *Charts on Biblical Prophecy & Eschatology* (Grand Rapids: Zondervan Publishing House, 1998).
6. For recent arguments for a pretribulational invasion see Zola Levitt and Tom McCall, *The Coming Russian Invasion of Israel*, rev. ed. (Moody Press, 1992); Hal Lindsey and Chuck Missler, *The Magog Factor* (Hal Lindsey Ministries, 1992) and "Magog Updates" in *Personal Update: A Newsletter of Koinonia House* (P.O. Box D, Coeur d'Alene, ID 83816-0347). A good survey of this position is also provided by Arnold Fruchtenbaum, *The Footprints of the Messiah* (Ariel Press, 1978), pp. 69-83.
7. Palestinian Authority daily newspaper *Al-Hayat Al-Jadida*, Dec. 1, 1997.
8. *The Voice of the Temple Mount* (Autumn 1995), pp. 2, 7.
9. Frances Kennett, *The Greatest Disasters of the 20th Century* (Secaucus, NJ: Castle Books, 1975), p. 7.
10. As reported by Stan Goodenough of the International Christian Embassy in Jerusalem News Service in Jerusalem, March 20, 1998.
11. *Jerusalem Post*, March 11, 1998.
12. The assertion to the mayor was communicated by him to me during an interview on November 25, 1996.
13. The Har Homa project required the appropriation of 1,400 dunams from Jewish landowners and 450 dunams from Arab landowners. The High Court of Justice upheld the government's right to appropriate this land in order to meet the burgeoning housing needs of the Jerusalem public at large.

14. The statement was made February 20, 1997 and cited in the publication "Building in Jerusalem—Background" (February 24, 1997), available from the "Virtual Jerusalem" internet site.

15. Associated Press article by Hillary Appelman, "Netanyahu cautions U.S. only Israel will make decisions on its security," *San Antonio Express-News* (Friday, March 20, 1998), p. 6A.

16. Grant Livingstone, spokesman for Christians Concerned for Lebanon, *Jerusalem Post*, July 1997.

17. Ibid.

18. John Loftus and Mark Aarons, *The Secret War Against the Jews: The Shocking Story of Israel's Betrayal by the Western Powers* (New York: St. Martin's Press, 1994), p. 1.

19. *Jerusalem Post*, March 13, 1998.

20. Johanna McGeary, "Nukes . . . They're Back: India's surprise nuclear tests shake a sense of security and could spark a new arms race," *Time* (May 25, 1998), pp. 32-42.

21. The London-based *Foreign Report*, cited in *International Christian Embassy Journal*, March 12, 1998; *Time* magazine, February 2, 1998; *Arutz Sheva* report, March 9, 1998.

22. Ari Sorko-Ram, "The Palestinian Authority: Getting Ready for War with Israel," *Maoz* newsletter, Tel Aviv, April 1998.

23. Statement made by Arafat after three Palestinians were killed when Israeli soldiers returned fire leveled at them in the Gaza Strip, as reported in the editorial "The Specter of the Holocaust," *Israel My Glory* magazine (April/May 1995), p. 4.

24. This is the verdict of Elie Rekhess, a professor of Arab affairs at Tel Aviv University after an analysis of contemporary clashes between these Arab groups and Israeli authorities; see Danna Harman, "Israeli Arabs call for general strike after brutal battles with police," Associated Press story, April 6, 1998.

25. As cited in Fatah's *Al Hayat Al-Jadeeda,* March 26, 1998.

26. Associated Press release of a speech by Yasser Arafat at a Land Day rally, Bagdad, Iraq, March 30, 1990.

Chapter 9: Redeemer to the Rescue

1. As cited by Benjamin Netanyahu, *A Place Among the Nations: Israel and the World* (New York: Bantam Books, 1993), p. 343.

2. Interview with David Dolan, Jerusalem, November 9, 1995.

3. For an exegetical defense of this position, see Eugene H. Merrill, *An Exegetical Commentary: Haggai, Zechariah, Malachi* (Chicago: Moody Press, 1994), pp. 249-57.

4. Although the Old Testament text being cited, Isaiah 59:20, reads, "A Redeemer will come to Zion . . . " it expresses the same idea; namely, that the Messiah will come to the Jewish nation (as symbolized by Zion, i.e., Jerusalem, its central city through the ages).

5. I believe that the plural use of armies here indicates that there are at least two separate armies in view: the angelic host (Matthew 16:27) and the redeemed saints (Isaiah 63:1-6).

6. See Arnold G. Fruchtenbaum, *The Footsteps of the Messiah: A Study of the Sequence of Prophetic Events* (Tustin, CA: 1982), p. 248, where he interprets the reference to the "tents" of Judah as indicative of the fact that these Jews are not resident in their native land, but somewhere else—that is, Bozrah.

7. The cataclysmic events described here and in Matthew 24:29 will attend Messiah's coming in judgment at the end of the Tribulation period.

8. As cited in George T.B. Davis, *Seeing Prophecy Fulfilled in Palestine* (Philadelphia: The Million Testaments Campaign, 1937), p. 76.

9. Rafael Eisenberg, *A Matter of Return: A Penetrating Analysis of Yisrael's Afflictions and Their Alternatives* (Jerusalem: Feldheim Publishers, 1980), pp. 61-62.

10. See Flavius Josephus, *Wars of the Jews* (Book IV): "But what more than anything else incited them to war was an ambiguous oracle [probably Daniel 7:13-14 or 9:26], likewise found in their sacred scriptures, to the effect that at that time one from their country would become ruler of the world. This they understood to mean someone of their own race, and many of their wise men went astray in their interpretation of it. The oracle, however, in reality signified the sovereignty of Vespasian, who was proclaimed Emperor on Jewish soil."

11. *Sefer Hassidim,* edited by J. Wistinetzki (1924), pp. 76-77, no. 212.

12. Throughout this article the term *Jewish messianist* will be used rather than Messianic Jew, although the latter is that most used in Israel. The substitution is made to avoid confusion with Jews who believe in Jesus as Messiah, commonly referred to as Messianic Jews, especially in the United States.

13. As cited in the article "Messianic Moods" by Elwood McQuaid, *Moody* magazine (inset box, n.d.).

14. Rabbi S. Stein, *Magog: The War of Russia with Israel* (Jerusalem, 1974).

15. The name "Chabad" is actually an acronym for H=*chokmah* ("wisdom"), b=*binah* ("understanding"), d=*da'at* ("knowledge"). The "a" vowels are only supplied for readability; the Hebrew consonants alone make the word.

16. *Jerusalem Post* magazine (August 15, 1997).

17. Two of the most widely circulated are Rabbi Abraham Stone, *Highlights of Moshiach,* based upon the Talmud, Midrash, and classical rabbinic

sources, and Rabbi Jacob Immanuel Schochet, *Mashiach: The Principle of Mashiach and the Messianic Era in Jewish Law and Tradition.*

18. While Chasidic magazines such as *Chai Today, Wellsprings,* and *L'Chaim* all carry articles relating to the present messianic expectation, a newsletter devoted entirely to the issue, called "Moshiach Matters," has recently been published by the International Campaign to Help Bring Moshiach.

19. For example, full-page ads in the *New York Times* announced "The Time of Your Redemption Has Arrived."

20. An introduction to the Jewish concept of the Messiah is available by dialing 1-800-4-MOSHIACH in the United States and 1-800-2-MASHIACH in Canada. The message, a four-minute mini-class (in English) is changed weekly. A more detailed daily message in English, Hebrew, or Yiddish can be heard by dialing (718) 953-6168. With all the hotlines, questions can be left for return-information calls. For those interested in contacting the international campaign headquarters in New York, call (718) 778-6000.

21. Lisa Beyer, "Expecting the Messiah," *Time* (March 23, 1992), p. 49; Kenneth Woodward and Hannah Brown, "Doth My Redeemer Live?" *Newsweek* (April 27, 1992), p. 53.

22. Zalman Herzl, "Ad Mosai?" *Beis Moshiach* 24 (weekly publication for Anash and Tmimim 26 Shevat 5755), p. 66.

23. From a Chasidic postcard with children on a "Geulah train" that had the caption: "The children first recognized him."

24. Although there is a minority group in Chabad that contends that the rabbi never died at all!

25. *Jerusalem Post* magazine (August 15, 1997).

26. Ibid.

Chapter 10: Regathering the Remnant

1. Emil Fackenheim, *Face to Face* (1979) as cited by Eliyahu Tal, *Whose Jerusalem?* (Tel Aviv: International Forum for a United Jerusalem, 1994), p. 289.

2. Mark Twain, *The Innocents Abroad or The New Pilgrims' Progress* (Pleasantville, NY: The Reader's Digest Association, Inc., 1990), pp. 358, 360-61.

3. Excerpted from the article "Arab Jerusalem . . . Its Walls and Its People," published by the Palestine Ministry of Information, December 10, 1997, via their internet site (http://www.pna.org).

4. There is a Hebrew inscription in the southern section of the Western Wall (quoting Isaiah 66:14), which was written either during the time of the Byzantine emperor Julian the Apostate or later. This was undoubtedly written by Jews returning to Jerusalem with the belief that the restoration was imminent (for this interpretation see Meir Ben-Dov, *In the Shadow of*

the Temple: The Discovery of Ancient Jerusalem (New York: Harper & Row, 1985), p. 219.

5. For this evidence, see *Ancient Synagogues Revealed*, ed. Lee I. Levine (Jerusalem: The Israel Exploration Society, 1982), pp. 3-4, 11-12; and "The Jewish Quarter: Ruins and Restoration" (Jerusalem: Israel Information Centre, September 1973).

6. For the archaeological evidence, see my book *The Stones Cry Out: What Archaeology Reveals About the Truth of the Bible* (Eugene, OR: Harvest House Publishers, 1997).

7. As recorded in Jerome's *Commentary to the Book of Zephaniah* (347-419). Petrologia Latina (Paris, 1845).

8. Dan Bahat, ed., *Twenty Centuries of Jewish Life in the Holy Land: The Forgotten Generations* (Jerusalem: The Israel Economist, 1975), p. 2.

9. See the statistical chart from 1820–1911 in Eliyahu Tal, *Whose Jerusalem?* (Tel Aviv: International Forum for a United Jerusalem, 1994), p. 94.

10. Walter C. Kaiser, Jr., "The Land of Israel and the Future Return (Zechariah 10:6-12)," *Israel, the Land and the People: An Evangelical Affirmation of God's Promises*, H. Wayne House, gen. ed. (Grand Rapids: Kregel Publications, 1998), pp. 223-24.

11. Rabbi Nisan Aryeh Novick, *Fascinating Torah Prophecies Currently Unfolding* (New York: Netzach Yisrael Publications, Inc., 1997), p. 72 (emphasis in the original).

12. From *Drishat Zion* (1862): cited in *The Zionist Movement*, ed. J. Kaplan (Jerusalem: Hebrew University Press, 1983), 1:6.

13. See my "Old Testament Tribulation Terms," *When the Trumpet Sounds*, eds. Thomas Ice and Timothy Demy (Eugene, OR: Harvest House Publishers, 1995), pp. 57-83.

14. Statement reported by Arutz Sheva news service on December 6, 1997.

Chapter 11: Watch Out, World!

1. Speech by Benjamin Netanyahu at the General Assembly of the American Council of Jewish Federations, November 16, 1997 (communicated by the Prime Minister's Media Advisor), p. 2.

2. As cited by Arnold Olson, *Inside Jerusalem, City of Destiny* (Glendale, CA: Gospel Light Publications, 1968), pp. 179-80.

3. This imagery of the fertile field also appears in Ezekiel chapters 16, 17, 21, 31, and 39 and indicates the scope and magnitude of God's power and its fruitful ability to accomplish its ends.

4. Marvin Lowenthal, *Diaries of Theodor Herzl* (New York: Dial Press, 1956), pp. 428-29.

5. Russell Bradley Jones, *The Latter Days* (formerly entitled: *The Things That Shall Be Hereafter*) (Grand Rapids: Baker Book House, 1961), p. 83.

6. Ibid. pp. 67-74.

7. In previous chapters I have dealt with several aspects of this first argument, especially those contained in the events leading up to and including the Olivet Discourse (Matthew 24–25, Luke 21).

8. For a more detailed study of this passage in light of Restoration Theology, see my "Prophetic Postponement in Daniel 9 and Other Texts," *Issues in Dispensationalism,* eds. W. Willis and J. Master (Chicago: Moody Press, 1994), pp. 132-65, especially pp. 134-40.

9. Each of these examples may be found in Eliyahu Tal, *Whose Jerusalem?* (Tel Aviv: International Forum for a United Jerusalem, 1994), p. 93.

10. Among those where I have seen an Arab-revisionist position assumed in reporting have been the major news networks, especially CNN, but also ABC, NBC, CBS, and NSBC, the newsjournals *Time, Newsweek,* and *U.S. News & World Report,* the geographical magazine *National Geographic,* and the encyclopedia *The Webster New World Encyclopedia* (1992), as well as anti-Semitic publications such as "Spotlight."

11. As cited by Marilyn Henry, "Impartial U.N. mask hides a hostile face," *The Jerusalem Post International Edition* (April 4, 1998), p. 3.

12. The other sessions concerned the 1956 invasion by the Soviet Union of Hungary and then later Afghanistan, the Lebanon crisis in 1958, and the crises in the Congo (1960) and Namibia (1981).

13. These statistics have appeared in a number of sources; this appeared in Dave Hunt, "Israel Update," *The Berean Call* newsletter, March 1996, p. 2.

14. Jeff Barak and Liat Collins, "U.N. chief has tough message for Israel," *The Jerusalem Post International Edition* (April 4, 1998), p. 32.

15. Wayne Malcolm, "A Word to Kings & Presidents: The Battle of Armageddon," *Prophecy Update* 2:1 (1998): 36.

16. Menachem Mendel Ussishkin, *Last Words* (1949), as cited by Eliyahu Tal, *Whose Jerusalem?* (Tel Aviv: International Forum for a United Jerusalem, 1994), p. 288.

Chapter 12: God Comes Home

1. For the theological argument on this see my book: *The Desecration and Restoration of the Temple As an Eschatological Motif in the Tanach, Jewish Apocalyptic Literature and the New Testament* (Ann Arbor, MI: UMI Publications, 1994).

2. For further explanation of this chronology, see my chapter "Prophetic Postponement in Daniel 9 and Other Texts" in *Issues in Dispensationalism,* eds. W. Willis and J. Master (Chicago: Moody Press, 1994), pp. 132-65, and my several articles on the interpretation of Daniel's seventy-weeks prophecy in the *Dictionary of Premillennial Theology,* ed. Mal Couch (Grand Rapids: Kregel Publications, 1996), pp. 75-81.

3. The word for "temple" here is the Greek word *naos,* which usually distinguishes the most sacred portion of the Temple from its less-sacred precincts (Greek: *hieros*).

4. Interview with David Dolan, Jerusalem, November 9, 1995.

5. Harold D. Foos, "Jerusalem in Prophecy," Th.D. dissertation, Dallas Theological Seminary, 1965, p. 230.

6. Various idealist and historicist schemes have been proposed in their commentaries on Ezekiel; however, from the Second Temple period onward, various sects in Orthodox Judaism continued to look for a literal fulfillment of the prophecy, as did Jewish apocalyptic groups (such as the Dead Sea sect) and as has futurist Christian interpretation.

7. For a further study of the Millennial Temple see the recent work by John Schmidtt and J. Carl Laney, *Messiah's Coming Temple: Ezekiel's Prophetic Vision of the Future Temple* (Grand Rapids: Kregel Publications, 1997).

8. Interview with Gershon Salomon, Jerusalem, November 27, 1996.

9. For further information on these groups see Richard J. Andrews, "The Political and Religious Groups Involved with Building the Third Temple," M.A. thesis, Indiana University, 1995.

10. Richard N. Ostling, "Time for a New Temple?" *Time* (October 16, 1989), p. 64.

11. As reported by Stan Goodenough of the International Christian Embassy in Jerusalem News Service in Jerusalem, March 20, 1998. Amnon Ramon of the Jerusalem Institute for Israel Studies replied to this survey, saying that the results "indicate just how important the Temple Mount is to Israeli Jews."

12. Yisrael Ariel and Chaim Richman, *The Odyssey of the Third Temple* (Jerusalem: Israel Publications & Productions Ltd., 1994), p. 102.

13. The author has discussed these plans and the possible prophetic purpose for the Ark of the Covenant in his book *In Search of Temple Treasures: The Lost Ark and the Last Days* (Eugene, OR: Harvest House Publishers, 1994).

14. Interview with Rabbi Shlomo Goren, Tel Aviv, November 1993.

15. "Genetic link found among Kohanim," *Jerusalem Post International Edition,* January 1997.

16. Kendall Hamilton (with Joseph Contreras and Mark Dennis), "The Strange Case of Israel's Red Heifer," *Time* (May 19, 1997), p. 16.

17. For direct information about this, contact Clyde Lott at his e-mail address: red@teclink.net.

18. *Message of the Christian Jew,* newsletter of The Christian-Jew Foundation (January-February 1996), p. 7.

19. For details, see "GSS [Israel General Security Service] Working to Delegitimize Temple Mount Effort," Israel Internet News Service Ltd. (March 16, 1998).

20. Ibid.
21. Ibid.
22. Arutz 7 News, January 8, 1998.
23. Zev Vilnay, *Legends of Jerusalem* (Philadelphia: Jewish Publication Society of America, 1973), pp. 42-43.
24. Bill Hutman, "Hussein gives $8.2m. to repair Dome of Rock," *Jerusalem Post International Edition*, September 23, 1995.

Chapter 13: God on the Throne

1. As cited by Murray Dixon, "Israel: A Biblical Perspective" (Prayer for Israel, New Zealand), p. 20.
2. For the extrabiblical data on this term see the articles in the *Theological Dictionary of the New Testament* (Grand Rapids: Eerdmans Publishing Co., 1979), 1:686-89.

Chapter 14: The Jerusalem Above

1. Aggadic saying cited in Zev Vilnay, *Legends of Jerusalem* (Philadelphia: Jewish Publication Society of America, 1973), p. 156.
2. The following texts contain references to the New Jerusalem concept among those works considered as Jewish apocryphal or pseudepigraphical (and apocalyptic): *Tobit* 13:8-18; *Testament of Dan* 5:12-13; *Sybilline Oracles* 5:420-27; *1 Enoch* 90:28-29; *2 Esdras* 7:26; 10:25-28; 13:36; *2 Baruch* 4; 32:1-4.
3. For the complete extant text of this document see Michael Wise, Martin Abegg, Jr., and Edward Cook, *The Dead Sea Scrolls: A New Translation* (San Francisco: HarperCollins, 1996), pp. 180-88.
4. Yitzhak I. Hayutman, *Realizing the Heavenly Jerusalem*, The Academy of Jerusalem Monographs—#3 (March, 1995).
5. Ibid., p. 459.
6. The predicate adjective τετράγωνος ("foursquare"), describing the city, is from τέτρα (Aeolic for τέσσαρες) "four" and γῶνος (a cognate of γωνία) "corner." This term was also used with reference to cube-shaped building stones, cf. *A Greek-English Lexicon of the New Testament and Other Early Christian Literature* by W. Bauer, trans. and rev. by W.F. Arndt, F.W. Gingrich, and F.W. Danker (Chicago: University of Chicago Press, 1961), p. 821, and indicates here a quadrilateral quadrangle or tetragonal structure.
7. The calculations are those of an Australian engineer by the name of Tammas, as reported by Wilbur M. Smith, *The Biblical Doctrine of Heaven* (Chicago: Moody Press, 1968), p. 246.
8. Interview with Noam Hendren, Independence Park, Jerusalem, Shavuot, May 1997.

9. Robert L. Thomas, *Revelation 8–22: An Exegetical Commentary* (Chicago: Moody Press, 1995), 2: 478.

10. J. Dwight Pentecost, *Things to Come: A Study in Biblical Eschatology* (Grand Rapids: Zondervan Publishing House, 1958), p. 580.

11. It should also be noted (as we argue) that if the Temple-city is the heavenly Temple's holy place descended to a restored earth, then the language displays the continuity between the Edenic Sanctuary and Ezekiel's Temple, both of which were patterned after the heavenly archetype and represented idyllic realizations. Thus, the Millennial Temple (Ezekiel's) realized the earthly ideal, which was lost at Eden, and unrealized by either the First or Second Temple, and the New Temple, represents the ultimate realization in an uncursed (new Eden) world.

12. George E. Ladd, *A Commentary on the Revelation of John* (Grand Rapids: William B. Eerdmans Publishing Co., 1972), p. 284.

13. As seen, the purified condition of the peoples would not require outer courts, which formerly served to provide separation or gradations of holiness.

14. Some have suggested this mimics the city planning of Near Eastern cities such as Babylon, which, according to Herodotus, was laid out as a square with each side 120 stadia in length, and Nineveh, which Diodorus Siculus described in a similar fashion. However, the adjective ἴσα indicates the shape of a perfect cube, which from the Jewish perspective, would have had reference to the Holy of Holies, as described in 1 Kings 6:19-20.

15. "The New Jerusalem" in *Songs of Faith: Keys for the Kingdom: A Progressive Piano Method for the Christian Student,* by Joseph Martin, David Angerman, and Mark Hayes (Delaware Water Gap, PA: Shawnee Press, Inc., 1997), p. 29.

Chapter 15: Jerusalem Is Ours!

1. Benjamin Netanyahu, "With God's Help, Israel Will Prevail," speech given to 4,500 Christians assembled in Jerusalem during the Feast of Tabernacles, *Middle East Intelligence,* digest of International Christian Embassy in Jerusalem (November 1995), p. 3.

2. Benjamin Netanyahu, *A Place Among the Nations: Israel and the World* (New York: Bantam Books, 1993), p. 259.

3. New Jerusalem Ministries "SOS" website: "Frequently Asked Questions: The Christian's Obligation and Involvement" (http://www.fan.net.au/~sos/obli.htm).

4. As cited in an ad published by Facts and Logic about the Middle East, *U.S. News & World Report* (March 30, 1998), p. 36.

5. Issued on May 18, 1997 as cited in *U.S. News & World Report* (March 30, 1998), p. 36.

6. Ibid.
7. Comment submitted by Noam Hendren, Kfar Saba, Israel, March 31, 1998.
8. Ibid.

Scripture Index

Jeremiah

Malachi

Matthew

Jewish Text Index

Subject Index

Jerusalem in Prophecy
Video

Filmed on location in Israel with prophecy and Middle Eastern expert Dr. Randall Price, the *Jerusalem in Prophecy* video gives a fascinating overview of Jerusalem's past, present, and future. This film includes material not found in the book, including exclusive interviews and footage not available elsewhere.

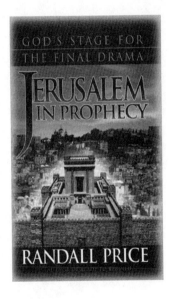

$19.99
(plus $3.95 shipping and handling)
Order your copy today from:

WORLD OF THE BIBLE MINISTRIES, INC.
P.O. Box 827
San Marcos, TX   78667-0827
(512) 396-3799 / FAX (512) 392-9080

Other Books and Resources by Dr. Randall Price

The Stones Cry Out
Recently uncovered ancient artifacts shed light upon the lives of the patriarchs, the Ark of the Covenant, the fall of Jericho, the existence of King David, and more. A fascinating survey of the latest finds in Bible lands, with more than 80 photos affirming the incontrovertible facts that support biblical truth.

Secrets of the Dead Sea Scrolls
Discover the new technology that helps translators with previously unreadable Scroll fragments, supposedly "secret" Scrolls in hiding, the furious debate about who rightfully owns the Scrolls, and the newest efforts to find more Dead Sea Scrolls. Includes never-before-published photographs.

In Search of Temple Treasures
Does the Ark of the Covenant still exist? Why is it so important? *In Search of Temple Treasures* takes you on a remarkable expedition into the Ark's mysterious past, its explosive significance today, and its implications in the timing of last days' events. Meticulous research and dozens of interviews with leading authorities in the Middle East provide a factual inside view of one of history's most fascinating quests.

Ready to Rebuild
A fast-moving overview of contemporary events which indicate that a significant move to rebuild the Temple is gaining momentum in Israel. Includes important pictures and charts. Co-authored with Thomas Ice.